The History of Medicine, Money and Politics

The History of Medicine, Money and Politics

Riding the Rollercoaster of State Medicine

Paul R Goddard MD

Published by: Clinical Press Ltd. Redland Green Farm, Redland, Bristol, BS6 7HF, UK.

British Library Cataloguing in Publication Data

A catalogue record for this book is available from the British Library

ISBN-13:   978-1-85457-050-5
EAN: 9781854570505

Contents

Acknowledgements

Many people have helped in the production of this book, some wittingly and some unwittingly.

I would like to thank, in particular, my wife Lois. She has helped at all stages. I have rehearsed all of the arguments and discussions with her and she has read the book in several forms and made pertinent comments and changes. The book could not have been written without her.

A special thank you must be extended to Barry Clayden of Coincraft (London) for checking the validity of my numismatic comments and to both Brian Potter and Coincraft for supplying some of the coins.

Jeremy Mann read the manuscript and made important contributions. Thanks also to Alf Troughton for putting up with my heated discussion either on car journeys or telephone calls and for Paul Aylard for encouraging me to write the book in the first place. Richard Ashcroft was invaluable with his work on the ethics papers quoted in the book. Other good friends have also helped me to hone the arguments.

Needless to say not everybody has agreed with all the points I make. I would not expect them to do so. The opinions expressed in the book are mine and not theirs and I take full responsibility for the book. I believe that the ideas needed to be put down in writing and aired to the public. Perhaps they will assist in the attempts to save the NHS for present and for future generations.

About the author

Professor Paul Goddard has always taken a keen interest in the relationship between politics, medicine and money. He has undertaken, with his family, large scale fund-raising for the NHS and a variety of charities. He was treasurer of the (Junior) Hospital Doctors Association in 1975 and 1980 and vice-president of the same organisation from 1985 to 1995, partner in a medical agency for ten years and director of Clinical Press Ltd. He has been President of the Radiology Section of the Royal Society of Medicine and of the MRRA(UK). He sat on the Council of the British Institute of Radiology and was Head of Training in Radiology for 10 hospitals in the South West of England.

In 1991 he was appointed as Civil Consultant to the RAF (Hon. Air Commodore) and in 2000 he was appointed Visiting Professor at the University of the West of England. He has won the Couch Award, the Twining Medal and the Kodak Scholarship of the Royal College of Radiologists and was awarded the Barclay Prize of the British Institute of Radiology in 2002/3 and was delighted to receive their Honorary Fellowship in 2007.

He is a retired NHS consultant, a member of the Bristol Medico-Historical Society and also a Fellow of the Higher Education Academy.

Preface

The first medical practices were probably shamanic arts 40,000 years ago but medicine has only developed as an ethical science over the last 4000 years. During that time its fortune has been intertwined with that of the state and with that of money. It has thus shown periodic highs and lows along with the prosperity and stability of the particular country or empire.

The intervention of the state in healthcare has seen a progressive rise over the last two hundred years via legislation and control of standards. Many countries have set up national health services since the 2nd World War. However, on reading newspaper reports about the UK's NHS one could be forgiven for believing that we have the only National Health Service and that only our health service is having problems. This is not the case. Most developed and many developing countries have a national health service of some form and some, such as Australia, even call it the NHS. Many health services around the World are in serious difficulties at present due to the rising cost of healthcare. Money and Medicine are entangled in many ways as we shall see in the book.

In the last 50 years, with the inception of the World Health Organisation (WHO), the various health related committees in the European Union and the advent of the European Health Insurance Card we are witnessing the rise of something greater than a National or State Health Organization. This is something which the WHO denies being but which it certainly acts as in many ways: the supranational health system.

- Why is our health service as it is?
- What is the history behind its inception?
- Why does it appear to be failing now and where has it gone wrong?
- What will the future trends be in health services?

These and other questions are addressed in the book. The first part provides an overview of the history of state intervention in healthcare. There is an enormous body of evidence to draw from and the choice has been eclectic. The second part will concentrate mainly on the relative decline of the British NHS compared with other healthcare systems in the world. It is based on my own perception of the situation and what it felt like to be a porter, doctor or nurse working in the NHS. I realise that this is only one perspective on the situation, mainly hospital orientated, but having gone through all these roles and sailed the rough seas of change and disaster, the perspective may be of some interest, however misguided.

Part 1
The Rise of State Medicine
A Chronology and Critique

Chapter 1

Introduction

'Histories make men wise' Francis Bacon 1561-1626[1]

Many people living in the United Kingdom, when asked about modern medicine, would date it to the start of the National Health Service. To some this is like a singularity or event horizon: before the NHS there was nothing and afterwards we had hospitals, general practitioners, antibiotics, X-rays, transplant surgery and gene therapy!

It was not really like that. Medicine had evolved over many millennia from the days of the shaman or witch-doctor, through the earliest efforts at rational explanation by the ancient Greeks such as Hippocrates and Galen, to the earliest experimental anatomists such as Harvey and the discoverers of germs and sterilisation (Pasteur, Koch, Lister in the 1860s to 1890s).

The apparent decline and imminent fall of the National Health Service (NHS) is an event interesting enough to be worthy of being recorded on its own. But the old adage 'history repeats itself' has considerable truth in it. From where did the NHS arise? The concept of a state health scheme did not appear overnight. The British National Health Service was not the first state-inspired provision of health care and the staff, providing the health-care free at the point of delivery, were not the first to declare that they despised the profit motive in medicine. Nor is it the first government sponsored medical provision to run into trouble.

Research has shown me that although the exact problems facing the NHS in particular and medicine in general are specific to this time and place there are considerable parallels at other times and in other countries. It is a fool who ignores history since it is only with knowledge of the past that we can understand the present and plan for the future.

Thus I have written a history of State Medicine, riding its ups and downs like a rollercoaster.

The book is in two main parts. The first part of the book is entitled *The Rise of State Medicine (A chronology and critique)*. This section provides a brief overview, since that is all it can be, of the enormous history of medicine, its rise and fall and the way in which it has interacted with politics and money.

Periodically throughout history the public faith and trust in doctors and nurses has had

1

peaks and troughs. A lifetime's work culminating in a few prominent successes, perhaps treating emperors or famous poets, and the trust in a particular doctor or medical practice rises. A single disaster or even just one disreputable or murderous doctor can ruin the faith in medicine for a generation or more. It is much harder to build a reputation than it is to destroy one.

State intervention in medicine has waxed and waned but this has not necessarily coincided with the alteration in public perception nor indeed with the rise and fall in fortune of the medical staff and their patients. States and their governments are remembered in history more for their activities that lead to reduced life expectancy than those which increase health. Thus the killing sprees, such as wars, pogroms and revolutions are recorded but the endowment of hospitals and the training, encouragement and regulation of healthcare professionals is much less newsworthy.

But what is a State and what do we mean by State Medicine? According to the Concise Oxford Dictionary[2] a State is "An organized political community under one government…" This could be part of a larger system such as a federation or perhaps a single, isolated nation. Medicine, in the same dictionary, is defined as "The science or practice of the diagnosis, treatment and prevention of disease".

State Medicine as a term could cover a broad range of possibilities but all would include some kind of government intervention in the running of health care.

Increased government intervention in healthcare can enhance or detract from medical services. Sometimes the intervention has been beneficial but at other times, despite good intentions, it has been harmful. In some eras the interference by government has been deliberately harmful.

Money and Politics have been included in the title because the research has thrown up several other interesting findings. Medicine relies on good economics. It does well when the economy of an area flourishes and suffers when the economy suffers. For advancement in medical science the nature of the philosophical and political environment is also extremely important and in recent years this has been transmitted to the health services by way of management.

Another interesting factor is the antagonism between those in medicine who wish to make a good living financially and those who believe health-care should, as far as possible, be free. Cynical government and management have often exploited the altruistic vocation of the latter group, as we shall see in later chapters.

Medicine or " healing" was initially practised by the local witch-doctor or medicine man. The commonly used term for this is the Shaman. He combined the role of priest and doctor since illness was considered to be a spiritual problem to be cured by religious ceremony whenever possible. In addition he would sometimes also act as a local ruler. This priest/doctor role survived into the civilisations of Mesopotamia and Egypt where healing was to be attempted initially by incantations, spells and prayers to the relevant gods and resort to physical cures, such as herbal medicines or surgery was undertaken only when the incantations failed. The kings and pharaohs were also considered to be important healers. Hammurabi, ruler of Babylonia, was a healer and some Egyptian pharaohs were physicians, combining the roles of healer, ruler and priest. As the god-like embodiment of the State the pharaohs would have undoubtedly have been the leader of all medical priests at the time representing some form of early State Medicine.

Jesus Christ as a historical figure was considered to be a healer, priest and disputed King of the Jews. Many monarchs since the ancient times have been considered to have miraculous powers for healing the sick. A famous example is that of Scrofula. Popularly known as the King's Evil, it was believed in the Middle Ages that the Royal Touch could cure this form of lymph node swelling. Traditionally the English or French monarch would heal the person with a touch and give them a coin. Such coins were considered to have healing power and were known as 'touch pieces'. Similar traditions persist amongst the credulous.

The religious and spiritual aspect of healing has continued right through to the modern day with, for example, provision of health care by religious orders. In the Roman Catholic Church these are well known with many holy orders including medical sections still running hospitals and hospices. In addition there are places, such as Lourdes, where healing by supernatural means is sought by millions of people annually. It is common in almost all religions to pray for God's intervention in healing the sick and to pray for God's protection from disease.

Throughout the religious provision of health-care is the belief that the providers of that care should be selfless and disinterested in the profit-motive. Thus monks and nuns running hospitals would not be individually permitted to own property and this may be reflected in the title of the order "The poor sisters of Saint Mary" or whatever. The leader of the religion (for example the Pope) would be at least nominally in charge of the healers.

However, from Greek times onwards there is also the development of the science of medicine. This completely discards supernatural intervention as the cause of disease and tries to find a rational basis for diagnosis and treatment. The protagonists of this would not be priests, monks or nuns and would need some means of financial support. They would be working for a fee and living in secular society rather than living in a convent or monastery.

Thus we have two major schools of thought with regard to health care. One would emphasise spirituality and supernatural means of achieving good health and the other would solely accept practical, physical causes for disease. One would eschew financial gain but the other would require it. One may be supported by religious government and the other by secular government. The secular government may exploit the spiritual beliefs of the altruistic group in health care and, conversely, a religious government may suppress advances discovered by rational scientists. High priests of the old system may fight against a new rational basis and vice-versa. Examples of all of these possibilities are included in the book.

Hippocrates had founded a school of medicine in the Greek Island of Cos around 420BC and his famous Oath includes the words "Whatever houses I may visit, I will come for the benefit of the sick"[3,4]. Galen, who lived at the end of the second century, taught that the doctor should learn to despise money.

40,000 years of history have gone into the making of medical science and many philosophers, scientists and governments have contributed to the ethics and provision of medical care. The first part of this book races through an overview of this worldwide endeavour in a brief history or chronological timeline. The choice of subjects in this section has to be eclectic and there is some overlap of time periods due to the overlap of different civilisations. I have picked out examples of State intervention in the provision of medical care and in addition highlighted a few of the major scientific advances. With some practices, such as an understanding of the importance of good hygiene, the knowledge has been gained and lost several times throughout history. Some advances could only occur when other discoveries had already been made. A good example of this would be the subject of pathology which was only possible in a superficial and gross way before the advent of the microscope. Another example is the discovery of X-rays in 1895, which would have been impossible without prior discovery of electricity, Crooke's tubes and such like.

The illustrations in the book mainly include busts of famous doctors and nurses or coins of the same era and place. The latter serve several purposes. Coins are genuine artefacts from the era in question. They are a primary source that tell us who the monarch or emperor was in that country at that time and thus remind us who was in charge of the state. They have something to say about the wealth of the era since well-made coins are usually available from a period of well-organised prosperity. The constant display of small coins is salient since there have been disagreements and bad feeling about the cost of employing doctors throughout history. There have been arguments about the profit motive in medicine from the earliest times right up to the present day and this is reflected in the chronology. People do not want to pay for a health service when they are well and when they are ill they do not wish to think about the cost, especially if the doctor fails to heal them quickly enough. Finally there is the belief, which persists even to the modern day, in the supernatural ability of some coins and medals to ward of evil and cure disease.

The second part of the book, entitled the *Decline of the NHS* will be discussed when we come to it.

4

Medicine in Prehistoric Times and in the Ancient World

The earliest medical practice: The Shaman

Science is the record of dead religions Oscar Wilde

Shamanic medicine

Shamanism probably extends back at least 40,000 years. The word 'shaman' hails from the Tungus people of Siberia, and means 'one who sees'. All diseases and death itself were regarded as spirit phenomena. Some historians and anthropologists do point out the considerable similarities in many different cultures. These include healing via the spirits or soul, drumming, vision quests, chanting, fasting and dance. The wearing of masks and the use of carvings representing the particular demon of disease is also a theme.

Toothache demon?

North African Drums

**Demons of Disease
19th century Sri Lanka
(British Museum)**

Other anthropologists such as Alice Kehoe[5] dislike the use of the terms Shaman and Shamanism since they imply a common culture which may not really exist and may reinforce prejudices such as the concept of the "Noble Savage".

Historically the shamans while functioning as priests, also worked as doctors and surgeons. The practical techniques they introduced include:

- herbal medicines: Many pharmaceuticals in general use today, were known to the shaman. Herbal based medicines such as digitalis (from the foxglove) or salicylic acid (willow bark) were used as plant extracts but it was their purification and detoxification that led to the modern science of pharmacology. In the case of salicylic acid, willow bark extract was undoubtedly utilised by the Greeks, Sumerians, Ancient Egyptians, Assyrians and native American Indians to ease aches and pains and reduce fevers. It was not, however, until 1899, that the rather toxic salicylic acid was acetylated to the much better tolerated acetylsalicylic acid, which was then marketed by Bayer as Aspirin.

- trepanning (or trephination / trepanation)…the drilling of a hole in the skull. Evidence of trepanation has been found in pre-historic human remains from Neolithic times onwards. Cave paintings exist indicating that people believed the practice would cure epileptic seizures and mental disorders (which it can if the problem is due to increased intracranial pressure, say from an injury and haematoma). Inca Indians are documented to have performed these operations successfully, as judged by skulls of Inca people with well-healed holes, 4,000 years ago. Hippocrates, the Ancient Greek founder of medical science, gave specific directions on the procedure.

- cauterisation—using a red-hot iron to seal the blood vessels and prevent bleeding after surgery. This technique (or similar techniques) were rediscovered by surgeons in the Roman Republic and later in Europe (1300, 1854 and 1906).

As astrologers the shamans learnt to predict eclipses and were thus also some of the earliest astronomers. The shamans (both male and female) were immensely powerful priests and sometimes doubled as rulers, thus providing the first examples of government and medicine being intertwined[6].

The belief that a ruler or a priest has the ability to heal the sick has persisted in some places in the world to the modern day and examples of kings and emperors who were considered as great healers occur throughout history.

Shamanic medicine: today. Witch doctors and the witch-hunt

Superstitious shamanic medicine is still practised all over the world, particularly in the poorer parts of the developing world. "Among the poorly educated rural residents, traditional healers and clairvoyants claiming supernatural powers hold broad sway…. hunger, poverty, and unemployment can create jealousies that can quickly turn to anger and vengeance."[7]. Approximately 30 percent of accused witches are male — reflecting men's prominence as *nangas*, or traditional healers. Anton La Guardia describes the case of "Credo Mutwa, southern Africa's best-known practising healer … [who] said he had been accosted by a mob and stabbed several times. He lay bleeding on the ground and waited helplessly to die as his assailants poured petrol and prepared to set it alight. Mr. Mutwa … said he was saved by the same superstition which was about to claim his life. 'A young man shouted, "His ghost will haunt you." They vanished, leaving me like a fish on dry land.'"[8,9]

The term witch-hunt is also used to describe inquisitorial investigation in which people are accused of wrongdoing on flimsy evidence. The term is particularly used when onlookers are afraid to intervene in case they also are accused.

Medicine and Money in the Ancient Civilizations
Mesopotamia in 3,500BC

Sumer, southern Mesopotamia, was an ancient region of Western Asia in present-day Iraq. From the 4th millennium BC it was the site of city states which later became part of ancient Babylonia. The Sumerians were the first known people to create writing using the cuneiform script on clay tablets. They had systematic record keeping and instigated social and economic organization. They invented the plough (plow) and probably invented the first money. They devised the units of time that we still use today by the division of a day into 24 hours and one hour into 60 minutes[10].

Sumerian Shell Ring Money 3rd Millennium BC. Major commerce in western Asia of the 4th Millennium did not generally use the medium of money. (Gold and silver coinage was a late 7th century BC invention). Instead they used barter: there was an exchange of different commodities. For small local transactions, and for the needs of daily life however, the Sumerians are believed to have used rings, usually carrying them on a necklace string. The rings may have included gold and silver but for minor transactions it is likely that they used shell rings, many of which have been found. Thus these shell rings are an early form of currency and may indeed be the earliest example of money.

The Babylonian and Assyrian Empires developed from the Sumerian civilization. Hammurabi c. 1810 BC – 1750 BC was the first dynasty king of the Babylonian Empire. Interestingly his name meant "the kinsman is a healer". The Laws of Hammurabi established the first known code of medical ethics, and laid down a fee schedule for specific surgical procedures He founded an empire that was eventually destroyed by raids from Asia Minor. Hammurabi's code of laws is one of the greatest of ancient codes. It is carved on a diorite column, in 3,600 lines of cuneiform; it was found (1902) at Susa and is now at Paris. The code, which addresses such issues as business and family relations, labor, private property, and personal injuries, is generally humanitarian but the punishments would be considered harsh by today's standards since it relies heavily on "an eye for an eye, a tooth for a tooth". [11,12] Hammurabi's Code of Law specified: "If a surgeon performs a major operation on an 'awelum' (nobleman), with a lancet and caused the death of this man, they shall cut off his hands". Hammurabi also specified fees for lifesaving operations: "Ten shekels of silver for 'awelum', five shekels for 'mushkenu' (poor man) and two shekels for a slave."[13] The shekel at this time was a unit of weight rather than a coin and shekel weights of silver (and their fractions) appear in the texts of cuneiform tablets as far back as 2100 BC, the third dynasty of Ur period.

The Assyrian empire, which existed from around 2000BC to 612BC like the Babylonian, developed from the Sumerian culture. Assyria was a region on the Upper Tigris River named from its original capital, the ancient city of Assur. Later it came to mean the northern part of Mesopotamia with the southern part being Babylonia. In

Marble slab of Asshurbanipal fighting a lion (Brit. Mus.)

700 BC the Assyrians built aqueducts to provide fresh water, a significant advance in public health. The library of the last great king of Assyria, Asshurbanipal (668BC to 626BC), was housed in the king's palace at Nineveh, and when the palace was burned by invaders, around 20,000 clay cuneiform tablets were baked (and thereby preserved) by the fire. 660 medical tablets from the library of Asshurbanipal were translated by Cambell Thompson in the 1920s. Several hundred other tablets also relate to medicine[14].

There were two distinct types of medical practitioner practising in Assyria which is in many ways comparable to the present physician/surgeon split.

Ashipu, (also called a "sorcerer.") The Ashipu diagnosed which divine entity was responsible for the ailment. The phrase, "the Hand of..." was used to indicate the divine entity responsible for the ailment in question, who could then be appeased by the patient. The Ashipu also attempted to cure the patient by means of charms and spells designed to entice away or drive out the spirit causing the disease. Otherwise, rather as a last resort, the Ashipu could refer the patient to the Asu.

Asu. A specialist in herbal remedies, who dealt in empirical, practical applications of medication. When, for example, treating wounds the Asu generally relied on three fundamental techniques: washing, bandaging, and making plasters. These techniques of the Asu appear in one of the world's oldest known medical document (c. 2100 BC)[14].

Ancient Egyptians

The major Nile Valley cultures in North-East Africa were united under one ruler, the first pharaoh, in 3150BC. The reign of pharaohs officially ended in 31BC when Egypt became a province of the early Roman Empire. Like the Assyrians, religion dominated the ancient Egyptians' view of healing. Doctors were priests who were thought to be able to communicate with the gods responsible for the health of different parts of the body. The Egyptians had doctor/priests who specialized in treating particular parts of the body and researched the properties of herbal medicines[15]. There were specialists for treatment of the eyes, teeth, internal organs, obstetrics and gynaecology and the treatment of animals (veterinarians)[16]. Several papyri exist that detail medical diagnosis and treatment and these form some of the first medical textbooks. Pharmacists prepared prescriptions to treat specific illnesses using ointments, potions, inhalers and pills by processing plant materials. Preparations included opium, cannabis, linseed oil and senna[16,17] Imhotep, who lived in the reign of Djoser, 2630-2611BC, was probably the author of the Edwin Smith papyrus. Imhotep was a doctor, chief minister and vizier, scribe, sage, poet and architect. As the latter he built the step

Step pyramid, Saqqara

Left: Amenhotep I (British Mus.)
Right: A papyrus on plants used in healing.
A Botanical treatise from the late period
(664-332) (British Mus.)

pyramid at Saqqara. Another example is the Ebers Papyrus (c. 1534 B.C.) dating from the reign of the pharaoh Amenhotep I, and this refers to medical practices as far back as the First Dynasty (c. 3000 B.C)[16,17,18]

Egyptian surgery was surprisingly sophisticated. Medical papyri tell us that the doctor was able to characterise different types of injury. Broken bones were re-aligned. Where necessary, amputation was performed. Early instruments would have been made of stone (flint or obsidian, both of which are very sharp) but later instruments were Iron or Bronze.

2,500-1500BC Indus Valley Civilisation

Contemporary with the Assyrian, Babylonian and Egyptian civilisations there were major civilisations in India and China where medical practises were being developed.

The Indus Valley civilisation had aqueducts for fresh water, sophisticated drainage systems, medical and dental services.

In Hindu texts from 1500 BC childbed fever or pueperal sepsis was recognised as a cause of maternal death. Advice was given on hygiene for birth attendants. It is dismaying to note that puerperal sepsis in the United Kingdom was spread by medical attendants with filthy frocks until its cause was re-discovered in the 1840s (Over 3,300 years after it had been described in India!)[19]

The First Coins

One of the world's earliest silver coins
Silver siglos of Kroisos
c.561-546BC
Obverse Lion and Bull
Reverse Incuse punch

Herodotus states that the first coinage was issued by Kroisos, King of Lydia 561-546BC. This was the ruler with fabulous wealth about whom the expression 'Rich as Croesus' became common parlance. Herodotus was not quite correct. Coins were probably invented by the early Anatolian traders who stamped their own marks so that they would not have to weigh the silver or gold again each time it was used. It does appear likely that Kroisos was indeed the first king to issue coins of pure gold and pure silver since earlier coins were made of electrum, an alloy of gold and silver which varied in content. Kroisos was defeated by Cyrus the Great, founder of the Persian Empire, who was in alliance with King Nabodinus of Babylon. Lydia then became a satrapy of Persia. Cyrus followed this by attacking and defeating Nabodinus.

Ancient Greece 3000-60BC

Homer

The earliest literary sources, such as Homer (about 850-800BC), show that in Ancient Greece sickness and disease was viewed as being of supernatural origin. This belief was similar to Egypt and Babylon. In the Iliad, for example, the plague that decimates the Greek army besieging Troy is represented as being sent by Apollo.

As the Greek civilisation developed their philosophers progressed beyond this way of thinking. They described the world in more rational terms and considered that most events had natural rather than supernatural causes. They included diseases in this debate, considering that disease was due to natural causes rather than the visitation of angry gods. Only a few of the many advances that the Ancient Greeks made in medical science and medical ethics are discussed in the following pages but they serve to illustrate the relevance of their science and philosophy to modern medical practice.

Parthenon marbles: Centaur and youth (British Museum)

In Greek mythology there were several gods of healing. Initially Apollo was regarded as the god of healing. The playwright Homer refers to Apollo's son, Asklepios (Asclepius, Roman Aesculapius) as a skillful human physician. In the mythology, Apollo is said to have entrusted the child Asklepios's education to the Centaur, Chiron who taught Asklepios the arts of healing. Asklepios was worshipped as a god in post-Homeric times, beginning in the fifth century BC. As the Greek god of healing he became the patron deity of physicians. Asklepios was the father of Hygieia (health) and Panacea (all-healing).

The term "a panacea" is still used today but has become a derogatory term to describe a supposed cure-all.

The staff of Asklepios with a coiled serpent became the traditional symbol of medicine. The correct symbol of Asklepios is a single snake but twin winged snakes, the symbol of Hermes or Mercury, are often incorrectly used as a medical symbol[20].

Illustration Left: Snakes and staff (Royal Society of Medicine)

Sophocles 495-406BC

Right: Sophocles 495-406BC

Silver Tetradrachm of Attica, Athens (2nd century BC) Obverse: Head of Athena, Goddess of Wisdom Reverse: the owl, symbol of Athens and of wisdom

Sophocles was an ancient Greek playwright, Athenian politician and general. He served for many years as an ordained priest in the service of two local heroes – Alcon and Asklepios, the god of medicine[21]. Sophocles asserted that the physician was merely a hired hand, a tradesman whereas Aristophanes (playwright c.448-380BC) contended that medicine was an art[22,23].

Socrates (470-399BC) noted that money was important. "Unless pay is added to the art," he wrote, "there would be no benefit for the craftsman, and consequently he would be unwilling to go to the trouble of taking care of the trouble of others."[22,24]

The Athenian Plague of 430-426BC is the first epidemic to have been recorded in any accurate detail. The epidemic broke out during the Peloponnesian War between Athens and Sparta, spreading rapidly killing tens of thousand. The Athenian general Thucydides gave a first-hand account of the 'plague' in his History of the Peloponnesian War. He was himself infected and described the symptoms as headaches, conjunctivitis, a rash covering the body, fever, retching and uncontrollable diarrhoea. He believed that there was a rational cause for the outbreak and discounted the idea that it was due to the wrath of a god. The signs and symptoms were not those of Bubonic Plague and it seems likely from DNA analysis of teeth that the Athenian Plague was due to Typhoid.[25]

Hippocrates

Born on Cos (Greek Island) 460BC

Hippocrates
(Bust: Gower St.)

Hippocrates is considered as the founder of medical science. He rejected the view that illness was caused by disfavor of the gods or possession by evil spirits. Instead he believed that illness had a rational explanation. His theory was that this was imbalance of the four humours: blood, phlegm, choler and melancholy. A theory of imbalance is similar to ideas being propounded by Traditional Chinese Medicine. Hippocratic writings contain salient references to such subjects as childbed fever (puerperal sepsis), and the view that the epileptic fits are not due to evil spirits but to a physical cause. Dissection of dead human beings was, however, a taboo so the study of human anatomy was hampered. Hippocrates founded a medical school on Cos. He developed the Hippocratic oath of medical ethics (probably partially Pythagorean in origin also)....*Whatever houses I may visit, I will come for the benefit of the sick, remaining free of all intentional injustice, of all mischief......"Primum non nocere" — "First, do no harm"*[3,4].

One of Hippocrates' tutors, Herodicus, was a Thracian physician of the fifth century BC. He has the reputation of having been the first named sports medicine practitioner having advocated the importance of regular exercise in the maintenance of good health![26]. Another Thracian, called Democritus (c. 460 BC- 370 BC.) was a Greek philosopher and mathematician from Abdera, Thrace (a site which now lies in the Xanthi Prefecture of modern Greece) His very significant contribution to science was development of the atomic theory, the belief that all matter is made up of various imperishable indivisible elements which he called atoma or atoms. (He was not quite the first person to put forward this idea since it had been a theory from India a century previously)[27,28]

11

Alexandrian Medicine in Hellenistic Egypt

**Bronze Coin of Ptolemy I,
305-283BC**

Obverse   **Reverse**
Alexander the Great   **Eagle**

By the Fourth century BC the main centre of innovation in medical science and practice had moved from Cos to Egypt. A new city known as Alexandria had been set up by Alexander the Great in 331BC. It was a major centre of learning under the Ptolemaic Pharaohs who were very supportive of scholarship. Alexandria housed the largest library in the ancient world with over half a million books. In addition there was a large museum and a medical school.

The philosophers Aristotle and Plato had put forward the supposition that the soul of a person left his body after death and that the dead body was therefore of little or no importance. Following these ideas there was no taboo over dissecting dead bodies in Alexandria. More worryingly, it is possible that vivisection was also permitted.

Praxagoras 320BC and Herophilus 280BC were Greek physicians who practised in Alexandria. Herophilus dissected the human eye, investigated the pulse and discovered the function and anatomy of the nervous system[29]. His theories were later developed and tested by Erastistratus who showed that the brain was the origin for all the nerves.

**Surgical Instruments Kom Ombo
(Photograph: Lois Goddard)**

Dissection and surgery at this time in Egypt were becoming very advanced and a range of instruments were available for the use of the operator. In an outer corridor wall of the Egyptian temple of Kom Ombo there is a depiction of 37 surgical instruments carved into the stone. These include shears, knives, saws, spatulas and spoons and probably originate from the Greco-Roman period[30].

The temple was built in the Hellenistic period. The earliest Pharaoh named on its wall is Ptolemy VI Philometor (180BC-163BC). The instruments shown can be compared with those from Pompeii later in this book.[30,31]

Traditional Chinese Medicine

Traditional medicine in China developed over a period of five thousand years. Chinese medicine "views humans as a microcosm of the universe and inherently connected to it, to nature and to all of life" and lays great store in keeping all of the factors in balance and harmony[32].

There are many examples of historical records of Chinese medicine and they include techniques and traditional medicines still in use today:

Nei Ching Su Wen, compiled between 475 BC and 24 AD, is a classical treatise of Chinese healing arts written as a conversation with the Yellow Emperor ((Huang Di Nei Jing) who was the legendary first ancestor of the Chinese nation and mythical ruler (2697-2597 BC) .

The text was compiled by several authors and the major contents of the treatise had appeared in the Warring States sometime between 475 BC and 221 BC. It was added to during the Qin Dynasty (221 BC - 206 BC) and Han Dynasty (206 BC - 220 AD), and was compiled for the public at the early time of the Western-han Dynasty (206 BC - 24 AD)[33].

Recipes For 52 Kinds Of Diseases These were found in the Mawangdui Han Dynasty tomb, dating from 168 B.C.
Artemisia annua, or "sweet wormwood," is mentioned in the work. The herb is recommended for use for hemorrhoids.

"Zhou Hou Bei Ji Feng" ("Handbook of Prescriptions for Emergency Treatments").
The use of sweet wormwood (qing hao) in an infusion for treating fever was described by a Taoist scribe in 340 AD[34].

Note that the same substance (Artemisinin) is becoming an important modern-day treatment of Malaria, having been used successfully in over a million patients.

There are seven major treatments in Chinese medicine:

1. Acupuncture,
2. Moxibustion to acupoints,
3. Tai chi, chi kung and meditation, therapeutic exercises using the power of inner energy
4. Cupping uses cups placed on the skin to treat disease by causing local congestion
5. Tuina massage is a special form of manipulation
6. Diet and nutrition teaches the energetic quality of food
7. Herbal medicine, is the use of raw herbs (usually a last resort) as pills, herbal creams, plasters, poultices.

MEDICINE IN ANCIENT ROME

The Romans noted the link between dirt and disease. They built baths, aqueducts and sewers and drained swamps to combat disease: all examples of successful State intervention in healthcare.

Again this depended on the attitude of the senate or the emperor. Some rulers believed in promoting public services, improving the water supply and cleaning up their cities. Others just gave their subjects access to the circus and ignored public works.

Roman Republic 510BC to 27 BC

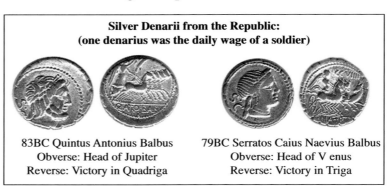

Silver Denarii from the Republic:
(one denarius was the daily wage of a soldier)

83BC Quintus Antonius Balbus
Obverse: Head of Jupiter
Reverse: Victory in Quadriga

79BC Serratos Caius Naevius Balbus
Obverse: Head of V enus
Reverse: Victory in Triga

In the early Roman Republic the only medical services were folk medicine.

The Romans adopted Greek religious ideas and cults. The response to a plague in 431BC was to build the first Roman temple of Apollo. Greek medicine was introduced to Rome by wound specialist Archagathus (219BC). He was initially highly regarded and was given a surgery at public expense : an early example of "state sponsored medicine". Later, due to his savage use of the knife and cautery, he was nicknamed the executioner. He, and all other Greek physicians, had then fallen into disrepute.

More successfully Asclepiades (c.129 - 40 BC) of Bithynia established Greek medicine in Rome. Asclepiades taught that all diseases occur because of an imbalance in the natural harmony of the human body. His doctrine of constricted or relaxed conditions of solid particles derived from the atomic theory of the philosopher Democritos (see page 11). Asclepiades treated mental disorders humanely, he had insane persons freed from confinement and treated them with natural therapy, such as diet and massage

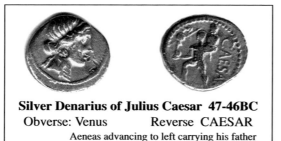

Silver Denarius of Julius Caesar 47-46BC
Obverse: Venus   Reverse CAESAR
Aeneas advancing to left carrying his father
Anchises and Palladium (statue of Athena)

The position of doctors in society was resurrected by Julius Caesar in 46BC. He was perhaps spurred on by the success of Asclepiades or with the considerable assistance that the Greek physicians gave to his wounded soldiers. Whatever the reason, Caesar made the bold move of giving citizenship to all physicians in Rome[35, 36].

Roman Empire 27BC – 5th century AD

Several important texts on medical practice were compiled during the period of the Roman Empire, some of which have survived intact or in partial form. There were possibly many more which did not survive. Unfortunately the Roman Catholic religious establishment in power during the thousand years that followed the fall of Rome considered many ancient writings heretical and destroyed them.

The references to medicine that do persist are very illuminating in that they provide us with an insight into the way in which medical science was developing and how doctors were perceived during this time.

Celsus (or Aulus Cornelius Celsus 25BC-50AD) was a Roman encyclopedia writer. Only his books on medicine (De medicina) survive. He recorded a history of Greek and Alexandrian medicine and books on treatment by diet, by pharmaceuticals and by surgery. In addition to general hygiene, Celsus recommended the washing of wounds with antiseptic substances, such as vinegar and thyme oil. And Celsus's four classical signs of inflammation – *calor*, *dolor*, *rubor*, and *tumor* (heat, pain, redness, and swelling) are still the standard today.

I think we would all agree with the quote from Book 7 " Now a surgeon should be youthful or at any rate nearer youth than age; with a strong and steady hand which never trembles" [37,38]

7BC-29AD*[39] Jesus Christ (*Dates are approximate)

Jesus Christ was a historical figure who lived during the early part of the Roman Empire and was referred to by non-Christian historians (Josephus 93AD, Pliny 112AD, Tacitus 115AD and the Jewish Talmud 70-200AD)[40-44].

As recorded in the Bible, Jesus was a healer of the sick and the disputed Priest/King of the Jews. Since much of his healing consisted of casting out evil spirits he was firmly in the tradition of the Shaman or the Assyrian Ashipu. He did not believe in making a profit from healing and exhorted his disciples to do the same as him: "Heal the sick, cleanse the lepers, raise the dead, cast out devils: freely ye have received, freely give" [45] (Matthew 10:8 AV)

The individual person to be blessed or healed was usually touched by the healer (Jesus or his disciple) in a ceremony of " the laying-on of hands".

Illustration from the Holy Bible Illustrated [46]

15

Despite the views of Jesus Christ that the healing should be freely given it is clear that he was not unaware of money and its significance. In the gospels [47] it is recorded that Jesus was asked 'Is it lawful to give Tribute to Caesar?' The tax or Tribute had been imposed on Judea when it was reduced to a Roman province in 6 AD and had to be paid by all males between the ages of 14 and 65 and all females between the ages of 12 and 65 [48]. The question was designed to put Jesus into a difficult position. The tax was much resented by the populace who believed that the land of Judea had been given to them by God. To suggest it should not be paid would have been interpreted by the Romans as a criminal act of revolt. He cleverly sidestepped the dilemma by asking for a specimen tribute coin to be handed to him. He held the coin up, asking whose image is this? His questioners replied that it was Caesar's. Jesus replied ' Render unto Caesar that which is Caesar's and unto God that which is God's!' Jesus is also recorded as himself paying the required Tribute tax [49]

'Tribute Penny'

The coin that Jesus Christ is most likely to have held was a silver denarius (penny) of the emperor Tiberius, who reigned during that period. The Tribute Penny [50] bears a laureate portrait of Tiberius, the Caesar, on the obverse and a seated figure of Livia, the emperor's mother, on the reverse. It is interesting to speculate whether or not a state or an empire can function without some form of taxation.

The Roman Empire certainly needed money in order to provide its armies and building programmes. These included the aforementioned baths, aqueducts and sewers and the draining of swamps all of which were so important for healthy living.

Tribute is a tax paid by the conquered to the conqueror. Before the advent of money this Tribute tax would probably have been in the form of service, slaves or goods but as soon as money was available it would have been used by the conquering state as the preferred means of taxation. When an Empire stops conquering other nations it has to tax its own citizens, which can be very unpopular and was certainly one of the problems later encountered by the Roman Empire.

Money was mentioned on other occasions in the Gospels. For example, Jesus was very vigorous in overturning the tables of the money-changers in the Temple [51] and Judas Iscariot famously betrayed Jesus for 30 pieces of silver [52]. The latter are likely to have been silver tetradrachm or shekels from Tyre. It is interesting to note that this was the same price as the penalty for letting your ox gore someone's servant [53] in the Laws of Moses and that a very similar penalty was laid down in the Code of Hammurabi hundreds of years before Moses [54].

Copper Coin of Pontius Pilate
(Roman Procurator of Judea 26-36AD)
(Obverse: Lituus, priest's staff)
This coin would have been well known to the money-changers in the temple

Silver Tetradrachm or shekel of Tyre, 1st century BC
The 30 pieces of silver were probably of this type

16

Britain under the Romans

Silver coin of Antedios, Celtic King of the Iceni and father of Queen Boudica (Boadicea)

In 55 and 54BC Julius Caesar had led successful invasions into the South East of England, leaving his own chosen vassal kings in place. Britain was at this time considered to be fairly wealthy due to the high fertility of the land, the equable climate and the trade with the continent of materials such as tin.

Dupondius of Antonia, the mother of Claudius.

Struck circa 41-54 AD. Many colonial imitations of official Roman issue were struck in Britain

The Romans did not return to Britain until 43 AD under Claudius. They eventually conquered England, Wales and Ireland but failed to

Hadrian, silver denarius 133 AD

pacify Scotland . . . hence Hadrian's wall was built to keep the Scots and the Picts north of the border.

Britain became fully part of the Roman Empire and of *Pax Romana (*the Roman peace). The Roman army would undoubtedly have taken physicians and surgeons with them when they invaded. Their role would have initially been to treat the Roman soldiers and keep them fit for fighting. Once the Roman rule had settled in the doctors would have extended their treatment to those members of the population who were able to pay. The Romans imported into Britain their love of bathing, clean water and sanitation. One of their most important sites was at Aquae Sulis, the famed spa of Bath. The healing powers of these hot baths were already legendary when the Romans invaded. Legend (and it is only a legend[55]) has it that the city had been founded in 863BC by the Celtic Prince Bladud, father of the King Lear of Shakespeare fame. Bladud had supposedly been cured of his leprosy by the waters and he dedicated the hot springs to the goddess Minerva. Aquae Sulis is the Roman name for waters of Minerva.

Simulated picture of a victorious Roman General
viewing the circular bath Aquae Sulis (Bath, UK)

Line drawing of the restored Roman Bath, Aqua Sulis
From the Bristol Med. Chi Journal 1897, Local Medical Notes p380

The complex at Aquae Sulis consisted of a temple and multiple hot baths (some very large) and cold plunge baths. The spring overflow and the great drain are in use today exactly as they were in Roman times. The Roman baths at Bath are the best preserved Roman religious spa from the ancient world.

Hot baths are still used to relieve pain from arthritis and immersion is known to lower blood pressure by instigating diuresis and naturesis. Nowadays they are also used to reduce stress.

Vespasian and the healing touch

Commemorative issue silver denarius Vespasian 80 AD

The Emperor Vespasian started the tradition of 'touch-pieces'. He is said to have given coins to the sick at a ceremony known as the 'touching'. This ceremony was practised up until the time of Queen Anne in England and until 1807 in France.

In the first century AD we note that writers were very scornful of medical practitioners. Doctors were not generally in high regard because of their low cure rate and high charges.

From Ancient Roman authors:

Martial writing in 80AD: *'You are now a gladiator, although until recently you were an ophthalmologist. You did the same thing as a doctor that you do now as a gladiator.'*[56] ....Presumably this consisted of the poking out of eyes!

Gargilius Martialis wrote in the 1st century AD: *'Some doctors charge the most excessive prices for the most worthless medicines and drugs, and others in the craft attempt to deal with and treat diseases they obviously do not understand.'*[57]

These views regarding doctors are very reminiscent of the attitudes and opinions propounded by some modern-day critics of medical practitioners. There is an interesting corollary. At that time the rational approach to medical practice was at the forefront but criticism of medicine was considered acceptable. Previously, when medicine was an arcane art practised by powerful priests or even kings, criticism had been muted ...nobody was going to argue with Amenhotep or Hammurabi as to whether or not their healing arts worked!

Today critics of doctors can be very fierce despite the fact that medical science is more advanced and effective than it has ever previously been. In the fairly recent past (such as the early Victorian era) the word of the doctor was considered to be true, criticism was relatively rare and the medical practitioner's position in society was extremely high even though their medical knowledge and skills were dubious.

The distrust of medical practitioners occurred at a time when surgical expertise was fairly advanced. When Pompeii was destroyed in the year 79AD a house, known to us as 'the surgeon's house', was overwhelmed. Sophisticated surgical instruments found within the house are very similar to instruments used today. Comparisons can be made with the surgical instruments carved on **Kom Ombo** temple wall (see page 12).

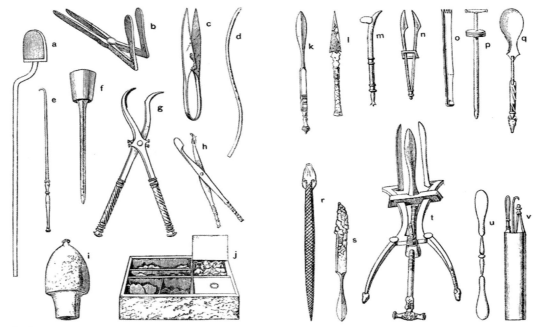

Surgical Instruments from Pompeii: (Illustration reproduced from the Bristol Medico-Chirurgical Journal [58])

a) cautery
b) bivalve speculum
c) scissors
d) male catheter
e) hook
f) point of injection syringe
g) forceps, each branch fitted with an engine-turned handle and a spoon-shaped blade
h) forceps with serrated bite
i) cupping-glass of bronze
j) medicine box with medicines
k) spatula

l) lancet
m) fleam for bleeding horses
n) forceps
o) toothed dissecting forceps
p) trocar
q) small spoon with bone handle
r) female catheter
s) bistoury
t) trivalve speculum
u) spatula
v) metallic case with instruments

Galen 131- 203 AD

Born in Pergamum, Mysia (now Bewrama, Turkey) Galen, by the age of twenty, had served for four years in the local temple as a *therapeutes* ("attendant" or "associate") of the Greek god of medicine, Asklepios[59].

Galen's first professional appointment was as surgeon to the gladiators in Pergamon. In his tenure as surgeon he gained experience and practical knowledge in anatomy from the combat wounds he was compelled to treat. After four years he moved to Rome where he attained a brilliant reputation as a practitioner and a public demonstrator of anatomy.

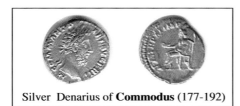

Silver Denarius of **Commodus** (177-192)

Among his patients were the emperors Marcus Aurelius, Lucius Verus, Commodus and Septimius Severus[60].

It is interesting to contemplate that Galen must have been a very successful physician indeed, since he lived to treat several emperors. For a doctor to survive the death of an emperor that he has treated is not that easy and to survive the death of several is very unusual! Their deaths were clearly not blamed on Galen or his reputation was so great that a few dead emperors could not dent it.

In his treatise entitled "That the best Doctor is also a Philosopher" Galen argued that the profit motive was incompatible with a serious devotion to the art of medicine. Galen considered that the doctor must learn to despise money and he accused his colleagues of avarice[60,61]. Galen studied anatomy by experimentation on animals but his dissection of human beings was limited due to prevailing social mores. This did lead to some significant errors in his understanding of human anatomy and physiology.

Galen advanced medical science considerably but in the Middle Ages rigid adherence to his writings held back clinical medicine in a way that the practical Galen would have found abhorrent.

The Fall of Rome

Within the Roman Empire medical services, including fairly advanced surgery, were available, at a price, even in fairly remote parts such as Britain.

Obverse Head of Caesar Constantius Gallus (actual size)
Reverse Soldier spearing fallen horseman (enlarged)
In the final years of the occupation many unofficial British imitations of the above and similar coins were minted showing the 'Soldier spearing fallen horseman'.

But the Roman Empire was coming to an end. Many reasons have been put forward to explain its demise. One reason may have been the splitting of the Empire into two, a Western Empire ruled from Rome and an Eastern Empire, Byzantium, ruled from Constantinople (now Istanbul). In addition the surrounding hordes of Huns, Ostrogoths, Visigoths, Vandals and other races had become more organised whilst the Roman Empire had become progressively more bureaucratic.

It has often been stated in the past that the end of the Ancient civilizations occurred with the sacking of Rome in 410AD. However, with the assistance of the Pope (Innocent I), Rome was restored to the Western emperor (Honorius) and the Western branch of the Roman Empire limped on for a few more years.

Certainly from this time onwards the Roman presence in Britain decreased considerably with the withdrawing of troops to the Continent by Honorius in 411 AD. A Romano-British administration continued for some time afterwards until interrupted by Teutonic invasions.

The troop withdrawal, the gradual decline of central administration and the Teutonic raids led to a rapid deterioration in the money supply. Local copies of the coins from the last few emperors were circulated including, in particular, variants on the coin shown with the 'soldier spearing fallen horseman' reverse. (Incidentally this design may have been gradually 'converted' into the St Michael and the Dragon seen on much later coins such as the gold Angel which were thought to be imbued with healing powers). It was probably not until late in the 6th century that renewed political, commercial and cultural links with the kingdom of the Merovingian Franks led to the appearance of small quantities of Merovingian gold tremisses (one-third solidus) in England. The Sutton Hoo ship burial included such coins[62].

Map of the Tribes and their Territories in Europe 476AD

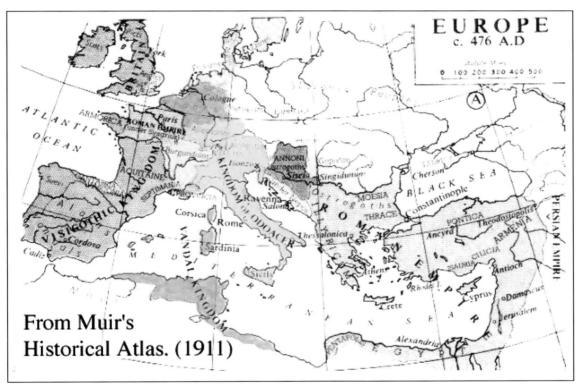

(Muir's Historical Atlas, Public Domain)

476AD is traditionally given as the date of the fall of Rome when Romulus Augustus, the last Emperor of the Western Roman Empire was deposed by the Ostrogoth Odoacer, who ruled as King of Italy. The Ostrogoths did, however, consider that they were continuing the Roman traditions. The Eastern Empire (Byzantium) and the civilizations of India and China continued unabated. In Britain the Celtic and Anglo-Roman settlements continued under nominally Roman control at least in style. All this was to change in the Sixth century AD.

21

Chapter 2

Medicine in the Middle Ages

In the period between 500 and 600 AD momentous changes occurred in Europe, Asia and North Africa[1,2,3].

In Britain the Saxons invaded. On the continent of Europe the Roman Empire shrunk back to a small Eastern remnant (Byzantium) and in the Middle East the prophet Mohammed started the Islamic religion. In India the Gupta Empire fell.

It has been postulated that these changes to a large extent were able to occur as a result of the Justinian Plague which started around 542AD. This in turn may have progressed into a catastrophic pandemic due to the so-called 'Summers without Sun'.

It is from this time that the Middle Ages (Dark Ages or mediaeval period) are dated by some sources: *The mediaeval period may be said to begin with the great plague* (bubonic) *which arose in lower Egypt in the reign of Justinian (AD542) and spread over the whole empire of the east and west. Nothing checked its progress*[4]

Justinian I 482-565 (Eastern Roman Emperor 527-565)

Large bronze Follis, Justinian regnal year XIII (539-540)

Justinian Gold Solidus

Obverse	Reverse
Head of Justinian (facing)	Angel holding long cross and globus cross

The coins from the part of Justinian's reign just before the plague, such as this Bronze Follis and Gold Solidus, are highly valued because they are of better style and size. They proved their users with a solid assurance of value.

Justinian had come from a humble background but was a very able man and his actions whilst emperor had profound effects on the history of Europe and the whole World. He undertook huge building projects, such as cathedrals, and set up the Justinian Legal Code (*Corpus Juris Civilis*). This code is still the basis of the civil legal system for much of Europe. The United Kingdom has had a different legal system, being based on precedent rather than a single code, but integration with Europe via the European Union must mean that the Justinian Code is becoming progressively more significant in the UK.

It is, however, for a great disaster that Justinian is widely remembered . . . the Justinian Plague.

When Justinian became Byzantine Emperor in 527AD he immediately set about regaining the fallen lands of the Western Empire. He was an excellent administrator and leader and his initial successes were considerable. He retook Spain, much of North Africa and a considerable part of Italy. He appeared poised to retake nearly the whole Empire but his campaign with nearly invincible armies collapsed due to a series of natural catastrophes. These included volcanic eruptions, a massive earthquake, sunless summers and the first-recorded pandemic of Bubonic Plague.

536-545 AD Summers without sun worldwide

In the ten years between 536 and 545 momentous events appear to have affected the entire world. Tree ring records show minimal growth in this period and contemporary historians record loss of power of the sun... the so-called " Summers without sun".

Flavius Cassiodorus wrote regarding the year AD 536 : *The Sun...seems to have lost its wonted light, and appears of a bluish colour*

Lydus : *The Sun became dim...for nearly the whole year...so that the fruits were killed at an unseasonable time.*

Procopius (Byzantine Historian): *.. the Sun gave forth its light without brightness*

Michael the Syrian : *The Sun became dark and its darkness lasted for eighteen months*

John of Ephesis, A Syrian bishop, *There was a sign from the Sun, the likes of which had never been seen or reported before. The Sun became dark, and its darkness lasted for about 18 months. Each day, it showed for about four hours and still this light was only a feeble shadow. Everyone declared that the Sun would never recover its full light again.*

China, *the stars were lost from view for three months*

Further sources state that in China drought caused the tax base to collapse and destabilized the ruling powers and that in South America the drought caused the collapse of the Teotihuacan empire[5]

23

Tree ring analysis show abnormally little growth in Irish oak in 536 and another sharp drop in 542, similar patterns are recorded in Sweden, Finland and Sierra Nevada Prof. Mike Baillie has shown five ages of minimal tree ring growth which correspond with "dark ages" in civilization including the period between AD 536 and 545[5].

It has been suggested that this may have been due to extreme volcanic activity or due to meteorites. The eruption of the Indonesian volcano Krakatoa (or a volcano previous to Krakatoa at the same site, proto-krakatoa) has been put forward by some scientists as the most probable trigger for all these events[6]. "Under a likely scenario, a large volcano, which Wohletz calls proto-Krakatoa, connected the islands of Sumatra and Java. When it erupted and then subsided, it created the Sundra Strait and left a ring of smaller volcanoes, including the present day Krakatoa. The ash, dust and water vapor blown into the stratosphere would disperse across both the Northern and Southern Hemispheres."

The twenty year period between 535 and 555 AD began with "significant solar darkening and a sudden, significant worldwide temperature decline. Floods and droughts, crop failures, plagues, and famines followed this global cooling of the climate"[7]

Justinian Plague 542

In 542 AD plague broke out in the capital of the Empire, Constantinople. The plague was reported to have begun in central Asia, spread into Egypt, and then made its way through Europe reaching Britain by 547AD. [8,9,10,11]. Bubonic plague is spread by rats and fleas and these may have been driven into close proximity with human beings by lack of food and the wet and cold conditions. The military campaigns of Justinian added to the spread of the plague with devastating outbreaks occurring throughout his armies. Procopius (Byzantine Historian) recorded that at its peak the plague was killing 10,000 people per day in Constantinople. This figure may be disputed but certainly so many people were dying that there was difficulty in burying the dead. Justinian ordered gigantic pits to be built outside the city and these also filled to overflowing,[11]. "The initial plague went on to destroy up to a quarter of the human population of the eastern Mediterranean. New, frequent waves of the plague continued to strike throughout the 6th, 7th and 8th centuries, often more localized and less virulent. A maximum figure of 25 million dead for the Plague of Justinian is considered a fairly reasonable estimate. Some historians such as Josiah C. Russell[12] have suggested a total European population loss of 50 to 60 percent between 541 and 700."

The symptoms and signs of the Justinian Plague are well described. Evagrius and Procopius, for example, had first hand experience of the plague. Evagrius was a lawyer and honorary prefect living in the city of Antioch at the time of the plague. He wrote his *Historia Ecclesiastica* covering the years 431-594 at the end of the sixth century, Procopius, the legal secretary of General Belisarius traveled with Belisarius throughout Justinian's campaigns in Italy, the Balkans, and in Africa. In 542, Procopius witnessed the plague in Constantinople.

Symptoms started with hallucinations, fever and fatigue with some people suffering from a sore throat and diarrhoea. These symptoms soon led on to the characteristic sign of Bubonic Plague: swellings or buboes in the groin and armpits. These suppurated or became gangrenous. Death occurred in the vast majority affected.

This is the first recorded plague that can with any certainty be ascribed to Bubonic Plague. It is due to *Yersinia* (or *Pasteurella) pestis* and transmitted generally by the black rat, *Rattus rattus*. The medical personnel at that time had no idea that it was spread in this way. Some people thought that it was spread by cats and dogs (which can catch the plague) and destroyed as many as they could. This may perversely have allowed the rats to flourish. Even Justinian was personally affected. He was treated successfully by Sampson (later called St Sampson), a physician from Rome. In gratitude the emperor built him a large hospital The Hospice of St Sampson.

As the world's first known pandemic spread throughout the empire (and beyond) the military campaigns of Justinian faltered and failed. At home Justinian had to suppress revolts against increased taxes. The plague and the failed military adventures led to financial ruin of the empire. The under-population led to major social change. The old world was dominated by empires with a slave workforce. This could not continue. Serfdom and nation states developed. Religious orders of monks were initially devastated by the plague since it spreads quickly in areas of high population and between people living in close quarters. Despite this, the Church benefited both financially and with power. The Justinian plague and the subsequent waves of the plague which affected each generation, were seen as evidence of God's wrath against sinful leaders and wicked people. The Roman Catholic Church gained ascendancy over the rational argument.

This is put very well by Miguel A Faria, Jr.[14]

> "The humbling of the medical profession because of its impotence to control the plague of the 6th Century, essentially halted the advancement of medical knowledge for centuries. Medicine regressed, and disease in general was equated with vice and sin, rather than with filth, poor hygiene, and natural causes. Yet, medicine was not the only profession in abeyance to disease. Other ancient professions, such as law, engineering, and the natural sciences (not to mention the liberal arts of the Greeks and Romans), were largely erased from the collective memory of humanity. All areas of human endeavor were doomed to intellectual dormancy. Progress stopped. The turning wheels of Western culture and civilization had ground to a shrilling halt as humanity became fully immersed in the Dark Ages".

European Medicine was dominated by the religious belief that illness was a punishment for sin. The secular medical profession disappeared to be replaced by religious establishments. Monasteries provided spiritual guidance and medical services. Hospitals were set up by the Church. Universities in Western Europe were all religious establishments, as many still are today.

25

After the fall of Rome and the shrivelling of Byzantium, medical and other sciences in Europe suffered under a cloud of civil unrest, repeated wars and religious bigotry. There was no coordinated medical advance for a very long time. Government intervention in health care consisted mainly of Kings using their 'healing touch' or proclaiming prohibition of playhouses and isolation edicts in times of Plague. For 1000 years there were constant problems of various plagues, pestilence and famine. Galen was the one acceptable source of medical knowledge. For a millennium science, or natural philosophy, was severely hampered and medicine, with its cautious adherence to dogma and authority, showed no progress and continued harmful practices such as blood-letting until the middle of the 19th century. In much of Europe any ancient texts disagreeing with Galen were forbidden and any doctors discovering new knowledge were considered as heretical. This was at a time when to be heretical was to be condemned to death.

Early Anglo-Saxon England

**Anglo-Saxon Sceat or penny
(Debased coinage of copper)
Obverse: facing bust,
Reverse: Runes**

Little is known about medicine in England in the early Anglo-Saxon period. From oral tradition it is likely that they used herbal remedies and leeches and wore amulets in an attempt to protect them from harm and keep them healthy. These may have included earlier better-formed coins, such as the 'soldier spearing fallen horseman' type (see the end of chapter 1). One extreme epidemic was described by the Venerable Bede. This was the Yellow Plague which arrived in the South of England in 664AD, overran the whole country and spread to Ireland. The exact nature of this plague is still unknown but possibilities which have been advanced include Yellow Fever, Hepatitis or Leptospirosis. The Yellow Plague continued at intervals until 685. Of the Irish it is said that two out of three died. Bede (c.672-735) recorded that the devastation from the plague caused the East Saxons to revert to paganism[15].

For advances in science and medicine we have to look at the Chinese Empire or the emerging Islamic world.

Traditional Chinese Medicine 600 AD

T'ang Dynasty One Cash Coin with crescent mark on reverse The legend is that The Empress 'Wende' stuck one of her fingernails into a wax model of the coin when it was presented to her. The Emperor retained the mark as part of the design [16]

T'ang Cash Coin issued 621-907 AD

In the early part of T'ang Dynasty Emperor Taizong's reign (January 23, 599–July 10, 649), the government opened medical schools and specialist subjects were devised and studied. Then during the reign of Emperor Gaozong (649-683) the government implemented the compilation of the T'ang Materia Medica. This had the distinction of being the first ever pharmacopoeia to be published by a state and it was not for some 800 years or so that a similar project was undertaken in Europe[17]

Islamic Medicine

Islamic silver coin 278 AH (900 AD) (Umayyid, Arab ruler of Spain 228—278AH)

The Islamic hospitals of the Arabic world at the turn of the first millennium (1000 AD) provided services to the rich and the poor and were more advanced than those of Europe. Most of the science was based on translations of the ancient writings of Hippocrates and Galen but in addition real advances were made by Islamic surgeons and physicians. Large hospitals were involved in the training and licensing of doctors and pharmacists. Islamic rulers realised the importance of licensing to maintain standards.

In 931 AD the Caliph Al-Mugtadir from the Abbasid dynasty, ordered the Chief Court-Physician Sinan Ibn-Thabit to screen the 860 physicians-of Baghdad, and only those qualified were granted license to practice. The counterpart of Ibn- Tbabit, Abu-Osman Sai'd Ibn-Yaqub was ordered to do the same in Damascus, Mecca, and Medina. The latter two cities were in need of such an act because hundreds of thousands of pilgrims visited them every year[18].

The Roman Bridge, Cordoba

The best medieval surgical encyclopedia was entitled "Al-Tastif Liman Ajiz'an Al-Ta'lif'"
The author was Al-Zahrawi (930-1013AD) who is also known as Abulcasis. He was a prominent Arabic surgeon and author who was born and practised in Cordoba, Spain. He stressed the importance of basic sciences "Before practising, the physician should be familiar with the science of anatomy and the functions of organs so that he will understand them, recognize their shape, understand their connections, and know their borders. Also he should know the bones, nerves, and muscles, their numbers, their origin and insertions, the arteries and the veins, their start and end. These anatomical and physiological bases are important, and as said by Hippocrates: 'There are many physicians by title and a few by practice.'"[19]

11th century Iranian copper crucible for indigo
(British Museum)
Abulcasis catalogued Indigo for medicinal use.

Ibn Sina (980-1037) known in the West by his Latinised name of Avicenna, was a Muslim polymath who outshone even Abulcasis. He was the foremost philosospher and scientist of his age. His first appointment after studying medicine, was that of physician to the Emir, who owed him his recovery from a dangerous illness. Avicenna discovered the contagious nature of diseases such as Tuberculosis, he instigated quarantine to limit spread of contagion, he introduced systematic experimentation and quantification into the study of physiology and medicine and described the concept of momentum in physics. In addition he was a statesman and soldier and at one time was raised to the level of Visier of Bukbara and Hainadan, the south of Persia.

Avicenna wrote 100 treatises, including the Canon of Medicine (Al-Qanon fi Al- Tibb), an encyclopedia containing more than one million words. Composed of 5 volumes:
Volume I- described the principles and theories of medicine.
Volume II- contained the simple drugs arranged alphabetically.
Volume III- described localized diseases of the body from the head to the toes.
Volume IV- was addressed to generalized diseases of the body e.g. fevers.
Volume V- explained compound drugs[19]
Many of his maxims for carrying out a drug trial remain true to this day such as:
- The drug must be free from any extraneous accidental quality.
- The time of action must be observed, so that essence and accident are not confused.
- The experimentation must be done with the human body, for testing a drug on a lion or a horse might not prove anything about its effect on man.

In the 12th century the reputation of Moses Maimonides, who like Abulcasis was also born in Cordoba, outshone all others. Born in Cordoba Spain in 1135. Maimonides became the Rabbi of the Jewish Community of El-Fostat city (part of old Cairo) the capital of Egypt at that time. He later practised medicine and was a particularly eminent and respected physician. He served both Kings Salah-El-Din (Saladin) and his elder son Sultan Al-Malik Al-Afdel

During Saladin's war with King Richard, the Lion-Heart, the latter fell sick. Although those two kings were at war, they respected and admired each other. Saladin sent Maimonedes to Richard to treat him. After being, cured. Richard asked Maimonedes to join his court. But the latter politely declined and preferred to stay with Saladin

Maimonides translated Arabic books, including the Canon of Avicenna, into Hebrew and they were then translated into Latin and other European languages. Maimonides' own books include
- "Magala fl Tadbir Al-Sihha" (Regimen Sanitatis) stressing proper diet, personal hygiene, and moderation in the pleasures of life.
- "Kitab" Al-Fusal fi Al-Tibb" (Fisul Musa). A collection of 1,500 aphorisms extracted from Galen writings together with forty-two critical remarks.
- A book on poisons and their antidotes. ([19,20,21])

England and Wales
Edward the Confessor and the Touch-Piece

Edward the Confessor from the Litlyngton Missal 1383 AD
With permission (Copyright: Dean and Chapter of Westminster)

Edward the Confessor, who reigned between 1042 and 1066, was the penultimate Anglo-Saxon King of England. He is said to have reintroduced the ceremony started by the Roman Emperor Vespasian in which the monarch touched the sick patient and gave him or her a coin as a 'touch-piece' to aid the cure.

Edward the Confessor Silver Penny
(Hammer Cross Type)

The coin would probably have been a silver penny since that was the only denomination in Edward's reign. This practice was continued by English and French Monarchs until the 18th and 19th centuries. Edward was made a saint in 1161 and his body was moved to a shrine in Edward's own cathedral, Westminster Abbey. He became the patron saint of England from Henry II's reign until 1348.

From the reign of Edward IV onwards the coin given during the touching ceremony was a gold piece known as an Angel. The Angel coin was introduced into the currency at one third of a pound or six shillings and eight pence with a weight of 80 grains (5.2gm).

This odd denomination had become the standard fee for professional work (including that of doctors) and a coin at that value had to be re-introduced when the old gold coin worth a third of a pound (the noble) was revalued to 8s 4d.

Hospitals

In England and Wales about 1200 hospitals, run initially by the Church, were set up after 1100AD and provided some help for the poor. The oldest surviving examples are St Bartholomew's Hospital in London (set up in 1123) and St John's Hospital, Canterbury (1184).

St Bartholomew's Hospital is situated in Smithfield in the City of London. It was founded in 1123 AD by Raherus or Rahere (died 1144), a favorite courtier of King Henry I. The hospital has a continuing current role as a National Health Service Teaching and District Hospital well as a long history and architecturally important buildings[22].

St John's Hospital, Canterbury was founded in 1184. The rules of the medieval hospital state 'sick and weak people should be admitted kindly and mercifully, except for pregnant women, lepers, the wounded, cripples and the insane[23].' According to the website about St John's Hospital 'there were almost as many hospitals as there were monasteries. The name hospital comes from the Latin hospes, which means guest, stranger or foreigner. Hospitals in the middle ages were not places where people went to be cured. They provided shelter for travellers, the elderly and the sick. Usually they were run by monks or nuns and would offer some general nursing skills. There were no doctors in medieval hospitals until after the Black Death'[23].

The clergy monopolized all the professions during this period and undertook the tasks of both physicians and surgeons. But the religious sentiment apparently became offended by the shedding of blood by the ecclesiastical surgeons and in 1215 Pope Innocent III put out a papal edict that no operations were to be performed that involved such a result. The clergy, no longer permitted to perform the surgical operations themselves, employed barbers to perform this task under their direction[24].

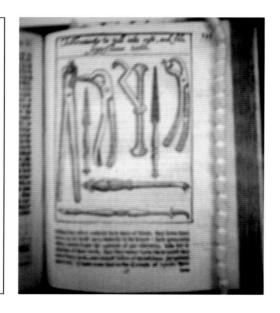

Illustration of Surgical Instruments in the Middle Ages and Early Modern Period
(Salisbury Cathedral, England)
Peter Lowe, A discourse of the whole Art of Chyrurgerie 3rd ed., 1634

Comparing the illustration of surgical instruments with those of Kom Ombo and Pompeii featured earlier in this book it is clear that there was very little change over a period of more than a thousand years. Several of the instruments are identical with those of Pompeii whilst some are cruder than the older instruments.

In the 13th century occultist, alchemist and learned physician Arnold of Villanova (c.1238-c.1310) searched for an effective anaesthetic. In a book usually credited to him, a variety of medicines are named and different methods of administration are set out, designed to make the patient insensible to pain, so that "he may be cut and feel nothing, as though he were dead." For this purpose, a mixture of opium, mandragora, and henbane was to be used. This method was similar to inhaling the vapours of the soporific sponge mentioned around 1200 AD by Nicholas of Salerno, and sporadically in different sources from the 9th to 14th centuries[25]. Also around 1300 the use of cauterisation was rediscovered by the French surgeon Henri de Mondeville (1260-1320).

The Black Death

Edward III (1327-77)
Silver Halfpenny
Minted in London
The Black Death started
during his reign.

In the year 1348 the second world pandemic of pestilence occurred (the first having been the Justinian Plague). The incurable plague known as the 'Black Death' swept across Europe killing a third of the population. The exact nature of the Black Death is not known. It was very probably a variant of Bubonic/Pneumonic plague but it has some unusual features. Other possibilities, such as Ebola virus or Anthrax have been postulated. The Black Death arrived in Britain on the 25th June through Weymouth. This is documented in the Grey Friars Chronicle. *"In this year 1348 in Melcombe, in the county of Dorset, a little before the feast of St. John the Baptist, two ships, one of them from Bristol came alongside. One of the sailors had brought with him from Gascony the seeds of the terrible pestilence and through him the men of that town of Melcombe were the first in England to be infected"*.

The plague spread to villages on the outskirts of Weymouth and villagers fled to the cities taking the Black Death with them. Edward III ordered that the movement of the villagers should be restricted but the Death spread killing between 30-50% of the total population. The plague struck several more times in the 14th century with 1361 (pestis secunda) 1369 (pestis tertia) 1375 (pestis quatra) and 1379-83 (pestis quinta) and 1390-91 being particularly bad years.

Geoffrey Chaucer (c.1340-1400), the English Poet, was a young lad at the beginning of the Black Death pandemic. His ambivalent attitude towards the medical profession may have been shaped by their obvious inability to deal successfully with the plague. In the Canterbury Tales he indicates that his 'doctor of phisyk', although exceedingly well read, was a charlatan relying on astrology to treat his patient. (Astrology had entered medical practice via Islamic physicians).

Note that Chaucer's physician was not interested in the bible. Perhaps if the first pandemic can be blamed for creating the so-called Dark Ages, the second pandemic may have assisted in changing the world order. The grip the clergy had on the practise of medicine was weakening, at least in England, by the time Chaucer wrote his poetry. The last few lines indicate that the doctor's greatest love was not heavenly saints but gold which he would have received as professional fees from the patients. I have included here an adapted modern English translation.[25,26,27]

'With us there was a doctor of medicine;
In all this world was none like him
For talk of medicine and surgery;
For he was grounded in astronomy.
He often kept a patient from the pall
By horoscopes and magic natural.
Well could he tell the fortune ascendent
Within the houses for his sick patient.
He knew the cause of every malady,
Were it of hot or cold, of moist or dry,
And where engendered, and of what humour;
He was a very good practitioner.
The cause being known, down to the deepest root,
Soon he gave to the sick man his boot.
Ready he was, with his apothecaries,
To send him drugs and all electuaries;
By mutual aid much gold they'd always won
Their friendship was a thing not new begun.
Well read was he in Asklepios,
And Deiscorides, and in Rufus,
Hippocrates, and Hali, and Galen,
Serapion, Rhazes, and Avicen,
Averrhoes, Gilbert, and Constantine,
Bernard and Gatisden, and John Damascene.
In diet he was measured as could be,
Including naught of superfluity,
But nourishing and easy. It's no libel
To say he read but little in the Bible.
In blue and scarlet he went clad, as well
Lined with a taffeta and with other silk:
And yet he was right chary of expense;
He kept the gold he gained from pestilence.
For gold in medicine is a fine cordial,
And therefore loved he gold exceeding all.'

**Chaucer's Doctour of Phisyk (Medicine)
Taken from the Ellesmere MS of the
Canterbury Tales**
Reproduced from the Bristol-Medicochirurgical J.

**Henry VI silver 4d (groat)
Issued between 1430-34**

National Epidemics of Plague in the 15th Century

Bubonic/pneumonic plague were epidemic nationally over the following periods and were locally epidemic in many years in between: 1405-1406, 1411-1412, 1428-1429, 1433-1435, 1438-1439, 1463-1465, 1467, 1471 1479-1480, 1499-1500
The plague continued into the sixteenth century which opened with 'a great pestilence throughout all England'. The plague story will be continued in the next chapter.[29,30,31,32,33]

Traditional Chinese Medicine 1518 AD

Li Shizen
                 Jade cup Ming Dynasty 16ᵗʰ-17ᵗʰ century (Brit Mus)

Li Shizen, was born in 1518 in a quiet village in today's Hubei province of China.
He compiled the Bengcau Gamu (The Great Herbal Compendium or Compendium of Materia Medica) which at the time was the world's largest and most comprehensive materia medica.

The work consisted of 52 volumes divided into monographs, which Li called "gang." His starting reference point was the 800 medical texts available in his time, supplemented by travelling and seeking out herbs and herbal remedies by himself.

The Compendium took 30 years to complete and included 1892 medicinal substances, over 300 of which were never before recorded. 10,000 prescriptions were included in the Compendium with the names of ingredients, their descriptions and preparation. Li Shizen corrected mistakes from other records and commented on the history of use of the herbs, their origin and utility. The Compendium was translated into European languages in the 17ᵗʰ century[34].

Li Shizen rediscovered the use of sweet wormwood (qing hao) in an infusion for treating malaria previously described by a Taoist scribe in 340 AD, in"Zhou Hou Bei Ji Feng" ("Handbook of Prescriptions for Emergency Treatments"). This was rediscovered yet again in 1972, when Chinese scientists took an interest in the plant's reputed qualities. They successfully extracted the plant's active compound, calling it 'qing hao su' – transcribed into artemisinin in conventional scientific terminology, after the herb's Latin name, Artemisia annua. This is now being used in the fight against drug-resistant malaria.[35]

In a malaria epidemic in the early 1990s in Vietnam, artemisinin reduced the death rate by 97%.[36,37]

Chapter 3
Medicine in the Early Modern Period

Renaissance

The Renaissance is usually said to have begun with the fall of Byzantium. Constantinople had withstood all attacks for over a thousand years but in 1453 fell to the invading Islamic forces. The Ottoman Empire achieved its first success against Byzantium in 1301 and had grown in strength and boldness over the next century and a half. The Greek and Roman churches were fiercely divided and Byzantium received no help from the West. The fall of Constantinople ushered in 150 years of greatness for the Ottomans with the high point being the reign of Suleiman the Magnificent (1520-1566). During his reign culture flourished. Mosques were built of magnificent size and beauty rivaling the cathedrals of Europe.

The knowledge of Byzantium had been sequestered for a millennium. Western Europe had been under the thrall of the Roman Catholic Church in which heretics were punished with particularly nasty deaths and any work deemed heretical was ceremonially burnt. Some cities, particularly in Germany, had appointed town physicians and midwives to help look after citizens and to advise the authorities on matters of public health. These examples of intervention in healthcare on the part of political masters and rulers were isolated and were not organized at a national level[1].

Byzantium, under the Orthodox version of Christianity, was different. The ancient texts had been preserved and much of the art and science of the Greeks and Romans was suddenly available again. In addition knowledge from the Arabic world, such as mathematics, was presented to much of Europe for the first time. The Renaissance started in Italy and spread through Europe, reconnecting the west with classical antiquity. Printing presses had just been invented and the dissemination of knowledge during this period was exceptional.[2]

From an old printed MS reproduced in the Bristol Med-Chi J. (December 1912)

"Of the Woundes in the Heed come by cuttynge and brekynge."

"Yf there be cuttynge and brekynge of the heed yet not to the percing of the braine panne, this wounde may not be sewed in the myddes of ye heed because she maye not clense by herselfe. Therefore she must be dryed with tentes and other thynges to sucke out ye matter or elles there myght abyde corrupcyon in the myddes of ye ii tables to the hurtynge of the bones."

The Middle Ages were dark not because the history of Greece had been forgotten but because the art and culture of classical times had been lost. With the Renaissance Europe began to shake of the fetters of ignorance and art was at the forefront of the revival. Medicine benefited from the resurgence of art particularly with regard to the illustration of anatomy. (The Debt of Medicine to the Fine Arts, Bristol Med Chi J, Vol 40 pp1-29, 1923).

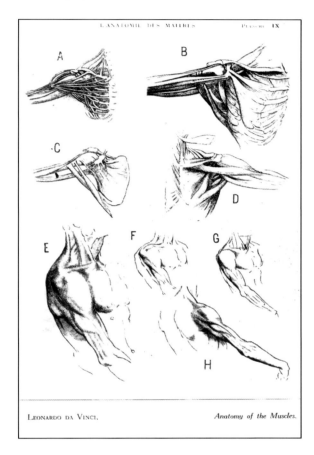

When Leonardo da Vinci, perhaps the greatest renaissance man of all, was born in 1452 Europe had roughly 30,000 books. By the time he died in 1519 it had many millions. Leonardo da Vinci was passionate about nature. He collaborated with the anatomist Della Torre by illustrating Torre's anatomical treatise and also wrote and illustrated anatomy from his own observations. He kept many of his anatomical observations secret and lived by his paintings and inventions for patrons such as Duke Lodovico Sforza, and Giuliano de' Medici, brother of Pope Leo X.

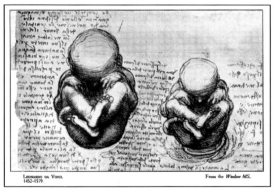

Above and right
Anatomical drawings by Leonardo da Vinci

In Britain the Renaissance and the Early Modern Period did not really start until the end of the War of the Roses and the accession to the throne by Henry VII in 1485.

The Renaissance sparked Reformation in the Church led by Martin Luther and John Calvin. In 1517 Martin Luther, an Augustinian monk in Germany, protested against Rome by nailing his 95 theses to the Wittenberg church door decrying and demonstrating the faults he perceived in Roman Catholicism. This resulted in the formation of the Protestant church. Calvin started his own protestant movement, and took over the government of Switzerland as a religious dictatorship.

1518 England. The College of Physicians was founded in London with a charter from Henry VIII. A standard for entry was set and formally assessed.[1] The physicians had to be educated gentlemen able to supervise barber-surgeons and apothecaries. In 1533 Henry VIII broke away from Rome for personal reasons rather than religious. He sacked the monasteries and undoubtedly many hospitals run by monks would have been adversely affected. Certainly St James's Hospital (a leper hospital) in London was closed and Henry built himself a palace in its place (St James's Palace).

On the plus side the 'Company of Barber-Surgeons of London' was set up as a craft guild in 1540.

Henry VIII presenting a charter to the Barber Surgeons of London
(From the painting by Holbein, as reproduced in the Bristol Med. Chi J Dec. 1887)

St. Bartholomew's Hospital was put in a precarious financial position by the closing of the monasteries until it was re-founded by Henry VIII in December 1546, on the signing of an agreement granting the hospital to the City of London, which was reaffirmed in the Letters Patent of January 1547 endowing it with properties and income.

Henry VIII Groat (4d)
Minted in Bristol in 1547
Consisting mainly of copper with only a small silver component. The blanched silver surface soon wore away to reveal the copper alloy underneath earning Henry the nickname of 'Old Coppernose'.

By the end of his reign in 1547, Henry VIII and the country were bankrupt. He debased the coinage and set up several extra mints to keep up with the demand for money.

The Reformation, the break from Rome by Henry VIII and the start of the early modern period in Europe allowed more freedom of thought and permitted progress in medical science to go ahead. Previously dissenters from the wisdom of Galen and Aristotle had been in danger of being considered as heretics and even faced death.

36

Many Continental Europeans still had to be careful or face the wrath of the Catholic Church (or the similarly dangerous ire of Calvin!) Despite these considerable problems scientific discoveries occurred at an accelerating pace as shown in the next few pages.

The Renaissance was an intellectual and ideological change affecting a select few. For the majority of people many of the negative factors of the "medieval" period may have initially worsened. These included poverty, ignorance, warfare, religious and political persecution. Outbreaks of plague in England, particularly in London, certainly intensified until the great fire of 1666. This was also the age of the Wars of Religion, the corrupt Borgia Popes, the intensified witch-hunts of the 16th century and, of course, the Spanish Inquisition. This ran from 1478 until it was stopped by Napoleon between 1808 and 1812. It was then reinstated by Ferdinand VII of Spain until it was officially ended in 1834.

In 1513 Niccolo Machiavelli, a senior civil servant, wrote a study of political power called *The Prince*. This placed expediency above morality and advocated the use of deceit and cunning to retain authority. The work was published posthumously in 1532. Although at the time considered acceptable by his political masters his publications were considered by many to be immoral. To be Machiavellian was almost synonymous with being evil until very recently when many of his ideas appear to have been rehabilitated and taken up by the new proponents of subjects such as *Human Resource Management*.

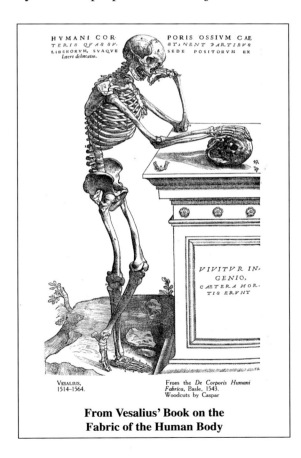

From Vesalius' Book on the Fabric of the Human Body

Andreas Vesalius (1514-64) exposed the anatomical errors of Galen in his book of 1543 entitled *De humani corporis fabrica*$_3$ (Fabric of the Human Body). He was able to do this and avoid the inquisition by stating that he was demonstrating the glory of the human body as designed by God. He established the importance of good illustration in the teaching of gross anatomy.

Avoiding the religious bigots and their murderous tendencies was not always that easy. On October 27th 1553 John Calvin, the founder of Calvinism and dictator of Switzerland, had Michael Servetus, the Spanish physician, burned at the stake just outside Geneva for his doctrinal heresies of anti-Trinitarianism and anti-paedobaptism.

Servetus was hated by both Catholics and Protestants because of his intelligent arguments about doctrine. Servetus had corresponded with Calvin by letter and made the fatal mistake of believing that Calvin was more progressive and open-minded than he turned out to be. In his medical and anatomical studies Servetus had discovered that the difference between the arterial and venous blood was the air that we breathed. He described the pulmonary circulation accurately; 'It is during its passage from the one system of vessels to the other that the blood comes in contact with the air, assumes a scarlet colour and is purged of its impurities, which are expelled by expiration'. Servetus' treatise *On the restoration of Christianity* which contained his discovery, and of which only a few charred fragments remain in the Imperial Library of France, was burned with him. The discovery was lost for 6 years[4] until in 1559 the pulmonary circulation was rediscovered independently by Realdus Columbus, a professor of Padua[5]. One cannot help wondering how many more discoveries were made in this time of great change only to be lost for a while due to the persecution of scientists by organized religion.

In 1574 Fabricius d'Aquapendente, also in Padua, discovered the valves of the veins. Harvey was one of his pupils[5]. In 1590 Hans and Zacharias Jansen in the Netherlands invented the compound microscope with two or more lenses.[1] The simple (one-lensed) microscope was preferred at this time since the compound microscope was hampered by chromatic aberration.

Elizabeth I Poor Law Acts (1598 and 1601)

In England before the Poor Law acts were brought in under Queen Elizabeth, medical services for the majority of common folk consisted of 'magical' touching and muttered spells by a village 'cunning man' or 'wise woman'[6]. Magical healing, which is in the tradition of the Shaman, was against church doctrine and the healer would include a Christian prayer to appease the church. Toothache, for example, was treated by the sufferer writing down three times: *Jesus Christ for mercy sake, Take away this toothache*.

Elizabeth I half-groat (two pence) issued from 1582-1600

Queen Elizabeth kept up the tradition of the healing touch for Scrofula (King's Evil) giving each sick patient a gold Angel. This was now worth ten shillings (120 old pence) which was a considerable sum at a time when a night's lodging in a feather bed might have cost just one penny a night and a loaf of bread cost a half-groat (two pence). The healing ceremony was included in the prayer book (Book of Common Prayer).

State sponsored medicine, perhaps present under the rule of the Roman Empire but not afterwards, was partially re-introduced into England and Wales by Elizabeth I, via the Poor Law Acts of 1598 and 1601. The acts empowered parish officials to pay nurses and midwives, surgeons and apothecaries to attend the sick poor. Nursing care was mostly provided within patients' homes but in some parishes infirmary wards were constructed, especially for the elderly[3, 5]. In Europe this is one of the very first examples of a secular system of medicine and nursing set up by State instigation since continental nursing orders were nearly all under the auspices of the Catholic Church.

Reverse (Actual size)
Enlargement of James I silver penny 1603/4

Costumes worn by physicians of this era to protect them when visiting the plague-stricken (From the Bristol-Med.Chi J. March 1898)

The Plague of 1603 coincided with the accession of James I to the throne of England. The plague began in the parish of Stepney at the time of Queen Elizabeth's death in March and by the date of the coronation of James, July 18th, the deaths had reached 1000 a week. "The victims came mostly from the crowded lanes of the sinfully polluted suburbs" wrote James Bamford, minister of St Olave's. He found that the infection was most rife among "such as do not greatly regard clean and sweet keeping and are pestered together in alleys and houses". All those who could flee from the city did so, including almost all the doctors. James I, a believer in the divine rights of kings but a Presbyterian, was persuaded to continue the practice of 'touching' to cure the King's Evil on the grounds that it would not be a popular act if he stopped what had become a form of 'Royal Health Service'. He presumably did not try 'touching' to cure the plague!

William Shakespeare

In 1603 one physician who honourably stayed at his post in Warwick Lane was Dr. Thomas Lodge. Lodge was better remembered as a poet having written *Rosalynde,* the source of William Shakespeare's As You Like It. In 1603 Lodge published *A Treatise of the Plague.*
Towards the end of 1603 King James granted a licence to reopen the Curtain and Boar's Head theatres as soon as the plague decreased to thirty deaths per week in London.[7,8]

The plague of 1625 coincided with the accession of Charles I. Dr Thomas Lodge died when fighting the plague in 1625 and the same plague killed another of Shakespeare's collaborators; John Fletcher (1579-1625)[7,9] Charles I was the last king to give Angels as 'touch-pieces' when using the royal touch to cure scrofula.

Charles I Shilling

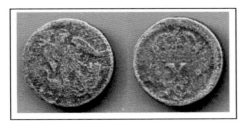

Brass Coin weight for the Charles I Angel. On the obverse the Archangel St. Michael, defeating the devil depicted as a dragon (or heraldic Wyvern). On the reverse a crown over the figures X/S (for ten shillings). Coin weights were used to check the weight of gold and silver coins. Normally they would correspond to the lowest weight at which the coin remained legal tender thus guarding against clipped, worn and counterfeit coins. The Angel had been revalued to ten shillings (half a pound) and this coin weight shows that the weight of gold in the Angel had been officially reduced to 50 grains (3.24gm).

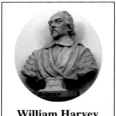

William Harvey
(Roy. C. of Surgeons)

In 1628 William Harvey published his theory of the systemic circulation with the heart acting as a pump. The anatomists had been getting closer and closer to this theory over the intervening years between the time of Vesalius and Harvey. Another great scientific event of this era was the formation in 1645 of what was to become the Royal Society[10].

On 30th January 1649 King Charles was beheaded. Oliver Cromwell took over as the Lord Protector of the Commonwealth of England, Scotland and Ireland. This was a period of great unrest in England (and especially in Ireland!) and there appear to have been few, if any, advances in medical care, either social or scientific, except experience in dressing and nursing wounds![11] On the 3rd of September 1658 the Lord Protector died, probably of malaria contracted in Ireland.

Commonwealth half-groat

In 1660 the monarchy was restored under Charles II and the Royal Society was founded only a few months after the Restoration. Charles re-started the tradition of the Royal Touch for King's Evil but with a slight twist. He had special medallions made, with the design from the Angel coin on them. The king then touched the medallion and gave the 'touch-piece' to the person who was sick with scrofula, but carefully avoided touching the patient! The medallion was worn as an amulet. In the first four years after his Restoration Charles II "touched" nearly 24,000 people with scrofula.

Charles II Farthing Pattern, 1665

In 1663 the hammered coinage was replaced by excellent coins milled using Blondeau's. machinery This is a silver pattern minted in 1665 for the copper farthing which was struck from 1672 to 1679. Note the allegorical seated figure of Britannia used for the first time since the Roman era. The hole indicates that this coin may have been warn as an amulet.

In 1665, London, the capital, was gripped by an epidemic of bubonic plague which was the worst since the Black Death. In September 1665 deaths reached a peak of 7,000 per week. In Westminster all the doctors were killed by the plague[9].

On Sunday 1st September 1666 a great fire started in a baking house in Pudding Lane and spread to 400 acres of the city. It destroyed 87 churches and 13,000 houses. It was finally brought under control by the Duke of York (later to be James II). He personally super-vised navy gunpowder teams blowing up buildings in the path of the flames. The Great Fire of London is reputed to have stopped the plague[9]. If Christopher Wren had not gained fame for the rebuilding of London and as the architect of St Paul's Cathedral, he should still be re-membered for his anatomical work. Thomas Willis, one of the founders of the Royal Society, went to Wren for help in illustrating the anatomy of the brain. Wren was one of the finest draughtsmen of the era and the results were astounding[3].

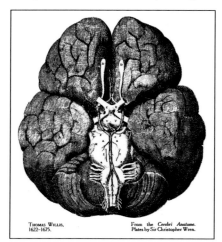

Cerebri Anatome by Thomas Willis
Plates by Christopher Wren[3]

THOMAS WILLIS, 1622-1675.   From the *Cerebri Anatome.* Plates by Sir Christopher Wren.

The 'glorious revolution' in 1688 saw James II flee to France to escape from William and Mary. On the 3rd January 1689 James landed in Ireland with a French army. His battles with William of Orange did not go well and he resorted to melting down the cannon to make coins, known as gun-money, from the metal in order to pay his soldiers.

Obverse IACO II   **Reverse** SOLI DEO GLORIA
Ship: Sovereign of the Seas   St. Michael killing the dragon

James II Gold Touch-piece for healing Scrofula

James II Gun-money shilling

Between 1661 and 1691 Malpighi, Hooke, Swammerdam and Leeuwehoek undertook excellent work using compound and simple microscopes. Their work was published either as books or as letters to the newly established Royal Society and remarkable strides in the biological sciences were made. These included the discovery that the organs of the body had complex structure and the demonstration of red blood cells, spermatozoa and microscopic creatures. Then the microscope was abandoned for 150 years. The probable reason, as bemoaned by Hooke in 1692, is that there was no money to be made in microscopy. Using the microscope, after the first flush of interest, led neither to status or wealth. Socrates, as described earlier in the book, was correct " Unless pay is added to the art, there would be no benefit for the craftsman."

William and Mary Farthing 1694

Mary died in 1694 and William continued to reign on his own until his death in 1702.

Queen Anne Silver Sixpence 1711

William III stopped the practice of the healing touch since he did not believe in its efficacy. He was succeeded by the daughter of James II, Queen Anne who re-started the ceremony and, famously, touched Samuel Johnson for scrofula when he was only two years of age. He is said to have worn his 'touch-piece' around his neck for the rest of his life. Meanwhile, St.Paul's Cathedral was completed in 1711 and Wren applied for his back pay of £200 a year. Parliament in 1697 had decided that he should only be given half-pay until the building was finished.[9] The money to pay for St Paul's came from the church of St Peter hence the phrase 'robbing Peter to pay Paul'.

George I, who followed Anne in 1714, once again stopped the touch-piece ceremony because it was too steeped in Catholicism.

Guineas were introduced as a coin of the realm in 1663. Unofficially named after the African country of Guinea, where the gold was mined, they varied in value from twenty shillings to thirty shillings (£1 to £1.50) until set at twenty-one shillings in 1717. Most invoices for professional fees (including most doctors' fees) were now issued in guineas.

Gold Guinea George I 1716

The Pretenders to the throne continued to " touch" in exile. Bonnie Prince Charlie's rebellion failed in 1745 and in the same year the surgeons split from the barbers as the Company of Surgeons. This eventually became the Royal College of Surgeons (RCS) in

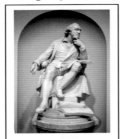

Statue of Hunter (1728-1793) RCS

1800. One of the most important figures in the Company of Surgeons was John Hunter, a leading surgeon and anatomist. He taught Benjamin Bell, Astley Cooper, Everard Home and Edward Jenner. Hunter's clear and concise teaching and publications were based on hours of careful dissection. Hunter's publications included: *The Natural History of Human Teeth and A Practical Treatise on the Diseases of Teeth in 1771, The Digestion of the Stomach after Death (1772) A Treatise on Venereal Disease (1786) and A Treatise on Blood, Inflammation and Gun-Shot Wounds (1794).* [12]

The French Revolution and the First French Republic

On the 14th July 1789 a mob of Parisians stormed the Bastille. The Revolution was under way and led to the formation of the First Republic. This was saved in 1792 when the Duke of Brunswick's Prussian army, weakened with dysentery, was turned back at Valmy by 50,000 Frenchmen.

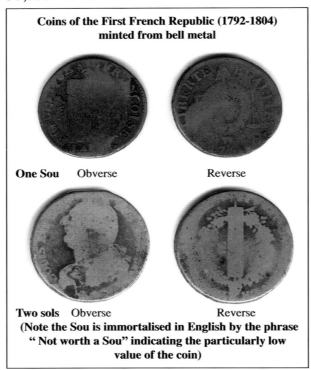

Coins of the First French Republic (1792-1804) minted from bell metal

One Sou   Obverse   Reverse

Two sols   Obverse   Reverse

(Note the Sou is immortalised in English by the phrase " Not worth a Sou" indicating the particularly low value of the coin)

French Hospitals were nationalised by the State in post-revolutionary France[13], the first example of true State Medicine in the modern era. Some medical historians date the start of modern medicine to the establishment of 'clinics' or medical schools in France at this time. Trainee doctors were systematically educated on the wards studying the diagnosis and treatment of patients. The patients who died were sent for autopsy and the pre- and post-mortem diagnoses were compared. The lack of efficacy of traditional medicine was highlighted by the use of statistics. The humane treatment of the insane was a major achievement. They were treated as invalids often amenable to improvement by patient care rather than as secret criminals cursed by God[14].

BUT Antoine-Laurent Lavoisier (the world's most eminent chemist at the time, hospital and social reformer and co-discoverer, with Priestly, of oxygen) had his head chopped off on the guillotine in 1794[15].

French Revolution Twenty Francs Note, backed by confiscated land

Jean Baptiste Lamarck (1744-1829) was a French botanist and zoologist who devised a theory of the evolution of species based on the inheritance of acquired characteristics[16]. This was revolutionary and heretical at a time when religion taught that species were created by God and immutable and Lamarck's theory paved the way for the later theory of evolution by natural selection propounded by Wallace and Darwin.

Edward Jenner   (Bristol Med Chi J)

1796 Edward Jenner: Vaccination for Smallpox
A most important discovery and a significant State intervention

Smallpox was a severe, frequently fatal disease. Inoculation with weakened virus from a smallpox-infected human being had been practised by the ancient Chinese and was customary in Constantinople. It was introduced to the UK in 1717 but Drs Robert and Daniel Sutton reported in 1760 that in 30,000 inoculation cases there were 1200 fatalities. Near the end of the 18th Century Edward Jenner made one of the most important discoveries in medical science. Jenner noted that milkmaids in Gloucestershire, having contracted the mild condition known as cowpox from infected nipples of cows, believed that they were subsequently immune to smallpox.

The beauty of milkmaids was legendary, probably because they did not suffer the facial ravages of smallpox. In the late 1790s Jenner subcutaneously inoculated patients with the milder cowpox virus successfully in 23 trial cases.

George III Guinea 1786
Gold was replaced by banknotes during the Napoleonic wars. One last issue of guineas occurred in 1813 to pay the soldiers.

Parliament in 1802 and 1807 voted Jenner £30,000 to improve and spread his method.[17] This was one of the most significant State interventions in the history of medical science. The disease has now been eradicated after a successful worldwide vaccination program. The last naturally occurring case in the world was in Somalia in 1977.

The payment to Jenner would probably have been in banknotes since notes replaced gold guineas during the Napoleonic wars although professionals (tailors and private doctors) continued to charge in guineas (21shillings).

The military knew the importance of good health in their men and provided health services. In 1805 at the Battle of Trafalgar each of Nelson's ships included a surgeon. Any seaman who was ill or injured had a duty to inform the surgeon and partake of treatment.[18]

This Naval surgeons kit in 1805 was very similar to equipment included in a modern-day surgical kit.
(Royal College of Surgeons)

State Intervention and Social Medicine in Nineteenth Century UK

Throughout the nineteenth century there were major legal developments in the UK which shaped the social structure of medicine and strongly influenced the attitudes and customs of present day medical practice.

These included the Apothecaries Act of 1815, the Poor Law of 1834 and the creation of the Registrar Generals Office and compilation of statistics on births, deaths and marriages 1836. These reforms continued with the 1858 Medical Act which established the Medical Register, a compendium of properly qualified practitioners and the General Medical Council (GMC) to supervise the doctors' professional and ethical behaviour [19].

The 1815 Apothecaries Act introduced the Licence of the Society of Apothecaries (LSA) as the legally required qualification for general practitioners (GPs) in the UK. The UK government, by legislating in this way, was controlling and licensing doctors. This was nearly 900 years after the Caliph Al-Mugtadir had decreed that physicians should be licensed in Baghdad, Damascus, Mecca and Medina.

University College, London

Jeremy Bentham, in 1826, was involved in founding the new London University, now known as University College London (UCL). The college was the first UK higher education institution to accept students of any race or religious or political belief. UCL retains its strict secular position today, and has no Christian chaplaincy or Muslim prayer rooms and was known at the time as the Godless Institute of Gower Street

The college had a medical faculty from the start and was also my medical school 142 years later. The foundation stone of a teaching hospital was laid in 1833. Initially called the North London Hospital, the name was changed in 1837 to University College Hospital. Robert Liston was the first professor of surgery. Meanwhile the last victim of the Spanish Inquisition, schoolmaster Cayetano Ripoli, was garroted to death in Valencia on July 26th 1826 (allegedly for teaching Deist principles)[20].

In 1834 a new Poor Law Act for England and Wales created central authorities in the persons of Poor Law Commissioners (after 1847, Poor Law Boards). The boards unified tax gathering, built workhouses, organized outdoor relief and oversaw public medical assistance.[21]

**William IV 1834
Silver
Three-halfpence
(Colonial use)**

Nursing, provided in the UK under the old poor law act of Elizabeth I, had fallen into disrepute. Nurses were renowned for their slovenly behaviour and drunkenness.
This changed due to the efforts of two particular ladies: Elizabeth Fry and Florence Nightingale.

Elizabeth Fry and Florence Nightingale

1840 saw two very different innovations of crucial importance to healthcare. The adhesive postage stamp and Fry's new nursing school.

Queen Victoria on the Penny Black 1840

The Royal Mail had been available to the public since 1635. The letter recipient paid the postage (averaging one shilling per letter). In 1840 the mail was revolutionized, by Rowland Hill, with the sender paying a much reduced fee of one penny (heavier mail cost more). The postage stamp caught on-with Brazil and Switzerland adopting the technology in 1843 and the United States, a little later, in 1847. The significance of the postal service to healthcare is shown by a recent postal strike which is thought to have caused up to a million missed doctors' appointments.[22]

Elizabeth Fry (reverse of the £5 note, current issue)

Elizabeth Fry was a well-known Quaker and prison reformer. People had seen the success in France of scientific medicine aided by a flourishing religious sector of nursing and called on Fry to create an English order of the Sisters of Charity. In 1840 she started a training school for nurses in Guy's Hospital. This was followed by an Anglican order of nurses 'St John's House Training for Nurses' at Kings College Hospital in 1856 and Charing Cross in 1866.[23]

Florence Nightingale wrote to Fry to explain how she had been influenced by her views on the training of nurses. Later, when Nightingale went to the Crimean War, she took a group of Fry nurses with her to look after the sick and wounded soldiers.

Florence Nightingale instituted hygiene in military hospitals in 1854 (initially in the Crimea) then organized UK hospitals. Her actions completely revolutionized nursing. Previous to Florence Nightingale nursing was a lower class activity for women with no training. After her reforms nursing became an occupation suitable for the middle and even upper classes. She was also a

Florence Nightingale 1820-1910
Detail from reverse of £10 note

gifted mathematician and a pioneer of epidemiology. In 1860 Florence Nightingale opened a School of Nursing at St Thomas's Hospital in London[23,24,25]

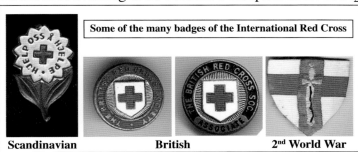

Some of the many badges of the International Red Cross

Scandinavian **British** **2nd World War**

The Red Cross and the Red Crescent: Inspired by the example of Florence Nightingale, five Swiss citizens founded the Red Cross in 1863, followed by the Red Crescent for Islamic countries.[26]

The Contagious Nature of Many Diseases:
Sanitary and Public Health Laws

Sanitary and public health laws were enacted in the UK every few years throughout the 19th century due to the growing awareness of the mortality risks of living in large cities and the growing knowledge regarding the contagious nature of many diseases. Some of these laws and advances are listed below. It is interesting to note that they resulted in a considerable measure of State and Local Government health provision including dispensaries and hospitals.

One major improvement that decreased mortality considerably was the provision of good water supplies and sewage disposal. This was taken out of the hands of private providers, mainly because the latter were not able to maintain standards. This is a lesson we may have forgotten. In discussion on a train just a few days ago I spoke of my concerns to someone from the Environment Agency. He initially dismissed them but then agreed that the present system of fines may not be sufficiently punitive to prevent the new private suppliers from cutting corners. This conversation occurred in a week when one of England's largest water companies - Severn Trent Water - was facing a criminal investigation by the Serious Fraud Office and another water company (Southern Water) could be facing a multi-million pound payout over irregularities in the handling and reporting of its customer enquiries and complaints.[27]

In 1842 Edwin Chadwick reported on the sanitary condition of the labouring population. Chadwick was a man of many talents. He was a botanist, lawyer, journalist and public health reformer. He became the Assistant Commissioner on the Poor Law Board in 1832 and Chief Commissioner 1833. In 1842 he published at his own expense his *Report on the Sanitary Condition of the Labouring Population of Gt. Britain*. Chadwick included figures to show that in 1839 for every person who died of old age or violence, eight died of specific diseases. Cholera, typhus, typhoid, and influenza were more or less endemic at the time. Chadwick advocated separating water and sewage supplies[28].

Also in 1842 Thomas Watson, Professor of Medicine at King's College Hospital, London, wrote: "Wherever puerperal fever is rife, or when a practitioner has attended any one instance of it, he should use most diligent ablution …to prevent the practitioner becoming a vehicle of contagion and death between one patient and another."

1843 in Boston, Dr Oliver Wendell Holmes published his classic essay *The Contagiousness of Puerperal Fever*. The essay contains eight rules for the obstetrician, which included not only hand-washing and changes of clothing, but also the avoidance of autopsies if obstetric cases were being managed. The reader will have noted that the significance of hygiene in the avoidance of Pueperal Fever was well recognized in ancient history having been recorded first in 1500BC in Hindu texts.

The appointment of Medical Officers of Health (MOHs) was made compulsory in cities with a death rate of over 25 per thousand under the Public Health Act of 1848. This was extended to all London's districts in 1855 under the Metropolis Local Management Act.

In the ancient past, the Indus Valley civilisation, the Assyrians and the Romans had all noted the importance of clean water supplies and good drainage systems. It is salutary to note that in the United Kingdom the relationship between contaminated water supplies and disease was only becoming apparent to a number of physicians in the 1840s and 50s and many of their contemporaries would not believe them.

1849 Queen Victoria Four Pence (groat)

In 1849 John Snow (1813-1858), published a brief pamphlet, *On the Mode of Communication of Cholera*. Snow, a London physician and obstetrician, believed that cholera was a contagious disease caused by a poison that reproduced in the human body and was found in the vomit and stools of cholera patients. He conjectured that the main, but not only, means of transmission was contaminated water. His idea was not generally accepted (most believed it was bad air). He proved his case in 1854 when he carefully mapped an outbreak around the Broad Street water pump in London. He removed the pump handle and the epidemic was contained[29,30]

In or around 1852 William Budd established the relationship between contaminated water supplies and Typhoid (Enteric Fever). In 1897 Dr J.G. Swayne spoke to the Bristol Medico-Chirurgical Society of his own experiences of Typhoid, forty-five years previously, when he was attended by Dr. Symonds and Dr. Budd. He told the Society that Budd had attributed his condition to well-water contaminated by a cesspool between York Place and Richmond Terrace in Bristol. Dr Swayne had been treated with leeches and quinine and had survived to tell the tale![31]

In France, Louis Pasteur (1822-95), a research chemist, had been asked to find out why fermented beer was turning sour in a factory. Using microscopy he demonstrated the presence of myriads of small living organisms which he surmised were the cause of the problem. He looked also at milk, wine and vinegar and became convinced that the liquids were contaminated by air-borne spread. He established that the organisms could be killed by heating the fluids. This process is now called Pasteurisation in his honour. In 1865 Pasteur became convinced that organisms could spread disease in human beings: the germ theory of disease. Pasteur knew about Jenner's success with vaccination for smallpox. He conjectured that it might be possible to find vaccines against other diseases. He proceeded to develop vaccines against chicken cholera, rabies and anthrax.

5 Centimes of Napoleon III
President of the French Republic 1848-52
Emperor of France 1852-1870
Napoleon III had socialist leanings and tried to reduce poverty by State Intervention. He replaced the unhygienic medieval streets of Paris with wide boulevards, created sewage systems and built parks and apartment blocks for the masses[33].

Louis Pasteur exhorted people to use laboratories to study disease:

"I beseech you to take interest in these sacred domains so expressively called laboratories. Ask that there be more and that they be adorned for these are the temples of the future, wealth and well-being. It is here that humanity will grow, strengthen and improve. Here, humanity will learn to read progress and individual harmony in the works of nature, while humanity's own works are all too often those of barbarism, fanaticism and destruction." — Louis Pasteur[32]

47

The Pasteur Institute was established by decree on June 4th, 1887 and financed by an international fund. Alexandre Yersin joined the recently created Pasteur Institute in 1889 as Roux's collaborator, and discovered with him the diphtheric toxin.

Chinese Cash   **Dutch India 1857**

British India 1862   **British Hong Kong 1863**

French Cochin-China 1879 (South Vietnam)

Coins from China and India during the 3rd plague pandemic

A third pandemic of bubonic plague had started in China in 1855 and spread round the world, killing 12 million people in India and China alone. It continued to appear in ports for 50 years. The organism responsible for plague was isolated in 1894 by Yersin when working in French Indo-China. The organism was originally named *Pasteurella pestis* but this was changed to *Yersinia pestis* in 1962. The discovery of the flea as the vector for plague was made in 1898 by Paul-Louis Simon.[34,35]

In 1882 Robert Koch, a German physician, published his classic work describing the Tubercle bacillus. At last the cause of Scrofula, Consumption and Phthisis was known.

Sanitary Acts, Antisepsis and Charitable Dispensaries

With Snow and Budd having established the importance of clean water supplies and good drainage, the UK Sanitary Act was passed in 1866. This enforced connection of all houses to a new main sewer, set limits for the use of cellars as living rooms and established the definition of overcrowding. This was followed by the 1867 Metropolitan Poor Act. Following these two acts and in view of the Pasteur germ theory of disease isolation hospitals for infectious diseases were created.[36,37]

Also in 1867 Joseph Lister revolutionized surgery (and much other medical practice) by announcing the results of his work on antisepsis. Lister had been a student at University College Hospital and worked his way up to Regius Professor of Surgery at Glasgow University. He knew about the germ theory of disease and was an established microscopist using the compound microscope with aberration correction which had been invented by his father. Lister hoped that

Joseph Lister (1827-1912) (Bust: Portland Place)

it might be possible to kill the germs in surgical wounds using carbolic acid.

Mortality rates in his ward for major amputation cases dropped from nearly 50% to 15%.[38,39]
The Lister Institute of Preventive Medicine was founded in 1891 as the first UK medical research charity.

48

Charitable dispensaries, offering diagnosis and treatment, had already been set up in Lancashire and West Riding. Under the provision of the poor law a programme of providing dispensaries for the poor was initiated. This resulted in the establishment of 44 dispensaries in London and a few in the provinces before it was curtailed for financial and moral reasons.[40] Apparently the prevailing view was that helping the poor pandered to them and led them into immoral and slothful ways. In 1871 the Poor Law Board was abolished and responsibilities for the service replaced by Local Government Boards. Although hampered by Treasury constraints on spending they did manage to raise medical standards in Poor Law institutions. Appointment of Medical Officers of Health (MOHs) were made compulsory for all urban and rural districts under the Public Health Act of 1872. The same year the Food, Drink and Drugs Act permitted local authorities to appoint public analysts (for food and drugs) and medical officers to order analyses. 1873 saw the publication of Budd's monograph on Typhoid Fever (a classic in public health literature).[41]

Advertisements 1886-1903 stressing the purity of the products[42]

In 1875 a further Food and Drugs act was passed to increase purity. Chemical adulteration continued to be a problem well into the next century. A further Sanitary Act was also passed in 1875 to make sanitary enforcement powers more explicit.

Under the terms of the Public Health (Waterworks) Act 1878 local authorities were able to obtain finances to buy the local waterworks. In 1879 only 415 urban authorities owned their own supply but by 1905 more than two-thirds of the 1138 authorities had taken control over local waterworks. Local Government control improved quality and supply[43].

Comment

The development and spread of ideas which started with the Renaissance had gathered pace over the following four centuries and medicine became a science as well as an art. Industrialisation in the 18th and 19th centuries had initially brought misery to the cities with a much lowered life expectancy than in the countryside. However the reawakening of ideas of sanitation and clean drinking water and the improved purity of foods improved the conditions for millions by the end of the nineteenth century. 19th Century pioneers had shown that epidemics of disease could be controlled using cleanliness and a scientific approach to medicine. Hospitals had changed from being places of filth and disease into clean, antiseptic environments. Government intervention in the United Kingdom had ensured that vaccination programmes reduced the incidence of smallpox and legislation had enforced the provision of sanitation. The Victorian legacy of public waterworks and sewerage is still relied upon in many British cities of the 21st century

Chapter 4

Modern medicine and the build up to the UK National Health Service (NHS)

Professional medicine

All professions are conspiracies against the laity
George Bernard Shaw 1856-1950 (Doctor's Dilemma)

The 1815 Apothecaries Act had introduced the Licence of the Society of Apothecaries (LSA) as the legally required qualification for general practitioners in the UK. This was followed in 1858 by the Medical Act establishing a compendium of properly qualified practitioners known as the Medical Register. Qualification had to be obtained from a recognised medical school. The General Medical Council (GMC) was established to keep the Medical Register and supervise the doctors' professional and ethical behaviour. " Proper" doctors could now be looked up in the register.

Anne Hardy in *Health and Medicine in Britain since 1860*[1] states that in the years between about 1860 and 1914 orthodox medicine in the United Kingdom " became professional". Certainly the training became increasingly scientific and recognised qualifications were necessary in order to be registered by the GMC.

262   *THE STRAND MAGAZINE.*

The Strand magazine of 1891 contains not only *The Adventures of Sherlock Holmes* but also an article about "the irregular individuals who may be seen at street corners, and on almost any night of the week"[2]
The author remarks that "a curious fact about these itinerants is observable; the majority are selling medicines or compounds to cure the ills of the flesh".

The individual in the illustration was said to be a New Yorker who, having arrived in England, decided to be the "greatest doctor of the London Streets" and proceeded to sell packets of hop-bitters at one penny a time. The Strand cynically remarked that these were claimed to cure "a splendid list of every ailment that could possibly afflict suffering humanity".

" THE GREATEST DOCTOR OF THE LONDON STREETS."

"Street Doctors", now considered as "quacks", were still prevalent on street corners in London at the turn of the century but they could not legitimately claim to be members of the medical profession. The public knew that they were not qualified and did not consider them to be "proper doctors".

Food and Drug purity laws had been enacted in 1872 and 1875. These permitted analyses of food and drugs but proved ineffective in preventing chemical adulteration or in stopping street vendors.

The recognisable division between general practitioners (GPs), surgeons and physicians had started with the distinction between physicians, barber-surgeons and apothecaries in the reign of Henry VIII. The apothecaries had become GPs whilst, from the early 1800s onwards, the physicians and surgeons were progressively hospital based as consultants. The separation of hospital consultants and general practitioners was in place by 1900[1] although their work overlapped considerably with much general primary care taking place in the hospitals and general practitioners still undertaking surgery in patients' homes.

Nursing also was becoming increasingly professional with the establishment of nursing schools at Guy's by Elizabeth Fry and at St Thomas's by Florence Nightingale. The new, trained nurses had almost completely replaced the old poor law nurse who had gradually fallen into disrepute since their inception under the old poor law act of 1598. The professional nature of nursing was further established by the introduction of the General Nursing Council in 1919 and the register of qualified nurses.

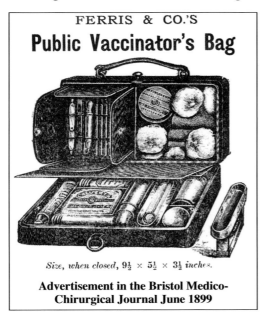

FERRIS & CO.'S
Public Vaccinator's Bag

Size, when closed, 9½ × 5½ × 3½ inches.

Advertisement in the Bristol Medico-Chirurgical Journal June 1899

Medical science was now at the centre of the fight against infectious diseases. Jenner's vaccination programme had been very successful in decreasing the incidence of smallpox. Compulsory vaccination had gradually been introduced between 1840 and 1870 despite active opposition. In 1871 Public Vaccinators were appointed: doctors providing vaccination free to all children. Rational science could combat plagues and one did not have to resort to irrational or supernatural comfort. Darwin and Wallace's new version of the theory of evolution, survival of the fittest, indicated that man was an animal evolved from the apes. It looked as if science would very soon be able to explain everything.

At the beginning of the 19th century the death rate was still rising, particularly in the larger cities. Overcrowding and un-sanitary conditions were largely to blame and the investment in new and improved waterworks and in sewage disposal brought about vast improvements in the latter half of the century. A lamentation that many people make even today is our dependence on the legacy of the Victorian infrastructure in these areas but this infrastructure has proved very durable and has certainly served the cities well. The advent of the germ theory by Pasteur at about the same time as the discovery of the role of contaminated water in both Cholera and Typhoid (Snow and Budd) had made an enormous impact. Deaths from puerperal sepsis were decreasing after 1842 and 1843 following the publication of the contagious nature of the condition and how to avoid it.

Medicine in Germany and Austria: Late 19th and Early 20th Century

German postage stamps of the 1880s

In the 1880s Social insurance schemes were pioneered in Germany[1]. Medicine in Germany and Austria was highly advanced and the establishment of social insurance schemes certainly put pressure on the government of the United Kingdom to introduce something similar. In addition to the social advances, practical innovation and discovery moved on at a pace in Germany including:

1882 Robert Koch, German bacteriologist and physician published his classic work describing Tubercle bacillus

1889 Minkowski and von Mering (Strassburg, Germany) proposed that the pancreas was crucial for sugar metabolism. Dogs had all the signs of diabetes mellitus when the pancreas was removed

1895 Roentgen discovered X-rays

1856-1939 Sigmund Freud (Austria)

1906 Diathermy: Nagelschmidt

X-Rays

1895 It was on the 8th November 1895 that Roentgen, working on emissions from a "Crooke's Tube", discovered X-rays. He worked feverishly over the next seven weeks and presented his work on 28th December. The results were described at the time as a medical miracle. Roentgen, who won the first Nobel Prize in physics in 1901, declined to seek patents or proprietary claims on the X-rays, even refusing to allow eponymous descriptions of his discovery and its applications.[3]

The discovery of X-rays could not have occurred earlier, except by a year or two, because the preceding inventions and discoveries of magnetism, electricity, batteries, vacuum tubes and such like, were all needed before X-rays could be produced and discovered.

It is from that period in the 1890s that I date modern medical science. Before that time there was no way of looking into the body without cutting open the subject of study and that surgery had been conducted on patients without anaesthetics or antiseptic agents.

We have indeed come an enormous way since then with other astonishing advances such as antibiotics, magnetic resonance imaging, transplant surgery and the unraveling of the human genome.

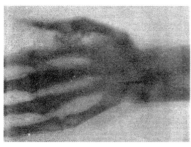
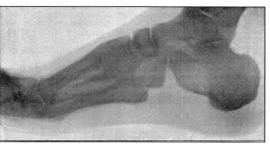
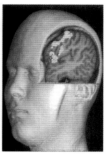

1)   2)   3)

100 years of medical imaging

1) X-ray of the hand and wrist showing a needle in a wrist February 10th 1896 [4]

2) X-ray showing a needle in a foot June 7th 1896 [5]

3)Functional Magnetic Resonance Imaging of the Brain at 4T, 1996. [6]

The scientific approach that was established at that time led the way. Despite major criticisms of medicine and its practice most people are aware of the differences in what can be done now compared with five decades ago, or even just five years before the present. The main worry is whether or not their local hospital or GP will be able to obtain these advances for their patients or whether the doctors will be ignorant and unaware of treatments discussed openly on television or on the Internet.

Sigmund Freud 1856-1939

Austrian physician Freud published works on psychiatry and psychoanalysis. Describing the Id, Ego and Superego, Freud argued that many of our actions and psychiatric illnesses are due to subconscious desires due to childhood sexual traumas. Right or wrong, his work freed the thinking of many people whose religious upbringing had forbidden them from talking or even thinking about such ideas.

1906 Diathermy: Nagelschmidt

German 1/2 Mark 1905

Cautery was first practiced by the Shamans and was rediscovered several times in medical history. In 1854 surgeon Albrecht Theodor Middeldorpf (1824-1868 Professor of surgery and ophthalmology and director of the outpatient clinic at the University of Breslau) had published the first monograph on the application of electrical current in surgical operations ("galvanocautery"). Modern diathermy (a form of cautery) with high-frequency alternating current was introduced into medicine by the dermatologist Franz Nagelschmidt from Berlin. He used the concept of "diathermy" to explain the creation of heat in the body by molecular agitation and oscillation caused by high frequency currents. The prototype apparatus used a 50 Hz power supply at 120 volts. Voltage was raised to 2000 volts by a transformer and four metal plate condensers were discharged across a spark gap[7].

Charity Hospitals in the United Kingdom

With malice towards none; with charity for all. Abraham Lincoln 1809-1865

The majority of hospitals in the 19th century were funded by charitable donations. Nearer the end of the century there were around 1100 charitable and local authority hospitals in the United Kingdom, the former including many of the hospitals originally set up by the Church.

The patronage of Royalty was very important when raising money for the charitable

Gold sovereign

Obverse   Reverse

Victoria   St George
(young head)   and the dragon
Pistrucci's design

hospitals. In 1870 at a fund-raising dinner for St George's Hospital, the Duke of Westminster, who had donated the land on which the hospital was built, spoke about a 3000 bed hospital in Milan in which various portraits of donors were displayed, the size of the portrait depending on the size of the donation.

The Prince of Wales quipped: 'I have one suggestion to make in that respect….that you should all contribute very largely that circular golden portrait representative of the Queen which this Hospital needs most.'[8]

Keir Waddington[8] states that in the 1890s London's hospitals were facing a financial crisis which was so severe that some feared the state would have to intervene. Charity was proving insufficient to meet the spiralling cost of care, despite the ability of those running the hospitals to pick the pockets of the benevolent.

By the time King Edward VII came to the throne in 1901 there were charity and local authority hospitals in all the large towns and cities of the United Kingdom. The finance of these hospitals remained precarious and was still based on donations by philanthropists and collections from the public.[9]

The sixpence issued in 1887 had to be withdrawn half way through the year because they were so similar to half sovereigns that confidence tricksters were gold plating them and using handicapped people to buy something small in a shop. They would then receive, from the unwillingly benevolent shopkeeper, the change due from ten shillings.

Albert Edward, Prince of Wales 1841-1901 and King Edward VII 1901-1910

Edward VII Sovereign
(Many thanks to Dr H Sims-Williams)

Medals for the opening of the King Edward VII Memorial Infirmary
(Bristol Royal Infirmary)

In an article in the Windsor Magazine in 1901[10] the virtues of the London Hospital's approach to health care were extolled. But despite being the second largest hospital in Europe, providing services to 1.5 million people and treating 200,000 patients a year they remained seriously underfinanced. I quote " The whole work of the London, as the staff themselves admit, is hampered at every turn by the old buildings and by lack of funds".

It was these hospitals, still in existence providing free care to millions of patients a year, which were to form the backbone of the NHS experiment.

The split between the type of general care provided by GPs and specialist care provided by hospitals had not yet occurred although by necessity high technology was concentrated in the hospitals. This included X-ray equipment and the new, clean operating theatres.

Poor people had access to health care via the poor act. A letter of introduction for admission to hospital was necessary at the beginning of the 19th century but by 1900 this had almost completely disappeared as a necessity. The wealthy could clearly pay for their healthcare but what of the working class? They largely contributed to sick clubs or friendly societies on a subscription basis out of their wages. Hardy states that a third of adult males and more than 45% of working class men obtained medical attendance through friendly societies by 1900[1].

A major change occurred in 1911 with the passing of the National Insurance Act, which came into effect in 1913. This was copied partly from the friendly society sickness provision but also from the pioneering social insurance schemes, which had been implemented in Germany (under Bismarck's direction) from the 1880s onwards. The aim was to stop the workers from tipping into poverty due to ill-health. It funded GP services for the insured workers and TB sanatoria for anyone with tuberculosis. It also paid for research into the health of the British people under the auspices of the Medical Research Council (MRC).[1]

1913 Implementation of the National Insurance Act

National Insurance (NI) was a contributory scheme with workers under £160 a year only having to put in 4d a week (equivalent to less than 2 pence in decimal coinage) but topped up to 10d by employer and government contribution.

The MRC (Medical Research Committee (now Council)) was also founded in 1913 using funds from National Insurance.[1]

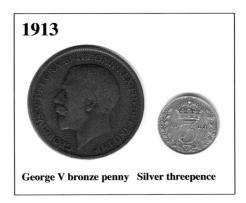

1913

George V bronze penny   Silver threepence

The First World War 1914-1918

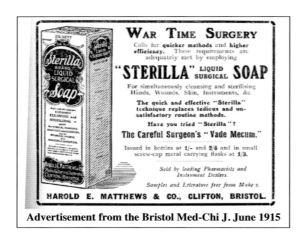

WAR TIME SURGERY
Calls for quicker methods and higher efficiency. These requirements are adequately met by employing

"STERILLA" LIQUID SURGICAL SOAP

For simultaneously cleansing and sterilising Hands, Wounds, Skin, Instruments, &c.

The quick and effective "Sterilla" technique replaces tedious and unsatisfactory routine methods.

Have you tried "Sterilla"?

The Careful Surgeon's "Vade Mecum."

Issued in bottles at 1/- and 2/6 and in small screw-cap metal carrying flasks at 1/3.

Sold by leading Pharmacists and Instrument Dealers.

Samples and Literature free from Makers.

HAROLD E. MATTHEWS & CO., CLIFTON, BRISTOL.

Advertisement from the Bristol Med-Chi J. June 1915

The National Insurance scheme had hardly been put into effect before the country was plunged into war with Germany.

The First World War had enormous psychological impact on the nation as well as obvious physical health effects. The importance of good sanitary conditions amongst the soldiers was emphasised by outbreaks of contagious diseases wherever the conditions were poor but not on the Western front where good hygiene was observed.

In August 1916 an outbreak of bubonic plague unexpectedly appeared in the centre of the City of Bristol in a rag warehouse. Four cases occurred, all directly related to the warehouse. The place was infested by rats and swarming with fleas, rats were killed and proven to have plague. The decision was made by Lieut-Col. D.S. Davies, (Medical Officer of Health, Bristol) that the contents of the warehouse should be destroyed by fire. The rats were fed to prevent them from migrating and the staff were inoculated against the plague. The bales of rags were disinfected and taken in closed vans to a city destructor. The work took ten days, sixteen tons of disinfectant were used and two tons of lime. The people employed to do the work were bathed and their clothes baked daily to avoid carriage of the infection by fleas. A large area of the surrounding district was mapped out and rat catching carried out for six months. 9,000 rats were caught but the only plague rats were those in the warehouse. One of the plague rats in the warehouse was an ordinary brown rat but in place of the rat's proper flea (Ceratophyllus fasciatus) there was found the flea (Xenopsylla Cheopis) which properly belongs to the Indian black rat and is known as the plague flea. No further human cases of the plague occurred due to the measures taken[11].

As the war progressed the surgeons became more adept at the prevention of sepsis in war wounds and in July 1917 the Professor of Surgery from the University of Bristol, Lieut.-Colonel James Swain, could confidently write 'Early treatment is highly desirable, and as this can be commenced in France soon after the infliction of the wound, most of the cases are rendered "sterile" and closed with about 99 per cent of successes in the course of five to twenty-five days.'[12]

Advertisement from the Bristol Med-Chi J. April 1917

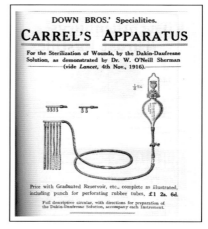

DOWN BROS.' Specialities.

CARREL'S APPARATUS

For the Sterilization of Wounds, by the Dakin-Daufresne Solution, as demonstrated by Dr. W. O'Neill Sherman
(vide Lancet, 4th Nov., 1916).

Price with Graduated Reservoir, etc., complete as illustrated, including punch for perforating rubber tubes, £1 2s. 6d.

Full descriptive circular, with directions for preparation of the Dakin-Daufresne Solution, accompany each Instrument.

At home the death rates rose amongst the elderly during the war years, probably related to overwhelming grief. Respiratory disease amongst the young women was also a major problem.

1917 Russian Revolution

Soviet Russian Worker's Medal

1917 the Bolshevik revolution. This eventually consolidated into the USSR (Union of Soviet Socialist Republics). The communist government set up a comprehensive medical service paid for by the State and intended for the entire population

The communist model adopted by the USSR never included equal wages. There was considerable prejudice against people who were considered as capitalist (landowners etc.) or intellectual (including teachers and doctors). An engineer was on a state wage four times that of a doctor. Workers of the world unite!

The inter-war years 1918 – 1939

1918-1919 saw the pandemic of influenza which killed more people in two years than any other epidemic before or since[13]. This was probably due to a mutated bird flu and some estimates put the total deaths at 37 million.

The General Nursing Council (GNC) for England and Wales was set up by the Nurses Registration Act of 1919. General Nursing Councils of Scotland and Ireland were set up at same time. The GNC was established to compile and maintain a register of qualified nurses and act as the disciplinary authority of the nursing profession (further acts were passed in 1979 and 1983).

The National Insurance Act of 1911 had an increasing effect in the inter-war years as working people were covered for visits to their general practitioners (GPs). They were progressively encouraged to go to their GP for minor or chronic ailments and discouraged from visiting hospitals with these ills. Thus the range of conditions seen at the hospitals changed from closely resembling the GP surgery to the more specialised services provided nowadays. Only the children and unemployed (mostly women) were seen for minor ailments in the hospital outpatient departments.

The approach to medicine in the Western World became progressively more scientific and more international. The isolation of Insulin and the development of antibiotics are two famous examples.

In 1910 Sharpey-Shafer of Edinburgh had suggested a single chemical was missing from the pancreas in diabetic people. He proposed calling this chemical 'insulin'. American scientist E. L. Scott was partially successful in extracting insulin with alcohol.

R. C. Paulesco, a Romanian, made an extract from the pancreas that lowered the blood glucose of dogs. In 1921 Frederick Banting and Charles Best (Toronto, Canada) with the help of a biochemist colleague named J. B. Collip, were able to extract a reasonably pure formula of insulin from the pancreas of cattle from slaughterhouses.

Canadian Five Cents 1923

In 1922 Banting and Best (Toronto, Canada) used pancreatic extracts of insulin for diabetes mellitus in a teenage diabetic patient.

The University of Toronto immediately gave pharmaceutical companies license to produce insulin free of royalties. In early 1923, about one year after the first test injection, insulin became widely available, and saved countless lives.

In 1928, Oskar Wintersteiner (Columbia University, New York) proved that insulin was a protein[14].

Also in 1928 Fleming described the mould penicillium notatum inhibiting growth of bacteria and in 1939 Howard Florey and Ernst Chain isolated penicillin.

In 1932 Domagk was working at the new research institute for pathological anatomy and bacteriology built by the I.G. Farbenindustrie (Wuppertal). He made the discovery that a red dye-stuff called prontosil rubrum protected mice and rabbits against lethal doses of staphylococci and haemolytic streptococci. Prontosil was a derivative of sulphanilamide (*p*-aminobenzenesulphonamide) which the Viennese chemist, Gelmo, had previously synthesized (1908).

German stamp featuring Paul von Hindenburg (President 1925-1934)

Domagk's own daughter became very ill with a streptococcal infection, and Domagk, in desperation, gave her a dose of prontosil and she made a complete recovery. By 1937 five brands of Prontosil were widely available. The identification of the anti-bacterial activity of sulphonamides earned Domagk the Nobel Prize in Physiology or Medicine for 1939.

These discoveries led on to the modern era of antibiotics[15,16].

Medicine in the USSR

The Western World was very interested in the USSR (Union of Soviet Socialist Republics) in the inter-war years with an increasingly popular communist following in many countries, including the United Kingdom. In 1933 Sir Arthur Newsholme reported on the provision of medicine in the USSR and was, to modern eyes, surprisingly impressed. " The Soviet Union is the one nation in the world which has undertaken to set up and operate a complete organization designed to provide preventive and curative medical care for every man, woman, and child within its borders" " What Russia has accomplished in its courageously original schemes for the health and social wellbeing of its people constitutes a challenge to other countries"[17,18].

1938 Emergency Medical Service EMS

One Penny (George VI 1938)

In 1938 and 39 with war looming the Emergency Medical Service (EMS) was set up under the Ministry of Health because of the possibility of major air raids and subsequent expected casualties. They took over the running of 10% of the hospital beds, moving the long term sick and elderly out into more peripheral nursing homes and making the acute facilities available for the casualties expected from the coming war. This was supplemented by an Air Raids Precaution Scheme, Public Health Laboratory Service (PHLS), and Emergency Hospital Scheme (EHS)[19].

Royal Army Medical Corps

1939-45 2nd World War

United Kingdom

War was declared in September 1939. In April 1940 doctors aged under 41 were conscripted. In 1941 the limit was raised to 46 and women doctors under 31 included. By the end of 1945 a total of 15,701 medical personnel had been recruited, about 1/3 of the UK's doctors.[20]

The Second World War increased people's expectation that a health care system would be instigated after Germany and Japan were defeated. Sir William Beveridge in his report of 1942 recommended the establishment of a system that would include education, health care and pensions. The public now expected a complete Welfare State to be instigated after the war.

USA

The United States of America joined the 2nd world war rather late [1]*.

One major medical advance to occur during the period of WW2 was the discovery and development of Streptomycin, the first specific agent effective against tuberculosis (TB). The discovery was led by Selman Abraham Waksman, Ukrainian-born American biochemist working at Rutgers University, New Brunswick, the State University of New Jersey. At last an effective treatment was available for Scrofula that did not require the rather dubious Royal touch and a gold coin. Streptomycin was also, and perhaps more importantly, effective against pulmonary TB (consumption) and when other agents were later discovered, was used in tandem with two other anti-tuberculous drugs in the very successful triple chemotherapy.

---

[1]* As they had done for the first world war. Recent events in Iraq and Afghanistan have prompted some to say that the USA are determined not to be late for WW3.

Nazi Germany and Austria

Social programmes of healthcare insurance had been instigated in Germany well before those in most other countries. In addition, during the 1930s medical science in Germany and Austria was amongst the most advanced in the world.

Nevertheless, in Nazi Germany you only prospered if you were a member of the Nazi Party. During the Second World War some of the doctors working for the Nazis proved to the world that any group of society, however illustrious, could be perverted into truly evil practices if given the encouragement to do so. Scientists and medics are no exception and Nazi doctors violated the trust placed in them by breaking the most important rule of Hippocrates: *First do no harm*.

Starting on December 9th 1946, as part of the Trials of War Criminals before the Nuremberg Military Tribunals, twenty-three Nazi doctors were prosecuted at the Doctors' Trial. Sixteen doctors were found guilty.

Directed to do so by Hitler's government, the doctors had conducted appalling experiments on live victims which will not be detailed here but resulted in unbearable suffering and many deaths. German physicians also planned and carried out direct medical killings, the "Euthanasia" Programme, under their 'Life unworthy of life' policy and performed between 200,000 and 350,000 forced sterilisations.

Some doctors objected to carrying out such work and were themselves eliminated. Indeed in 1939 an amendment to the Nuremberg Laws had nullified the medical licenses of all Jewish doctors.[21,22,23,24]

There were, apparently no protests from the medical organizations in Germany but presumably they had fallen under the control of Nazi ideology. As Jack Boozer wrote in 1980 it does raise the question of the status and effectiveness of a professional standard like the Hippocratic oath against the power of the State.[25]

We must not consider that doctors are any less likely to obey the State blindly than any other group in society. In my experience doctors like to be part of the establishment and to have and hold a high place in the hierarchy. Perversely they may thus be more likely to obey the State than some other groups who are more anarchic.

However, when instructed to act in a manner that is against their training and ethics, some doctors will undoubtedly object. They are easily removed from practice by the State and by the action of other doctors who do obey their political masters, leaving only those who will obey. In our present political climate when we are instructed by managers to meet targets rather than work as we have been taught, doctors would do well to remember these conundrums.

1945

1945 saw the end of the war, the establishment of the United Nations and a general election in the UK. The Labour government of 1945 was elected with a landslide victory, much to the disappointment of Winston Churchill who presumably expected some gratitude for all his wartime efforts. But the people wanted a change and the Welfare State was the long-awaited Promised Land.

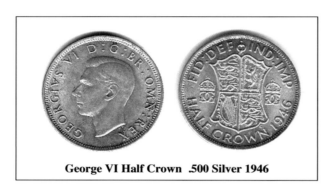

George VI Half Crown .500 Silver 1946

In 1946 the National Health Services Act was passed. The act was based on the Beveridge report and layed down the laws for creating the NHS and the Welfare State.

Comment

Throughout the recorded history the role of the State as a supplier or regulator of health-care has waxed and waned with greater provision often being made after a revolution or major war but gradually drifting back towards previous individual provision. The provision of healthcare depends crucially on economics and without the intervention of the state or charity the poor generally receive little healthcare.

One clear factor is the way that medicine has become professional over several periods…under the Greeks and Romans, in the early Islamic period and in the Modern era. This has been most effective when backed by legislation laid down by the State. The professional approach, with entry requirements, examinations and ethics, has not always been maintained and it cannot be assumed that it will be in the future.

The fight between the 'spiritual' approach (supernatural, religious) to medicine and the scientific rational approach must also be emphasised. If there is a big failing of one system, for example a devastating plague or a catastrophic war, the people will swing in an opposite direction.

The importance of psychology and ethics in health has not always been acknowledged by the scientific establishment whilst the role of good scientific evidence has frequently been ignored by the religious/supernatural proponents of healthcare.

Chapter 5
The Welfare State

No one can be perfectly free until all are free; no one can be perfectly moral till all are moral; no one can be perfectly happy till all are happy . Herbert Spencer (1820-1903)[1]

Born in the January of 1950 and conceived in the Spring of '49, I am a true child of the United Kingdom's National Health Service (NHS) .

**This is a photograph of the author as a baby in 1950 with his sister, Ruth.
My sister had been born in 1947, just before the advent of the NHS. My father
can remember receiving a bill from the doctor for his attendance on the delivery of
my sister at home. The bill was made particularly more memorable by the
doctor's mistaken addition of a fee for circumcision!**

Apart from a year or so working and holidaying overseas, I have lived all my life in the womb of the Welfare State, secure in the knowledge that I will be looked after by the State. I share this blissful condition with approximately 80% of the UK population[2]. Unless they are foreign nationals relatively few of the remaining 20% can remember the stress and worry of not being able to pay for a doctor or the fear that hospital admission may pauper the family.

The Welfare State was a courageous experiment undertaken by the Labour Government after the Second World War. After a gestation period considerably longer than my own, the NHS officially started on 5 July 1948[3]. Thus my own conception and the inception of the NHS occurred within a few months of each other.

**George VI Half Crown 1948
Base metal (cupro-nickel)**

On 5th July 1948 the Local Government and Voluntary hospitals were nationalised. This amounted to a total of 3118 hospitals of which 1100 were voluntary/charity institutions and the remainder were Local Government or Emergency Health Service.

The NHS was intended to provide a cradle to grave comprehensive health service free at the point of delivery. This was to be only part of the Welfare State, the construction of which was outlined by William H Beveridge. Like all the massive managerial changes wrought on health care over the last six decades the NHS was initiated without trial, prior experimentation or pilot studies. It is interesting and informative to contrast this with the enormous pressure on medical practice to prove that it is "evidence based" and the perceived necessity for rigorous trials before implementing any change in clinical practice.

WHO

Another momentous occasion in 1948 was the formation of the World Health Organization (WHO), which was established as a special agency of the United Nations.

The Beveridge Report

Lord Beveridge was an economist who was highly influenced by the Fabian Socialists. After being Director of the London School of Economics from 1919 to 1937 he worked on a wartime study, published in 1942, which became known as the Beveridge Report[4].

The post-war socialist government took the Beveridge Report as a blueprint and legislated the Welfare State into existence. The welfare state was meant to be a form of insurance paid by the National Insurance stamp. This is made clear in the report, which runs to some 300 pages in length. Amongst many other similar assertions it included the following statements:

"It is, first and foremost, a plan of insurance - of giving in return for contributions benefits up to subsistence level, as of right and without means test, so that individuals may build freely upon it.

Medical treatment covering all requirements will be provided for all citizens by a national health service organised under the health departments and post-medical rehabilitation treatment will be provided for all persons capable of profiting by it.........."

"The first view is that benefit in return for contributions, rather than free allowances from the State, is what the people of Britain desire. This desire is shown both by the established popularity of compulsory insurance, and by the phenomenal growth of voluntary insurance against sickness, against death and for endowment, and most recently for hospital treatment. It is shown in another way by the strength of popular objection to any kind of means test. This objection springs not so much from a desire to get everything for nothing, as from resentment at a provision which appears to penalise what people have come to regard as the duty and pleasure of thrift, of putting pennies away for a rainy day. Management of one's income is an essential element of a citizen's freedom. Payment of a substantial part of the cost of benefit as a contribution irrespective of the means of the contributor is the firm basis of a claim to benefit irrespective of means…….."

" (B) Comprehensive health and rehabilitation services for prevention and cure of disease and restoration of capacity for work, available to all members of the community;

(C) Maintenance of employment, that is to say avoidance of mass unemployment………."

It is interesting to note at this point that the provision of an insurance scheme in which the wealthier paid more for the same service, is unusual. From the beginning this was unlike any other insurance that you could buy.
1) it was compulsory,
2) the benefits were stated to be unlimited
3) the more you earned the more you had to pay.

You do not pay more for your car, property or life insurance because you are earning more…….. you only pay more if you are in a higher risk group or wishing to take out a higher level of insurance cover (say for a more expensive car). The Welfare State was definitely different since those who were at the highest risk (the lower socio-economic groups, otherwise known as the poor) paid the least. They had the greatest risk of unemployment, the worst health record and made the least provision for retirement

The wealthy, through the NI stamp and Income tax, paid vastly more for the Welfare State. They had private health insurance, private education and were healthier. I believe that they did not initially complain about the Welfare State because they felt included in it. Now there is a problem because many of the wealthier people do not feel that they are included and rather resent paying a perceived high price for services they do not necessarily receive. This is frequently a misconception but it is a common one.

There were no formal pilot studies and no trials for the inception of the NHS in the form it took. Other countries already had or went on to develop state-backed insurance-based health care provision and over the years they have worked efficiently and closely with the private sector of medicine. Despite naming the contribution as National Insurance back in 1911, the British scheme as inaugurated in 1948 was a tax-backed endeavour. There was no provision for topping up the NI with private insurance and, with regards to health care, no penalty for not having contributed.

For many people, especially in latter years those who have come to the UK as health tourists, it did indeed turn out to be a free allowance from the State. Despite the firm recommendations of the Beveridge Report *"that benefit in return for contributions, rather than free allowance from the State, is what the people of Britain desire"*

That is not what they got.

The Start of the NHS

Look to your health and if you have it praise God and value it next to a good conscience; for health is the second blessing that we mortals are capable of; a blessing that money cannot buy.
Izaak Walton 1593-1683[5]

The establishment of a Welfare State, and with it the start of the National Health Service, was greeted with great celebration by the public. In order to establish such a service the charity and local government hospitals, serving all the large towns and cities, were taken over by the State as Crown property. The smaller health charities, insurance schemes and nursing homes that were not required by the state were mainly grouped into the British United Provident Association in 1947 'to preserve freedom of choice in health care'[6]. Immediately previous to the inception of the NHS most people had some form of health insurance, even though this was often inadequate and charity based . It was a relief to the vast majority that health care was now a government responsibility and very few people retained private insurance.

There were initially great successes and as a child I remember being told that our health service was the envy of the world and what a great privilege it was to live at that time. I still believe that this is the case and that the Welfare State provided great benefit to the vast majority of people. In particular, families with a middle income were considerably better off under the scheme. The very poor had always been looked after by charities: these had originally been set up by the church but in addition there were institutes, hospitals and workhouses for the poor. The rich could afford to pay for health, education and retirement. The vast majority of people on a moderate income lived their lives in fear of hospitalisation and doctors bills paupering them and with regard to education, many decided that they could not afford to send their children on to further education after the age of fifteen. The Welfare State changed all this. Healthcare, education, unemployment pay and pensions were all covered by taxes and National Insurance.

For the babies of the Welfare State it is hard to imagine the situation prior to its inception. Apart from living abroad, perhaps the nearest one can get is to consider the legal system. It is often said that, when in dispute only the poor and the rich have access to the courts. The poor are covered by the legal aid system and the seriously rich can afford to employ lawyers. The rest of us, somewhere in between, find the idea of going to court to fight the perceived wrongs too frightening to contemplate. Even though we may consider ourselves to be completely in the right we know that a maverick judge or a potty jury can rule against us and the court costs alone could be enough to bankrupt us. Now extrapolate that to health, education, unemployment, pensions and general care in our old age. That was the situation before the Welfare State and, as the system is surreptitiously being dismantled by successive governments and particularly by our so-called socialist government, it is the situation to which we are returning. We can already see this with the nursing care of the elderly, the reduced value of pensions, the educational results from many of our state schools and now the privatisation of health care by stealth.

Moreover, unlike the pre-NHS days our freedoms of speech, movement and financial liberty are all being eroded at the same time as our benefits are being removed. The police, once our protectors, now patrol public areas with sub-machine guns and shoot to kill.

Unless we are extremely vigilant we will find that we are in a police state in which any dissent is dealt with by summary expulsion.

The public health measures of the Welfare State were excellent including, for example, immunisation and vaccination programmes, free orange and milk, dental and ophthalmological care for children. There was good funding for the education of health professionals and for medical research.

It is certainly true that many countries watched our NHS with a considerable degree of envy but it is also true that very few copied our exact system of health administration and funding preferring, in the most part, to provide a true insurance based system where money moves with the patient and often including some up-front payment by the patient at the time of delivery of care. In many cases the insurance is a benefit provided by employment and the main costs are borne by the employer.

For, despite its obvious successes, there were problems in the NHS that were developing immediately.

Within a short space of time it became clear that several of the predictions were awry. The Beveridge Report had implied that better healthcare and education would lead to healthier workers and a healthier economy. In addition the healthier workers would require less health care and the cost of healthcare would fall making the entire system economically viable.

What in fact happened was that people queued up to receive free cotton wool which, instead of being used for wounds, was used for stuffing cushions or washing pets[7]. They asked for prescriptions for the aspirin which they had previously bought for themselves for minor aches and pains. And large numbers of edentulous patients insisted on having new teeth free on the NHS.

The Beveridge Myth

Beveridge, or at least those who interpreted his report, had made the same mistake that many economists make. They had not sufficiently taken into account the profoundly selfish and illogical nature of human beings. Human beings do not act in a way that is most beneficial to the majority, or even the most beneficial to themselves. Some can be profoundly altruistic whilst others are determinedly selfish. The costs of the nascent and developing health service were vastly greater than predicted and this was at a time when the economy was in a poor condition.

Unfortunately it became clear that the NI stamp would not cover the costs and the extra expenditure would have to come out of general taxation where it would be competing with all the other government departments and expenses. Moreover cuts in the service would have to be made.

67

The NI stamp has never covered the cost of the NHS and Social Services but it has led to many a patient believing that, since they have paid their stamp, they have paid for the service (which they haven't) and that they are therefore entitled to receive the benefit. Indeed they **are** entitled to the service since they have been given numerous assurances on the subject by successive governments!

The costs of the NHS have always risen year on year and Beveridge's belief that expenditure would fall as people became healthier has never been shown to occur. It seems to be human nature that, once relieved of a major problem, they worry about something more minor. If, for example, your diabetes is being treated by the NHS you can then worry about your sprained ankle…..and, of course, demand treatment. In addition if you keep the patient with diabetes alive when they would otherwise have perished they will go on receiving treatment for the condition, have many complications and eventually succumb either from that condition or from something unrelated (which would usually involve further medical intervention). At no time would it save money.
This mistaken belief on Beveridge's part, or at least on the part of those interpreting his report, is known in some medical circles, perhaps unkindly, as the Beveridge Myth.

Dedication of the staff in the first twenty five years of the NHS

The dedication of the staff in the National Health Service has always been amazing. The doctors, dentists, nurses, porters, other paramedical and non medical staff (secretaries, clerks and even administrators) worked many hours more than they were paid to do.

People who were attracted to work in the early NHS were generally speaking an altruistic bunch. They knew the hours would be long for relatively little thanks but they felt that the work they were doing was not just necessary but vital. They were saving lives every day and making the world a better place to live in.

Doctors, for example, were very protective of their clinical freedom. They fought for the best treatment for each of their patients and would not accept political or financial interference at the clinical level. Woe betide any politician or administrator who tried to prevent a hospital in-patient having necessary drugs or an essential operation. This would have caused major ructions amongst the medical staff and the "admin wallah" would have been sent away with a flea in his ear!

This has been both the doing and undoing of the service. The cost of medical services does not stand still. Medical inflation is always above that of general inflation. For example one health insurance broker states "Present medical inflation therefore is usually 3-5% above UK inflation making premium rises of 8-10% per annum a norm"[8]. This is due to increased costs of new treatments, technologies and pharmaceuticals compounded with the general cost of inflation. This will be discussed again later in the book.

When a doctor insists on having the best for his patient, which is something he should do he runs with the highest level of medical inflation. If a National Health Service doctor works extra hours for which he is not contracted, **even though he is not paid for the work he is costing the health service extra money**! Despite the assurance that the health service is free at the point of delivery there is no such thing as a free lunch. Somebody is paying for the health service and that somebody is the tax-payer!

This pessimistic, if realistic, view of the rising cost of the NHS has to be put into context. It is not only in Britain and not only in the NHS that healthcare costs rise at a greater rate than general inflation. It is a general fact that the advances in medicine mean that more diseases can be diagnosed and treated. Much, but not all, of the time the newer techniques and drugs are more expensive than previous techniques.

Successive UK governments have despaired about the NHS costs, believing that they were spending too much and not getting value for money. This has led to the introduction of many major changes in the administration and management of the NHS from the 1960s onwards. These un-trialled alterations, brought in by political whim and fancy, will be discussed later. In fact compared with other countries the NHS has been a tremendous bargain. UK spending on healthcare as a percentage of gross national product (GNP) has lagged behind that of other developed countries all along. So we had at one time, before all of the political and managerial interference, one of the best health care systems in the world at the cheapest price. Why have we so carelessly thrown it away?

The cost of the health service was always going to be a problem because it so obviously comes out of the public exchequer. Whichever party is in power they will be put under pressure to please the voters by reducing the costs. The very large sums involved mean that the ministers in charge worry enormously that the costs will spiral exponentially out of control.

The first cuts came very soon. We will examine next the first evidence that the entirely laudable aim of providing a comprehensive, totally free "cradle to grave" health service was not ever going to be met. We shall then move on to the period of success in the 1960s and early 70s followed by the crux point or pivot in the NHS as it moved from its 'Golden Era' to a period of decline and then to the terrible failings we hear about every day at the present time. This will be followed by brief details of the emergency changes brought in by successive governments through to the present government. With this history behind us I shall take us into my speculation into why different professionals within the NHS have failed. These will include the major players: the doctors, dentists, nurses, managers and finally the patients. All have had a part in the story of the NHS and a role to play in its incipient failure as a bold experiment. In the final chapters we will examine the need for a health service (yes, there definitely still is a need) and what measures could be put in place to protect and maybe resuscitate it. Do not, however, be too hopeful. Resuscitation, for all its fame and prominence in TV medical drama, has always had a low success rate[9].

The First Cuts

Prescription Charges

Obverse   Reverse
One shilling

The Act permitting the introduction of prescription charges was introduced by the Labour government as an amendment in 1949 just one year after the advent of the Welfare State. It was implemented under Winston Churchill's Conservative Government in 1952. The charge was one shilling (5p) in respect of an item or items on any one form. In 1956 the prescription charge was increased to one shilling per item rather than per form.[10,11]

91% of patients in Scotland qualified for exemptions in 2005 according to Colin Fox MSP[12] and about 80% in England[11]. The disparity between England and Scotland is set to widen with the recent news that it is the intention in Scotland to introduce more exemptions for chronic conditions.

The present exemptions are illogical and unfair. In England a patient with diabetes mellitus is entitled to free prescriptions but chronic asthmatics are not. A chronic bronchitis sufferer with heart failure would still not receive free prescriptions. It is well known for patients to ask of their GP which of the several prescribed drugs is the most important because they cannot afford all of them. Moreover many drugs are cheaper bought privately than they are via NHS prescription.

The overall changes in prescription charge will be followed chronologically throughout the rest of the book.

Dentistry

Dentistry also suffered at a very early stage and has continued to be the Cinderella service of the NHS ever since. Reducing the fees paid to dentists did not sufficiently reduce the cost. So the government introduced a patient's contribution to the dental fee. Dental care would be provided free for children, for the poor (means tested) and during pregnancy.

At the time of writing, the patient's contribution to NHS dental care is about 80% (up to a maximum). However in many places this is irrelevant since you cannot find a dentist who is willing to treat you on the NHS, as demonstrated in the story on the next page.

GRANDMOTHER FORCED TO PULL HER OWN TEETH

Don't ask us to heal dental crisis, doctors warn Labour

The Daily Mail of October16th 2007 page 4 reported the story of a Grandmother aged 67 who had pulled out several of her own teeth over the years since she had lost her place at a National Health Service dental practice when it changed hands.

The Health Minister, Ben Bradshaw, had urged patients needing dental care to 'demand their rights' from their general practitioners (GPs).

The British Medical Association (BMA) had responded that GPs were not qualified to perform dentistry and that the patients should contact their primary care trust not their general practitioners. Laurence Buckman of the BMA said '… family doctors cannot pick up the pieces if there are not enough NHS dentists to go round'.

Optometry

The experience with opticians was similar. So many people wanted free spectacles that it could not be afforded. A system of patient contributions similar to that in dentistry was brought in for optometry. Children could have basic spectacles for free but adults had a somewhat subsidised service including a free eye test for those who qualified. Presently in England that includes those who are 60 or over, under 16 or under 19 in full time education, on income support, suffering from diabetes or glaucoma, at risk from glaucoma or registered blind[13]. Eye tests in Scotland are free[14].

Comment

The main contributors to the cost of the scheme, the taxpayer aged between 16 and 60, did not receive all their treatment for free. The principle of free treatment for all, from cradle to grave, had been violated almost immediately and those who paid the most tax also had to pay the most when they received treatment! This was initially acceptable since the National Health Service, despite its faults, provided good healthcare for the nation. However, it certainly created tensions. The politicians who set up the NHS were well aware of its imperfections but the initial goodwill of the public and of the NHS staff certainly allowed it to function more than adequately.

Advances in Medical Science

Throughout the 1950s the people of Britain were simply grateful that they had " the best health system in the world".

Major advances were occurring in the medical sciences and many of these were taking place in the United Kingdom reinforcing our belief in the NHS.

In 1953 the United Kingdom and the entire British Empire and Commonwealth celebrated the coronation of Queen Elizabeth II.

Coronation crown
5 shillings
1953

Bi-metallic two pound coin 2003
50ᵗʰ Anniversary of the discovery of
DNA structure

In the same year Watson and Crick described the double helix structure of DNA using Rosalind Franklin's data.

In 1956 a major prospective clinical trial, funded by the Medical Research Council and known as 'The British doctors study', provided convincing statistical proof that tobacco smoking increased the risk of lung cancer (the annual death rate from lung cancer in heavy cigarette smokers among doctors was about 40 times the death rate from that cause among non-smoking doctors). This prospective study heralded a new type of scientific research, showed the relevance of epidemiology and medical statistics in questions of public health, and vitally linked tobacco smoking to a number of serious diseases[15,16,17].

In 1957 Professor Sir John Charnley (1911–1982), a man whose contributions to surgery were huge, decided to research into hip replacement surgery. His efforts were extremely successful leading to the present day situation where hip replacements can routinely relieve pain but also provide full mobility and pointing the way for other replacement surgery[18].

With some justification on July 20ᵗʰ 1957, Harold Macmillan, the British Prime Minister, famously told the country 'Most of our people have never had it so good'[19].

A boom in the economy helped the dramatic rise in the standard of living and in 1959 the Conservative Party had a resounding victory putting it back into office and taking the country into the new decade, the Swinging Sixties.

Building Programme in the 1960s

When we build, let us think that we build for ever.
John Ruskin 1819-1900 (The Seven Lamps of Architecture Ch.5)

The 1960s were the first time that Government finance was available for new hospitals in the NHS. Up until then the National Health Service had existed entirely through the use of the old charity and local government hospitals that had been nationalised in 1948. In 1962 Enoch Powell published his Hospital Plan with the intention of levelling up the standards of service. 90 new general hospitals were planned and the remodelling of 134 more. Powell extracted a promise from the treasury that there would be capital spending in each financial year. Powell's priorities embraced disadvantaged groups such as the elderly, mentally disturbed and mothers with young children.[20]

In many ways this was the golden era of the NHS. Modern medical science was coming into practice with great advances in diagnosis and treatment and they were all being implemented in the NHS. The common feeling in Britain was that we had a health service second to none and that we were the envy of the world. Indeed it is true that many countries of the developed world had a very patchy record with regard to health care and that we were amongst the leaders of the world in medical research and teaching, punching well above our weight for the amount of money spent.

The division between provision of services in the north and the south of England was particularly marked but new hospitals were built or planned throughout the country with the intention of balancing the service on a truly national basis.

In 1963 Harold Wilson's Labour Government came to power after '13 years of Tory misrule'. This 'misrule' had set up the financial condition of the nation and the Socialists were able to put money into the health service including the hospital construction as planned by the Conservatives. The mid and late sixties became a time of considerable change in England with a feeling of considerably greater social and sexual freedom.

Half Crown (Two shillings and sixpence) 1967
(Last issue for circulation before decimalisation)

Prescription charges at two shillings were abolished by the Socialists in 1965 but were reintroduced at two shillings and sixpence (half crown) June 10th 1968 by the Conservative government led by Edward Heath.[21]
The Health Services and Public health Act of 1968 section 6(1) extended the powers of Regional Hospital Boards, Hospital Management Committees and Board of Governors to administer specialist patient services outside the hospital (at clinics or centres).

The hospitals were run efficiently by the matron, the medical superintendent and the hospital secretary. In particular the matron knew what was going on all over the hospital and was effectively in charge of all the departments apart from the medical practitioners. I found this out for myself when, in 1968 I took a post as a hospital porter for three months before taking up my place in medical school. A couple of weeks into the post I thought I was coming to grips with the job, which was a very demanding one in a large local hospital. I was asked to present myself to the deputy matron. I hurried along to see her feeling somewhat anxious since the matron and her deputies genuinely were significant figures. I could not imagine what I had done to upset her but considered various minor jokes and jollities we had perpetrated. The deputy matron took me to one side and told me that they were very worried about my friendship with one of the porters. I enquired what the problem was and she said that the porter in question had a bad reputation for drinking and they did not want me to spoil my chances at medical school by getting too friendly with him. I pointed out that I was very busy in the evenings anyway and although he had asked me to join him on a drinking spree or two I had not done so because of lack of time. I thanked her for the advice and thought no more about it since my shifts did not coincide with those of the porter in question for a few weeks. A month later I noticed a small piece in the local newspaper. Two days before the newspaper story, the porter had apparently been caught hopelessly drunk and breaking shop windows. It seems that he had started in the high street and the police had followed a trail of glass and blood until they had finally caught him in a red telephone kiosk where he was assiduously breaking each small, individual pane.

I reflected that I was glad I had been warned about his behaviour and that the matron and her staff really did know what was going on everywhere in the hospital. Even in a large hospital, the matron treated the staff as one large extended family and had the wellbeing of staff and patients foremost in her mind.

Inflation

1971 saw the decimalisation of the British currency and the start of a period of marked inflation in the UK. It was also the time when I started my clinical studies in medical school.

Decimalisation 1971   10 new pence   5 new pence   2 new pence   1 new penny 1/2 new penny
British decimal coinage had been first minted in 1968 to prepare the population for full decimalisation in 1971

The hospital building programme had only been going a few years when in the early 70s the oil crisis hit the world. Britain was thrown into turmoil with considerable exacerbation of inflation, the three-day week and rapid changes in government. Hospital building was put on hold. Only 40 of Enoch Powell's new general hospitals were built and there had been virtually no investment in modernising facilities for the mentally sick. By the mid seventies all public capital investment entered a long-term decline.[20] Prescription charges had reached 20 pence per item in 1971 (4 shillings in the old money) (and by the end of the decade had more than doubled at 45p per item.[21]

50 pence: celebrating accession to the European Economic Community 1973

The UK joined the European Economic Community (EEC) in 1973 calling it The Common Market.

The National Health Service Reorganisation Act of 1973 abolished boards of governors and created Area, District and Regional Health Authorities.

The miners were threatening to bring down the government. The Prime Minister, Ted Heath, went to the country to ask them who was leading it: Was he in charge or the unions? The answer seemed to be the unions since the Labour government of Harold Wilson was elected to replace Heath's.

During this period there was a growing feeling amongst a relatively small group of people that the NHS was poorly organised and administered. This partly emanated from the service side, in particular the nursing and ancillary staff whose unions were becoming militant. It was, however, also a civil service and government view that if they were spending so much on the NHS this should be reflected in a modern streamlined administration. There was little or no unrest amongst the public, negligence cases were very low in number and the patients had great respect for the doctors and nurses. Little did we realise that we were at the very peak of the National Health Service and that its golden period was coming to an end. At no time before or after was the NHS so loved and respected and at no time since then did it give such good value for money.

Part II

NHS failings
left 331 dead
from superbug

It's the doctors' fault the NHS is
in financial trouble, says Hewitt
11/03/2006 Daily Telegraph

Hospital Trusts Fail To Control Infection
By Thomas Moore_Health correspondent_Updated: 12:23, Thursday October 18, 2007
Sky News

Doctors' job system 'has failed
at all stages - and its review is a
fiasco too.
The Times May 14, 2007
College of Midwives News - 02/07/07
NHS ref Moree to fail if staff ignored says new report
More money but NHS fails to recruit doctors
LOUISE GRAY The Scotsman

Hospital bug deaths 'scandalous
BBC News 24 Thursday Oct 11 2007

Hard-up hospital orders staff:
Don't wash sheets - turn them over Daily Mail 29th Oct 2007

The Decline of the National Health Service

Part II

The Decline of the National Health Service

Introduction

A salutary tale

Andrew, the husband of Barbara had not been feeling well for some time. For a couple of months he had lacked drive and he had got to the point that he could hardly drag himself up in the morning. Although only 60 he put it down to old age and had decided to retire from his job. How could he possibly teach fitness classes if he was himself unable to summon the energy to get out of bed? Barbara was also worried about his loss of libido.

For the last week or so he had noticed another symptom: he had gone completely deaf in one ear. He thought that this was probably due to wax but in view of his general low condition and with his wife's prompting he decided to go and see his doctor.

The general practitioner was very thorough, taking his history and looking in his ears. He declared that there was no wax and in view of the profound unilateral deafness and his loss of energy Andrew needed an urgent appointment with the Ear, Nose and Throat (ENT) Specialist at the nearby district hospital. Thus saying the GP wrote the referral letter in front of Andrew and Barbara, stressing the urgency of the situation.

Six weeks later Andrew had heard nothing from the hospital and his health had further deteriorated. He was now confined to bed and seemed barely able to wake up. Barbara was very worried and decided that she had better call the ENT department in case they had not received the letter. On telephoning the department she got through to an admissions clerk and asked whether or not they had received the letter. The reply was in the affirmative. The conversation continued
'Could you please tell me where my husband stands on the waiting list?'
'Well, madam', came the reply. 'Your husband is not on the waiting list. He is on the pile.'

It turned out that the waiting list had reached a critical level set by some arbitrary Government target over which it was not allowed to go. In order that the new referrals still arriving did not cause the department to exceed the target the manager had decided that new cases would not be shown to a doctor to assess urgency but would simply be placed in a pile untouched until the waiting list was at acceptable levels. Andrew's referral letter was in that pile along with many other cases. Since the waiting list itself was for several months and the pile was growing enormous there was no indication that Andrew would be seen for a very long time if he ever made it at all.

Andrew was stoical and did not want to make a fuss but Barbara was very worried. Andrew was fading fast and she really did not think that he would last much longer. She was worried that he would die before he even had his condition diagnosed let alone treated. Luckily she knew a consultant in the NHS personally and spoke to him about the problem. He immediately understood the GP's concern and why the case was urgent.

Unilateral deafness of acute onset can be caused by a number of conditions but the one worrying possibility is a brain tumour.

Andrew needed urgent referral to determine whether or not he had should have tests for a brain tumour. Since the usual route of referral had been blocked by management the consultant took the liberty of arranging the Magnetic Resonance Imaging (MRI) scans himself. This was against the management rules since the patient was not in the correct area by postcode.

The scans were performed two days later and included the whole brain as well as the area of the acoustic nerves. Andrew had a very large tumour but surprisingly it was in the pituitary fossa and nowhere near the auditory nerves (but perhaps the hearing loss was due to a general distortion of the brain). In fact the tumour was pressing on the optic nerves and stretching them and Andrew was in imminent danger of also going blind. By breaking the rules Andrew had been scanned just in the nick of time.

Emergency referrals to endocrine specialists took place and then on to the neurosurgeons and within a very short space of time Andrew was undergoing complex brain surgery for removal of the pituitary tumour.

This was successful. The tumour, although growing quickly, was not malignant. Andrew made a very good recovery; his eyesight was fine and he regained his energy and libido. He was able to go back to part-time work. His unilateral deafness did not recover but did not worsen. The manager's decision to put all referrals in a pile rather than increase the waiting list had almost led to Andrew going blind or even dying.

This story has been told because it is an example of the problems facing patients in the present day NHS. This is a true story with the details changed for anonymity. But this is not a unique story and not everybody is lucky enough to know someone who is able to cut through the red tape and petty officialdom. Today, even if they know a doctor and the doctor agrees that the case is urgent, the medical person may be unable or unwilling to get involved. Doctors who take on the system are themselves at risk.

Mr. A, a hard-worked surgeon, died from a heart attack at the meeting convened to cut his hard-pressed surgical department. Professor B. was suspended because she was forthright with her patients about post-code prescribing. She told them truthfully that she could not give them the life-saving drugs they needed because the management was rationing the service. She was given no reason for her suspension as they trawled through the notes trying to find an excuse for excluding her from the hospital. Professor C. found that management had illegally used his research funds to keep the department in budget. When he tried to investigate he was immediately suspended. When Dr D complained that the training of junior staff was inadequate he was suspended and later sacked.

Meanwhile Mrs E died with terrible bedsores and a super-bug infection due to poor nursing in an NHS hospital. Mr. F died from another super-bug and so did the man in the bed next to him (and the man in the next bed). The list goes on and on.

Today's newspapers are full of gloom and woe about the state of medicine in the United Kingdom. They tell us that the costs have never been so high but that a third of hospitals have indicated that they will have to make desperate cuts. We hear that there are now more managers than there are beds. We are told about people who do not receive the drugs that they require even though the Government agency (NICE) has agreed they are appropriate. We hear stories of doctors who are unemployed even though there is a national shortage of medical staff. We know that it is virtually impossible to find an NHS dentist at all and we hear about medical staff making terrible errors.

And we are all scared of old age and of senility, for we know that the National Health Service (NHS) will not look after us and we will have to use up nearly all of our own hard earned savings to pay for second or third rate institutional care.

Compound that with your own experiences and difficulties in seeing your GP and you may believe that the NHS is failing in its task. You may be wrong. For many an individual it is not failing……it has already failed!

In the first part of this book we looked at the rise in state medicine and the inception of the British NHS. This was mainly a chronological report.

Part II of this book, the Decline of the NHS, is rather different. It does not set out to be a comprehensive history lesson. It is more of a personal comment on the present state of medicine and what I perceive as having gone wrong. There is more analysis of the various elements involved but because these factors are addressed from my perspective they are not as impartial and objective as in the first part. I have tried to see all sides of the arguments but know that this is impossible. You may, therefore, find yourself disagreeing vehemently with my debating point or disliking intensely the tone in which I have written a section. If so, please forgive me. The book has been written from a deep fondness for the NHS as we used to know it. My problem lies in the fact that the old NHS that we all loved no longer exists.

But an enormous amount of good work is done by the clinical staff in the NHS and without it we would be lost. Despite its bad points we all need the National Health Service and we need to save it. The pressure and PR from big business has, in my opinion correctly, not persuaded the majority of people in the UK that we should go the way of the USA.

In a later section of the book we will discuss healthcare systems in the world, see how we compare and discuss possible ways to help the UK's National Health Service.

But first we take up the chronological narrative where we left off, in the mid 1970s.

Chapter 6

Reorganisation and industrial action in the 1970s

Management Changes: the National Health Service Reorganisation 1974

The National Health Services Act of 1946 made the Minister of Health responsible for the constitution of Regional Hospital Boards, Hospital Management Committees and Board of Governors of teaching hospitals. The Health Services and Public health Act 1968 section 6(1) extended these powers to administer specialist patient services outside the hospital (at clinics or centres). This was one of the only significant management changes until 1974 when the NHS organisation was completely revamped.[1]

Put into action in 1974, the National Health Service Reorganisation Act of 1973 abolished boards of governors and hospital management committees and created Area, District and Regional Health Authorities.

Back in 1948, the service had taken over some 3,000 hospitals from local government and the voluntary sector. And it was these hospitals that attracted the funding, irrespective of the populations they were serving. The hospital plan in 1962 was the first attempt to reduce regional inequalities in healthcare provision. By 1966, with funding increasingly scarce, this ambitious plan was downgraded.[2]

The role of management in the NHS had traditionally from its inception in 1948 been one of administration. The hospital administrator was a facilitator who 'got things done'.[1] Professional staff, particularly the consultants and Matron, were responsible for the clinical service provided unfettered by management.

The reorganisation of '74 changed all this with establishment of management on a 'consensus basis' and putting considerable emphasis on the role of hospital treasurers. The Unit Administrator (hospital level) answered to the Sector Administrator who answered to the District Health Authority who answered to the Area Health Authority who answered to Regional Health Authority who answered to the Dept of Health and Social Security.

1974 was a time of shortages and industrial unrest throughout the UK. I was in my final year at medical school and spent some months in Nigeria on elective. Before I went away we had just settled into a new flat with some good friends. Whilst I was in Nigeria on March 3rd a Turkish Airlines DC10 crashed in Paris killing all 345 people on board, including, very sadly, both parents of one of the friends. They were only on the plane because of a strike by engineers at London airport and the subsequent cancellation of their British Airways flight.

I returned from Nigeria to a changed personal situation. The friends had left the flat and new flatmates had moved in. There were other, more subtle, changes. For example, a shortage of sugar in Nigeria had prompted me to give up sugar in my tea and coffee.

When I returned my fiancée had also stopped taking sugar due to a major supply crisis in the UK. Major changes had also occurred in the National Health Service.

The 1974 reorganisation of the health service was resented by NHS staff and considered to be disruptive[3]. The results may perhaps have been beneficial if the reorganisation had not occurred at such a time of financial difficulty. For the first time ever the NHS really began to feel the pinch.

The nurses thought the reorganisation gave too much power to the doctors, the doctors thought they had lost control and saw numerous administrators taking over their doctors' dining rooms and other facilities. In addition they thought that it was a terrible waste of resources and an excuse to bring in cuts in services.

Traditional strikes by porters and other staff played into the hands of the management. One manager confided in me some years ago that the "only thing that allowed us to stay within budget was the industrial action by the porters. Because we couldn't work we saved money. The strike action was very helpful". This is a good example of the NHS working in the opposite way to a conventional business.

The Regional Allocation Working Party (RAWP) brought into action in 1976 was one of the perceived problems. RAWP was designed to even up the spending on health care but, due to the financial crisis affecting Britain as a whole, it was used to institute cuts in areas considered to cost too much.

The Resource Allocation Working Party (RAWP) report
"Sharing Resources for Health in England"

In its report RAWP recommended the use of a formula reflecting relative need in order to secure equal opportunity of access to health care for people at equal risk. The formula included the use of mortality ratios, population, age and sex adjusted utilisation rates and fertility rates, but excluded caseloads; and suggested that the additional service costs incurred by the NHS in providing facilities for clinical teaching of medical and dental students should be recognised by the payment of a "Service Increment for Teaching" (SIFT)[4].

Unfortunately the formula was brought in just at the time that the economy was at its lowest ebb. RAWP was used as an excuse to cut funding thus leveling down rather than the leveling up which had been the original intention.

Inner city hospitals such as Bethnal Green in London, were targeted for cuts leading to extraordinary industrial disputes in which 24 hour *work-ins* were conducted by the staff at all levels preventing closures. These were eventually broken by the management taking legal action against "rogue" doctors working too much and forcibly moving nursing staff to other sites in the District. This is another good example of the NHS being the antithesis of a business since work-ins in most industries would simply lead to greater productivity.

The aggressive action taken shows that they were much more worried about staff working too hard than they were about staff going on strike!

It is hard to remember the power of the UK trade unions before the era of Margaret Thatcher. In the 60s and 70s the health service unions representing nurses, porters, cleaners (and eventually even the doctors) all undertook or threatened industrial action.

The nurses were reorganised into a civil service-like structure of numbered nursing officers under the Salmon Report (1966 but brought into action in the mid 70s). The effect was dire, leading to the removal of the most experienced nurses from the wards and operating theatres. This is described later in this book in the chapter about nursing.

The porters and cleaners and more junior administrators were in close discussions with the Labour Government of Harold Wilson via their unions (NALGO, COHSE). With Barbara Castle as Secretary of State for the Dept of Health and Social Services (DHSS) there was a very left wing bias. In this forum the junior doctors thought that they might have a sympathetic hearing for their problems. They could not have been more wrong.

Industrial Disputes
The Junior Doctors Dispute, 1975

My account of the junior doctors dispute, a previously unwritten piece of history, will not agree with official BMA and government accounts for reasons which will become obvious as you read this section.

In 1975 Labour was in power in the United Kingdom, and the country was in the grip of a recession caused by the oil crisis[4]. I was employed as a pre-registration house officer at the Westminster Children's Hospital working, like most other newly qualified doctors, an extraordinary rota, which is still ingrained on my brain (as their rota probably is on theirs). It effectively meant that I was on duty for an average of 120 hours a week. At night, when it might otherwise be expected that the duties would be lighter, I was the doctor on call for the children's casualty department. Thus I was up every night tending children with coughs and colds and the occasional real emergency such as meningitis or severe asthma. 120 hours spent working meant that there were only 48 hours left for catching up on sleep, meeting friends and general living. The duties were worked over a period of two weeks. One of the weeks would include continuous duties from the Thursday morning through to the Tuesday evening, a period of 128 hours with only the occasional catnap to keep me going, then back on again at 9.00am next morning.

I had been a keen and fit sportsman up until this time and this fitness allowed me to survive the incredible schedule. Unfortunately it did not permit any time for sport and I have never since then managed to regain the level of fitness or had time for regular sport.

The majority of patients were still grateful for the service we provided but there was a change in attitude appearing amongst the younger adults. I vividly remember whilst working in the middle of the night in the children's casualty, a mother complained to me vociferously that she deserved better than she was getting. After complaining that I had kept her waiting for fifteen minutes she launched into a diatribe about her living conditions. She had a young family to look after, the council had given her a free flat and to her disgust she had been given second-hand furniture. She very forcibly told me that she should have had new furniture! I had to bite my tongue since I was paying rent on a tiny little flat in a run-down part of Battersea and had just bought a pair of old second-hand armchairs *and* I was working as a slave.

Aged 25, and after 6 years of undergraduate and postgraduate study, two degrees (BSc. and MBBS) I was being paid less per hour than a first year student nurse. But so were all the other house officers. We were all on a contract that, although complex, basically required a working week of 80 hours physically in the hospital, beyond which overtime was paid at time and a quarter. There were payments for encroachment on off-time if it exceeded two hours and if this happened theoretically the entire period of up to 16 hours could be claimed (though I do not believe that this clause was understood or acted upon. It certainly was not at the Westminster Children's Hospital). The overtime forms had to be filled in by the junior doctor and then ratified by their consultants and by management (but getting the consultants to sign the forms was a difficult task in itself). No extra pay was available at all for on-call from home.

Not surprisingly the junior doctors wanted a better deal. The Junior Hospital Doctors Association (JHDA) was originally a breakaway committee from the BMA but in 1974 and 1975 it had become an active staff organisation in its own right. They were buoyed up by campaign for reforms of the General Medical Council (GMC). The Committee of Inquiry into the Regulation of the Medical Profession, under the chairmanship , of AW Merrison (later Sir Alec) had reviewed the regulation of medical education, fitness to practice, professional conduct and the structure and function of the GMC. Specialist registration by the GMC was to be a precondition for the independent practice of medicine. The committee stated that the Council should be independent and predominantly professional, financed mainly by the medical profession[8]. These changes were perceived as a considerable success for the JHDA.

The JHDA had vociferously pushed for a standard 40-hour week for the juniors for some time.

The BMA took the wind from their sails by announcing in early 1975 that they had secured a deal with the DHSS providing just that. The BMA had just signed a new contract with the government that gave us the desired 40-hour week with overtime payments for work in excess of 40 hours.

I was amazed. Partly this amazement was because I could not see how such a deal could be affordable. Surveys had indicated that the junior doctors were working an average of 86 hours a week. They were receiving overtime payments for just 6 hours! The new contract appeared to promise 46 hours of overtime payment for the same work.

Secondly, I did not share the views of many of my more left wing colleagues. They felt that we would be listened to sympathetically by Harold Wilson's socialist government for, after all, the Labour party were the ones who had set up the NHS. My left leaning friends thought that the socialists would be the ones to help the hospitals and that would include helping the junior doctors. I disagreed for I believed that doctors were perceived as Conservative voters and that they were hated by the ardent old-guard socialists.

The final reason for my amazement was that I had inside information. The husband of a close friend was working at the time as a civil servant in the DHSS. He warned me that he, in person, had heard Barbara Castle walking up and down the corridors of power and expressing with glee that "I will take the junior doctors to the cleaners!" (Note : this is a direct quote from the civil servant).

However it appeared that I was wrong. They had signed an agreement with the BMA on the basis of a 40-hour week and overtime.

I, along with nineteen thousand and five hundred other junior doctors, eagerly awaited the details of the contract.

The contract

When I saw the contract I was horrified. The contract had been duly signed by the DHSS and the BMA but it was un-priced. There were no details about the pay, either for the basic wage or for the overtime. Even the generic value of the overtime was not specified. Thus, I reasoned, the government could turn round and say that overtime would be at 50% of the basic rate. Or perhaps even less! In fact my quick calculations showed that this was highly likely since the government did indicate that they did not expect that the new deal would cost any more than the present contract.

I immediately conveyed my alarm to the BMA and to the JHDA. The BMA representatives on the negotiating committee told me that I was completely wrong. They were confident that the DHSS would not expect doctors to work overtime at less than normal time rate. They were, of course, wrong.

The contract when priced provided the following.

Basic pay for a forty-hour week.
A compulsory four hours free period (bringing the basic week up to 44 hours)
Overtime at 30% of time-rate for those working first on-call in the hospital after 44 hours or overtime at 10% for those second on-call in the hospital or on-call from home.

The vast majority of junior doctors were going to lose money on this new contract with a gain for the more senior of the junior doctors who were on-call from home. The contract had made things worse for the very doctors who were working the hardest, there was detriment to many and there would be no incentive for the management to improve the doctors' hours. Not surprisingly the most glaringly unfair examples emerged.

In my own case of 120 hours I had been paid for 40 hours for the basic salary, 40 had been for free (making a basic week of 80) then 40 at time and a half. So I was paid for 90 hours...the overtime more than doubled my income.

On the new contract I would receive the basic salary for 40 hours, then nothing for 4, then for the next 76 hours I would receive 22.8 hours pay. The total pay would be 62.8 hours which was only 70% of that which I had earned on the old contract. To receive the same income I would have to work over 210 hours per week. Since there were then (and there still are) only 168 hours per week this was clearly impossible. This is assuming that all my work in the hospital was considered as 'first on-call'. If it was thought to be 'second on-call' I would receive even less.

A casualty doctor working a 60 hour week (solid shift working doing no on-call) would be treated as though 16 of these hours were on-call and these hours of hard slog would be paid at 30% rate (not time and 30%, just 30%) and the first 4 hours after the basic 40 would be worked for free.

A dermatologist, working a 1 in 1 on-call rota from home, able to do such a rota because he was almost never called, would have a boost to his salary of 31%.

My calculations using a Sinclair pocket calculator (£14.00 by mail order) showed that over 70% of junior doctors would be in a detrimental situation. I could not accept that the government would even be paying the same amount on juniors' salaries as they had done in the previous year.

By this time I had attended numerous staff and union meetings and had been duly elected as the treasurer of the Junior Hospital Doctors Association (JHDA). I was also an elected junior doctors' representative for the British Medical Association.

Once again I conveyed my fears to the JHDA and the BMA but this time they were backed by cogent arguments and calculations. The JHDA immediately sent out a press report indicating that calculations by their treasurer showed that the DHSS had got their calculations wrong and the new contract would be a disaster for the doctors. The BMA, not realising that I was one of their representatives, put out a reply that the government had got the figures right and that the JHDA treasurer was a fool. They fully endorsed the new contract.

The DHSS did not have to make a reply at all since the BMA had replied on their behalf. I immediately resigned from the BMA realising that they were simply toeing the government's line (and I was not particularly enjoying being abused by them).
The press release was quoted in the newspapers and the JHDA executive committee were filmed by the TV news programmes as we entered one of our meetings.

At this point the proceedings took an interesting personal turn. The London School of Economics (LSE), a well known hotbed of radical activism, got in touch with me. They wanted me to speak at their weekly Current Affairs meeting.

This was a great opportunity but it could go hopelessly wrong. I knew that the LSE would not be on my side since the left wing newspapers had been reporting the dispute as being a fight by over paid junior doctors complaining about lack of private income. It seemed likely to me that the majority of students and many of the staff would consider me to be a rich conservative voter who they could shout down.

So I prepared well. I looked into the history of the General Strike of 1926. This was called by the TUC in support of the miners who had been given a longer working day and reduced rates per hour. Their slogan had been "Not a penny less, not an hour more".

I decided to adopt this slogan and prepared a poster. On one side it said

> *Not a penny less, not an hour more*
>
> *Miners Strike*
> *1926*

And on the other side I had scribbled

> *Not a penny less, not an hour more*
>
> *Junior Doctors' Dispute*
> *1975*

When I stood up to speak I realised that I had been quite right. The meeting did feel very antagonistic. The idea of militant doctors was obviously new to them and they did not like it!

I started to speak and hit them with the poster. "This is what it is about" I told the audience, "It's a repeat of the miners' action of 1926 which led to the General Strike".

They all looked knowingly as I showed them the first side of the poster, although they did not understand its significance. Turning the poster round they read the slogan and looked perplexed. " It's not about more pay and it is nothing to do with private practice. We just want to be treated like human beings and we do not want a contract which gives us less pay than we are presently getting and is an inducement to longer hours". I then explained about the overtime at 30% or 10%. There was general disbelief. " You surely mean time plus 30%" they asked and it took me some minutes to explain that this was not the case. " Then it's not overtime", " you are being offered an under-rate", "never heard such a ridiculous idea", were some of the comments I heard. I showed them the official documentation, passing it round for inspection by the participants.

The lecturers and the students were so incensed by the plight of the junior doctors that they decided they would help. Three heads of departments offered the assistance of post-graduate students who immediately came to meet the committee of the JHDA and to help me with my work. The students, named Peter Martin, Bernard Casey and Alan Cave, all took on different aspects of the dispute and we met with the heads of departments in a 'war cabinet' at least once a week whilst the dispute was at its height.

I showed them my calculations indicating that the government figures were wrong and they suggested that I needed to prove this. Since we had both the staff side (BMA) and the DHSS against us at the negotiating table (known as the Whitley council), they were right. We therefore wrote round to all the JHDA representatives asking them to obtain the information from their administrators. At that time many administrative staff were on our side and were happy to give us figures regarding pay to junior doctors in the previous year. We obtained a good smattering of the information before the supply dried up.
The information only ceased to be forthcoming because of government intervention.
They invoked the official secrets act and a D-Notice.

The official secrets act, legislation carried by Parliament in under an hour one Friday afternoon in 1911 was " One of the " first priorities" of the 'Intelligence Department' formed under the advice of the Committee of Imperial Defence during the tense build-up to the First World War. It gave very wide ranging powers to the government saying that no proof of intent of purpose 'prejudicial to the safety of interests of the State' is required, this can be inferred from the accused's 'circumstances', 'known character' or 'conduct'. The Act also contains provision to make an offence the "wrongful communication of information". This is extremely broad, including "any information which has been obtained by the accused 'owing to his position as a person who holds or has held office under His Majesty [or contracted to His Majesty in any way]'."[5]

This act, hated by socialists as being against civil liberty, was indeed used by Harold Wilson's government to stop the NHS administrators giving the JHDA and BMA representatives details of the previous cost of the doctors' payroll. The BMA had been slow off the mark and had only just started to request the information when the D-Notice was announced putting the data out of bounds and asking newspapers not to publish stories about the subject 'for reasons of national security'.

It is interesting to note that the official secrets act was replaced with a new act in 1989 which specifically removed the public interest defence. This defence had led to the acquittal of Clive Ponting in 1985. The case was a milestone in British legal history. D-Notices still exist and are now called DA-Notices.

Meanwhile the junior doctors around the country were up in arms. At various sites they called for strikes and in numerous hospitals they decided upon a 'work to rule' of a 40-hour week. Our hospital decided to undertake the latter, which gave me plenty of time to pursue the union role. The effect on the management was largely determined by the publicity gained in the media since the slow down in patient throughput will only have helped their finances. This is something which we did not realise at the time or we would have taken industrial action which increased their costs such as increasing operating theatre hours!

With the considerable help of the LSE the media coverage was excellent.

One of our problems with the story about the DHSS calculations on junior doctor expenditure was that at the time government figures were regarded very highly and most people, when questioned, would have said that government figures were usually correct. We needed to change the public perception about official figures for otherwise it was likely to be our information which would be considered as suspect.

The LSE working party suggested that we should actively search out examples of bad errors in government figures and put stories out about them. These need not be about the NHS, they just needed to be about inaccurate official figures.

Many official figures are accurate because they are based on past events. Finding examples of error was, however, fairly easy since predictions of future cost were usually highly inaccurate (just think of the overspend on building missiles if you want a simple example). This little campaign did upset the government and, with the union backed action as a backdrop, the JHDA were finally invited to meet the DHSS. This was a minor triumph in itself because the BMA have sole negotiating rights written into the original agreements about the NHS. We were allowed at this stage to meet the officials but not Barbara Castle.

At this meeting we finally achieved an agreement that the figures on overtime pay would be audited. This was something we had been fighting for from the beginning.

After some weeks I received a phone call from the auditors, Price Waterhouse.

"Dr. Goddard" they intoned " We now have the results of the audit. We believe we have reached a good compromise". I protested that a compromise was not what we were after but the spokesman continued " The figure we have reached is 14.2 million pounds"

This was a shock. The official figure had been stated as £12m and the expected cost (so my civil servant friend informed me) was £10m. My calculations had indicated that £18m would be a fair estimate but here we were being offered 14.2, roughly half way between the expected costs and my calculations.

I hotfooted my way to the LSE feeling that we had won at best a pyrrhic victory. We had obtained an audit but the money would not be sufficient to pay the junior doctors without detriment. We also felt that taking industrial action, which by this time had been called off, had antagonised the public and the government and that the gain was minimal.

The LSE listened to the tale of the telephone call with surprising glee. They dismissed my views that the results were a failure and told me that we had the government on the run. I explained that the figure would not cover a "no detriment" clause but they smiled. "Just change the ordinate," explained one of the students " If you can't change X, change Y". I still did not understand what they were saying but they made it simpler still

"If the figure is 14.2 million for all the overtime, tell them that the overtime worked was less than they thought. This will be the divisor (the number by which the 14.2 is divided) and with a smaller number for the divisor the pay per hour can be increased. Convince them that this is possible within the budget, they will agree to pay a higher figure to get themselves off the hook and when the figure is totted up at the end of the first year it will be vastly greater than they predicted, just like all their other predictions."

I agreed to look at this proposal. It went against the grain since all along I had argued that the doctors were working such long hours that they deserved more pay. To argue that they had been working fewer hours seemed wrong but I sat down and looked at the published figures on overtime hours.

From the start of the dispute the DHSS had been reluctant to believe that we were working so many hours but I knew that the official overtime figures did not reflect the hours spent. Many juniors were too afraid of their consultant to ask them to sign their overtime claim forms and I did not know of any instance in which a junior had been successful in claiming for working over two hours into an off period. But theoretically most of the claimed overtime could be for working just over two hours into an off-time period of 16 hours. If they claimed on the new contract they would only be able to put down the time actually spent (just over 2 hours). There was clearly a range of possibilities to explain the official figures. It could be that the doctors were only working just over two hours a night extra every night of the week giving an average of say 40 basic hours plus 11 of overtime. These 51 hours would have shown up as 120 hours because each night could be taken as 16 hours. Alternatively when the doctor claimed he was working 120 hours he could have been doing exactly that. I was pretty sure that the latter was the case but for the sake of argument I was, with complete rectitude, able to put the other possibility also.

To appear fair I stated that a mid-range figure would be reasonable. Thus rather than the 86 hours of average work one could say that this was achieved by working just approximately six hours extra but claiming for 3 nights of 16 hours. A midrange figure would be around 66 to 70 hours or so.

These calculations were carefully annotated and presented to the Doctors and Dentists Review Body as evidence from the JHDA. The evidence was accepted since it was mathematically correct. Even though I did not believe it to be true it was indeed possible.

The contract was re-priced and considerable improvement was considered affordable.

Virtually all overtime was to be paid at 30% with almost no 10% B units and the free period of 4 hours was removed.

The doctors who most benefited were once again those who were on call from home and doing the least work. So we set about improving the contract by another means.

It was one thing giving the junior doctors a new contract but completely another implementing it. There were no guidelines issued by the DHSS to the managers and they had no idea how to calculate the Units of Medical Time (a four hour period). These UMTs were the new name for overtime and had to be agreed in advance on each doctor's contract. So at the JHDA we sat down and wrote the guidelines. We spelt out that if the number of UMTs was not an integer (whole number) they should be rounded up and that for doctors on call in the hospital an extra UMT should be applied to all contracts ":for flexibility" to cover the odd period when another doctor did not appear on time or when there was an emergency. As far as I know these were not discussed by the BMA with the DHSS although we (the JHDA) had talked in general terms about them to the DHSS officials. The guidelines were printed and sent out to all the personnel managers without any indication of where they had come from. Nearly all contracts were then settled on the basis of the JHDA guidelines and when I spoke to the personnel departments they expressed themselves as being very grateful for the help!

In the first year the overtime did not cost £10 million, the government's original estimate, it did not cost £12m, the official figure, it did not cost £14.2m, the Price Waterhouse compromise and it did not cost £18m which was my original figure. It was almost twice as much at £30.5 million! To put this into perspective you would probably have to multiply by between 10 and 20 for today's costs.

So what did the experience of the Junior Doctors Dispute teach me and does this have any bearing on the imminent collapse of the NHS?

I learnt a number of things:

- It was very easy to gain 'power' through a union system and that this power had a corrupting influence (on myself as well as on others!)

- There were very clever civil servants in the DHSS. For perhaps the first time in my life I was aware of people who were brighter than myself. There were also some very clever guys at the LSE.

- The hospital management were out of their depth throughout the dispute.

- There was no central body of information in the NHS. It just muddled along not knowing what it was doing.

- The politicians found it almost impossible to believe that the doctors were working as hard as they were. It was this reluctance to understand our ridiculously long hours which permitted the DDRB to re-price the contract so erroneously.

- Unless an agreement was written down it was never adhered to. Whilst most of us live our lives on a basis of honour and keep to our word, the politicians and NHS management certainly do not.

- Doctors made very poor negotiators. We cared too much about the subject and about our jobs. We were too easily put under pressure by the politicians. It was only when we had the help of the LSE that we were able to progress. Unfortunately the BMA has continuously refused to use professional negotiators for consultants and juniors.

During the period of dispute one of the problems constantly thrown at us by the DHSS was the £6 a week pay rise agreement. The government had negotiated with the unions a broad and solid agreement that there should be no pay rises greater than £6 a week whatever the wages of the worker. So a professional earning £10,000 a year was only allowed a £6 pay rise just the same as the student nurse on £1,500.

It is interesting to note that the junior doctors' new contract broke this agreement from the very start. Some of the doctors were to have a 30% rise even on the original pricing and this was not permitted. We checked up on this by presenting the Department of Trade with a hypothetical case in which the pay increase over the entire shop floor of a factory was averaged at £6 but in which some workers gained much more than this limit whilst others might even lose. We were told that even if a cabinet minister sanctioned this it would break the agreement and the minister would be out of line with cabinet policy and would have to resign.

But what do I believe the long term effect were of this dispute with the government? I think that it certainly permitted many doctors to have a better lifestyle than they would have done if we had been forced to accept the original pricing. A much better way of doing this and lowering the hours would have been to negotiate a decrease in the required number of hours before punitive overtime payments were made. Thus a decrease from 80 to 70 hours for the normal working week would have been very beneficial for those working the longest hours. This could have been followed up by further reductions in hours in following years whilst maintaining overtime rates at higher than time rate. Unfortunately the BMA had already accepted the contract un-priced before the 19,500 junior doctors ever had a chance to see it.

The industrial action taken by the junior doctors may have been the only way of making the government listen to our legitimate claims but it has been argued that it had little effect on the dispute as shown in the abstract from Susan Treolar's article[6] reproduced below.

'In late 1975, for the first time in the history of the National Health Service, junior hospital doctors in the United Kingdom took industrial action. Their pay and working conditions were basic issues, but the dispute was complex. .... The ambivalence, confusion and ignorance about the new contract and the question of breaking government pay policy, problems of representation, and conflicts of interests within the profession are highlighted. It is suggested that the significant economic gains of the junior doctors were not achieved by industrial action.'

Having been 'in the thick of it' I have to disagree. Before we took action neither the Government or the BMA were listening to the junior doctors. As far as they were concerned it was all done and dusted. The industrial action reopened a debate, which the Government thought they had already won. This could only have been because of political pressure and public reaction not for fiscal reasons. As I argued earlier, because the NHS works in the opposite way to a business our industrial action certainly did not hurt the management or government financially.

On the negative side I believe that the industrial action, although deemed essential at the time, had a detrimental effect on our professional image. This was predicted by many of my colleagues and in view of the loss of esteem of the medical profession over the past 30 years they were probably right.

It showed the government that they could not easily control the doctors and that the management systems of the NHS introduced the year before, did not really work. The civil servants had been wrong footed and did not like this. Coupled with other health service disputes at the time it paved the way for the later government of Margaret Thatcher to introduce line management into the NHS in an attempt to control the medical profession.

The Paybeds Dispute

Whilst the juniors were having a dispute over contracts their seniors, the Consultants, were having a hard time over their private practice. The NHS trade unions COHSE (the Confederation of Health Service Employees) and NUPE (National Union of Public Employees) had long hated the way in which consultants were permitted to bring private patients into paybeds in the NHS hospitals. This was a right established at the inception of the NHS but the trade unions called it 'queue jumping'. The simple fact that the payments for using the beds very greatly supported the finances of the hospitals did not seem to bother them. Private medicine was queue jumping and they wanted to stamp it out.

Now the six pounds a week pay rise agreement with the trade unions mentioned a few paragraphs above was a very interesting thing. Many people were amazed that Harold Wilson had managed to organise this with the trade unions since they were very powerful at the time. In fact it was a trade-off. Wilson agreed that the unions could each have a bill of their own choice through parliament if they kept to the £6 pay rise.

For COHSE and NUPE the choice was a bill about pay beds

But the pay beds have never been queue jumping. They represented a second queue: a queue for private medicine. In many NHS hospitals the pay beds were in a separate private wing and they provided up to a third or more of the hospitals income, which was not replaced.

Barbara Castle hated private medicine and vowed to remove it from the UK. She also many times stated that she had never had private medicine herself until it is reputed that one day when she was talking on a radio programme a doctor phoned in to say that she had undoubtedly had private treatment. She threatened to sue him until he announced that he was her private surgeon and she still had not paid him!

Despite such successful point scoring Barbara Castle, NUPE and COHSE had their way. The Government issued a consultative document, "The Separation of Private Practice from National Health Service Hospitals", which set out proposals to reduce the number of pay beds in NHS hospitals and to control developments in private practice[8]. Most of the private medicine was expunged from the NHS by act of parliament in 1976. It then reappeared in the multitude of small private nursing and convalescent homes that were upgraded into private hospitals. Operating theatres, intensive care units and x-ray departments were put into the private hospitals and the rich private patients did not have to enter the portals of the NHS. Neither, unfortunately, did their money or their legacies.

On a separate historical point it is interesting to note that not all of the unions succeeded in obtaining the bill of their choice. I was in the visitor's gallery of the House of Commons on the day that the Dock Workers Bill was debated. This would have made any loading and unloading within 50 miles of tidal water into dock work, to be undertaken by members of the dockers' unions. The bill was an enabling law, which would have permitted the minister to change the number of miles at his discretion without coming back to parliament. The MPs sponsored by other union noticed that there was a problem with this bill. All manufacturing and most shop work involve some loading and unloading and the definition was very loose. So all workers in the country could, at a minister's whim, be turned into dock workers. The dockers already had guaranteed jobs for life due to the National Dock Labour Scheme (NDLS) which had been introduced by the Labour Government in 1947, thus they were already better off than most other workers. The other trade unions would have been redundant and the dockers' unions would have had a monopoly.

The bill was narrowly defeated due to a rebellion by backbench MPs. I believe that this was the first time that Harold Wilson's government had been defeated.

Also in 1976 a Royal Commission on the National Health Service was set up.

St George's Hospital Medical School, London, moved to Tooting. To the surprise of the DHSS the building at Hyde Park Corner reverted to the original donor when not used for health. This was the Duke of Westminster whose family had donated the site for medical use in 1870 as related earlier in the book (page 54). It is now a hotel.

Further Disputes in the NHS

The British economy was so weak in 1976 that a loan was sought from the International Monetary Fund. James Callaghan took over as Prime Minister and David Ennals replaced Barbara Castle at the DHSS

There were further major industrial disputes affecting all industries and culminating in the "winter of discontent". In the British winter of 1978–79 there were widespread strikes by Trade Unions demanding larger pay rises for their members. "The strikes were a result of the attempted enforcement of a government rule that pay rises be kept below 5%, and began in private industry before spreading to the public sector; many of them seriously disrupted everyday life. Whilst the strikes were largely over by February 1979, the government's inability to contain the strikes earlier helped lead to Margaret Thatcher's victory in the 1979 general election and legislation to restrict unions.
The most notorious strike, although it only affected a small part of the country, involved gravediggers and prevented burials for several weeks.[7,8]

Strikes also paralyzed refuse collection and hospital care. One friend of mine was involved in a road traffic accident at this time. The ambulance took him to a local hospital where he was met by striking porters. " You can't be admitted because there are no porters working" he was told. He replied that he was able to walk and got off the trolley. Before he knew what was happening he was bundled back onto the trolley and he reports "I was given a shot of something and woke up in a bed in a hospital many miles away from the first one."

These politically inspired catastrophes were bad enough. The NHS roller coaster was to become steeper and wilder under Thatcher and even worse under Blair.

Medical Training

It was around 1978 that, whilst sitting as chairman of the Junior Hospital Doctors' Association terms and conditions of service committee, I received an extraordinary document from the Department of Health. I no longer have this in my possession but it was entitled something along the lines of "On the Planned Reduction in Dependence on Overseas Doctors".

Overseas doctors had played an increasingly important role in staffing the junior doctor ranks of the NHS. They were expected to come over from their country of origin, take a relatively poorly paid junior hospital post and go back to their home country after a few years having ostensibly been trained in post-graduate medicine or surgery. In fact they were made to work excessively long hours and training was minimal causing much heartache. I believe the implicit but not stated argument was that female doctors could take the place of the overseas doctors and, just like the overseas counterparts they would not be expected to progress as a career, except at a snail's pace.

The plan was to double the UK intake into medical school and by 1984 produce 4,000 doctors per annum compared with the 2000 of 1979. They would do this by setting as 50% the minimum proportion of female medical students in training in each medical school. The percentage of female students rose very quickly until it hovered around 60 to 70%. The number and quality of students of the male persuasion applying for medical school became a progressive problem as medicine was more and more seen to be a subject for girls rather than boys and the poor working hours of the doctors were noted. In recent years the drop out rate, during training and in the junior doctor years, has become a serious worry.

The Royal College of Radiologists booklet Changing Working Lives (published December 2005)[9] addresses the contribution of female doctors on page 8… " *it has been estimated that the total contribution to work in a lifetime is approximately 25 years for a female doctor as opposed to 35 years for a male.*"

This must be taken into account when undertaking manpower planning.

Chapter 7

Fundamental Changes in the NHS

The Thatcher Revolution

There are bad times just around the corner, there are dark clouds hurtling through the sky
And it's no good whining about a silver lining, for we know from experience they won't roll by.

Noel Coward (1899-1973)[1]

Many people, when questioned about Maggie Thatcher, throw their hands up in horror and say " She was mad". They seem to forget that a majority of them voted for her in 1979, 1983 and 1987.

The initial effects of Thatcherism were like a breath of fresh air to most people in the UK. In particular the curbing of the power of the trade unions was well received since most of the public were fed up with the unions' bullying tactics. Later her moves to privatisation of previously nationalised industries were very controversial and I, like many others, think she went too far. I quote from Wikipedia[2]:

"The profound changes Thatcher set in motion as Prime Minister altered much of the economic and cultural landscape of the UK. She curtailed the power of the trade unions, cut back the role of the state in business and dramatically expanded home ownership, which were intended to create a more entrepreneurial culture. She also aimed to cut back the welfare state and foster a more flexible labour market which she believed would create jobs and could adapt to market conditions.
Exacerbated by the global recession of the early 1980s, her policies initially caused large-scale unemployment, especially in the industrial heartlands of northern England and the coalfields of South Wales, and increased wealth inequalities. However, from the mid-1980s a period of sustained economic growth led to an improvement in the UK's economic performance. Thatcher's supporters claim that her policies were responsible for this."

Margaret Thatcher and her policies were, and remain, highly controversial and polarising. Her supporters contend that she was responsible for rejuvenating the British economy, while her opponents argue that she was responsible for - among other things - mass unemployment and a vast increase in inequality between rich and poor."

Plagues

On the world stage, with regard to health, two major events occurred. The World Health Organisation (WHO) announced in 1980 that smallpox had been eradicated worldwide. One plague on humanity had been removed thanks to Edward Jenner, the enlightened intervention of funding from the UK government in the early 1800s and subsequent vaccination programmes.

In 1981 the first Acquired immune deficiency syndrome (AIDS) case was reported in the UK. It was to be the start of a new worldwide plague.

Thatcher and the Health Service

You never give me your money; you only give me your funny paper.
Lennon and McCartney[3]

The first health service reforms of 1982 were fairly minor, reorganising the areas and districts by enlarging the role of the latter and more or less removing the former. However the global recession of the late 1970s and early 80s meant that the inflation in the cost of medical care, always greater than general inflation, was particularly noticeable and the 'overspending' of the health service was seen as a major problem.

Small-sized pound notes introduced 1978

The answer from the medical profession was to ask for more money. They pointed out that the UK was paying the least on healthcare of any nation in Europe and they argued that the patients needed treating and therefore the money should be spent. Perhaps this would require a change in the method of financing but whatever was required it appeared in the eyes of the profession that the NHS was under-funded.

Thatcher thought otherwise. She had set up a working party on the financing of the NHS and this reported in 1982. I quote from Professor Chris Ham (1997[4])

" As the Secretary of State at the time, Norman Fowler, explains in his memoirs, the government decided not to move away from a system in which the NHS was financed largely from taxation, on the basis of the working party's report. This was because other European countries were faced with similar problems to the UK and a centrally funded service like the NHS appeared to be most effective in controlling costs."

Indeed the spending on health care as a percentage of gross national product has always been lower in the UK than in other comparably developed nations. In 1982 the UK's percentage expenditure on health care was 5.8%, the EU average was around 7.3% and Germany's was 9.2%. Switzerland spent about 10% and the USA topped the bill at around 14%. In terms of actual spending per capita the UK proportion was (and is) even lower[5].

There was therefore no desire to change the system but would the doctors have their way and receive extra money for the NHS? The reply was to be in the negative.

Thatcher asked **Business** (with a capital B) to supply the answer. Being a grocer's daughter it is not surprising that she turned to the Deputy Chairman of Sainsbury's to provide a report on the NHS. He criticised the lack of management and performance monitoring. He also questioned the clinical freedom of the doctors and stated that managers should be appointed with wide ranging powers to bring in 'cost improvements'.

From 1983 onwards the Griffiths managers were appointed to run the hospitals. Clinical directors, doctors having both a clinical and management role, were appointed to run departments (from then on known as directorates). Management by consensus and democracy was over in the NHS although most of the staff failed to realise this at the time.

Several other important events occurred in 1983 including:

- **The Medical Act** This act was concerned with the running of the GMC and fitness to practice. It reiterated previous legislation that a person must be registered as a medical doctor if they wish to use the title doctor for medical work.

- **The United Kingdom Central Council for Nursing, Midwifery and Health Visiting (UKCC)** replaced the General Nursing Council, the Central Midwives Board and seven other statutory nursing bodies. The main function was to maintain a register.

- **The Royal College of Physicians** published "Smoking or health"

- **1st April 1983** Prescription charges stood at £1.40p per item[6]

The twenty pence coin was introduced in 1982 and the first circulating base metal £1 coin in 1983

- **1st April 1983 Appointed as a Consultant**

1983 was the year that I was appointed as a consultant radiologist at the Bristol Royal Infirmary (BRI). At my job interview and in discussions when applying for my post, I had been promised a Magnetic Resonance Imaging (MRI) scanner at the BRI or one of its sister hospitals but on starting the post I had been firmly told to get on with the plain film reporting in the new "general reporting area" and to forget about my aspirations for MRI. Later in the year, having won the Kodak Scholarship of the Royal College of Radiologists, I spent two months with my wife, Lois, and son, Jeremy, touring the Radiology Departments in 13 cities of the USA. I came back convinced that Magnetic Resonance Imaging was the future of radiology in a number of important areas.

I was also convinced that I would be better off if I never again saw another burger bar.

I had the opportunity whilst in the USA of examining the X ray services in their three main methods of healthcare provision: private establishments, university hospitals and veterans' hospitals. The first two, private and university, were not surprisingly excellent. The USA government pays as much per head of population on just the university hospitals and on medical research as we do for our entire health care and at least some of the money is well spent. I had been warned, however, that the veterans' hospitals were grim. In fact I felt very much at home in them…they were much like the NHS with similarly rather old buildings but the equipment was generally newer than our own. Years of under-funding had left our healthcare system at a level somewhat below that of the worst hospitals in the USA.

Fundraising for MRI

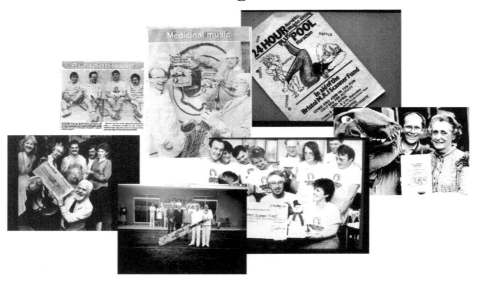

In 1984, since the money was not forthcoming from the NHS, I took the bold step of starting a fund raising committee for an MRI scanner. By 1987, with the help of my committee and my fund-raising jazz band *Dr Jazz* (all of whom I would like to thank) and with the considerable assistance of Bristol philanthropist Mr John James we had sufficient funds to buy the machine and build the centre. This opened in April 1987 and with the other trustees, Drs. Gordon Thomson, Clive Johnson and Terry Beddoe, we ran the centre from then onwards until it was taken over by the NHS in 1992. We were responsible for funding the entire running costs from the laying of tarmac and foundations to the tiles of the roof and for the cost of employing cleaners, secretaries and radiographers.

We were to provide a free service to our three local district health authorities, Southmead, Frenchay and United Bristol Hospitals (Bristol Royal Infirmary and sister hospitals). The centre was located at Frenchay Hospital, which was also the main Regional neurosurgery centre.

I was worried that other doctors encouraged by the managers might try to take over all of the space on the scanner and I wanted to provide time for all the important specialties such as neurology, oncology, orthopaedics, cardiac and paediatric medicine and surgery. When the charity document was being written, our solicitor had been careful to use the names of the three radiologists (from the three hospitals) as trustees and to ensure that they each received a third of the time. Dr Beddoe was the exception and, as a GP and considered as neutral, he acted as chairman.

After spending three years fund-raising with collecting tins, bands, fancy dress and whatever, it seemed only fair that the trustees should be involved in the running of the centre but we did indeed have to fight off several take-over manoeuvres from medical and management colleagues before the centre had even been opened.

These colleagues were used to getting their own way and were quite amazed when I showed them the Trust documents. These, as described above, named myself and the two other radiologists but did not name the hospitals. We had the sole rights over organisation of the new MRI centre (for which we had, of course, raised the money entirely without their help). I had not expected the attacks to come so soon and from the particular people involved but the forward thinking of our excellent solicitor, Nigel Burnell, had put us in good stead. The MRI scanner opened on time with myself in charge of the Bristol Royal Infirmary sessions but the opposition to our management of the centre reminded me yet again that when you have any dealings with NHS management everything must be in writing since they may not feel obliged to keep to their word if it does not suit them.

Over the next five years our scanner centre had a dynamic effect on MRI in the UK and the world. We were able to provide services to the local NHS free of charge on a state of the art machine. We were not dominated by a single specialty as many scanners were and we were able to innovate. We published hundreds of papers, books, journals and videos from the centre. We talked at numerous meetings and started several courses. In many ways for my own practice of radiology, they were Halcyon Days.

Meanwhile:

Not surprisingly, since the NHS runs in the opposite way to any normal business, the Griffith's managers failed to deliver the goods except in containing the costs. Between 1982 and 1990 there was no significant increase in the percentage of GNP spent on healthcare in the UK. It had crept up to 6% from 5.8 compared with a European Union rise to 7.7% from 7.3. It is interesting to note that the percentages for all of the EU countries broadly move up and down together although some countries spend considerably more than others and their systems of healthcare delivery vary substantially.

In the UK the growth of private providers outside the NHS over this period indicates that the percentage of Gross National Product spent on the NHS actually fell.

Unfortunately the impact in the NHS hospitals was felt very acutely. The directorates were now obliged to confront the cost of their services on a regular basis and the role of the finance officers in the hospitals became progressively more important. Every year they were asking the directorates to provide a 3% cost improvement. This could only be achieved by making cuts in staff numbers, reducing pay or outsourcing. The latter was undertaken in areas such as cleaning with a reduced number of the staff taken back on by outside contractors who paid, on average, 20% less. The quality of services provided waned with increasing problems such as long waiting lists.

Thatcher arranged another Ministerial review in 1988 followed by splitting up of the Department of Health and Social Security.

Two pound coin (Nickel-Brass) celebrating the Tercentenary (300 years) of the Bill of Rights On the 1st April 1989 Prescription charges stood at £2.80p per item [6]

Kenneth Clarke was appointed as the Secretary of State for Health in 1988 and he published first a white paper, *Working for Patients* in January 1989, followed by the *NHS and Community Care Bill* in November

William Waldegrave took over the mantle of Secretary of State in the November of 1990 and started putting the NHS and Community Care Bill into action.

The reforms set out in *Working for Patients* and then instituted in the *NHS and Community Care Bill* were, according to Chris Ham[4]:

"….a response to acute funding problems that developed during the 1980s. Although the reforms in themselves did not tackle the long term underfunding of the NHS they did seek to provide a way of ensuring that existing rersources were used as efficiently as possible and that increases in productivity were rewarded and not penalized."

The aim was to ensure that money would follow patients by separating the purchaser and provider roles and the creation of contracts with self-governing trusts. The GPs would have more say via a fund-holding role.

NHS Trusts and GP Fundholders

When we debated the advent of Trust status at the Hospital Medical Committee, I raised a question based on my own experience from running the MRI Centre as a self-governing Charitable Trust. The Griffiths manager had been appointed to be the Chief Executive when the Trust took over, and I enquired of him what would happen if a doctor wanted a patient treated but his management did not have the money to pay for it? Would we then be forced to refuse necessary treatment?

I cited the example of doctors wishing to have NHS patients from outside our area scanned in our MRI Centre. If the health authorities refused to pay our fees, which we already subsidised by charity, we were obliged, by fiscal necessity and the need to save time for our own three health authorities, to refuse the scans. This went against the grain for doctors steeped in the traditions of the NHS but we had found no way round it.

"That is a complete fiction and will never happen" was the reply I received from the manager. Nobody else in the room had experience of running a centre under tight financial stringency and nobody spoke up in support of my well-founded anxieties.

The first and second waves of NHS trusts and GP fund-holders did well out of the original allocation of funds. The real spending on health and the percentage of GNP rose significantly in 1991 and 1992 under the benign guidance of William Waldegrave before plateauing again between 1993 and 1999 whilst directed by Virginia Bottomley and Stephen Dorrell (Conservatives) and, after the ' 97 election, Frank Dobson (Labour).

Doctors and the public saw all this as a move towards the market economy. It was initially billed as an **internal market** but it was later said by the Dept of Health to represent a **managed market** because they wished to include players from outside the NHS. Although there were some beneficial effects initially, it is questionable as to whether or not the improvements were the effect of the reforms or simply due to the cash injection. In our own department we were able to replace X-ray equipment, some of which had become obsolescent ten or twenty years before. In 1992 we were able to purchase a new MRI machine with NHS money rather than charity funds.

It became clear over a period of time that one of the major outcomes of the reforms, whether intended or not, was to shift power from doctors to managers and from the specialists (the consultants) to the GPs[4]. In many respects the GPs and the managers were not equipped to deal with this new power. The latter in particular had to undergo a steep learning curve in many facets of health care and in particular, as reforms progressed, in the area of primary care.

In addition, as the initial waves of reform settled down and the expenditure levelled off, it was clear that the opposite had happened to that which was intended. Rather than the money following the patients, the patients had to follow the money.
Perhaps to counteract some of the potential ill effects of competition before and during the reforms the government had issued the Patient's Charter in 1991 and this was updated in 1995. The problems with the charter were that although laudable in its aims many of the so-called rights were unavoidably unobtainable from the NHS without considerable increase in funding and personnel: For example:

- a **right** "to be referred to a consultant acceptable to you"
- The Charter states that nine out of 10 people can expect to be seen in the hospital outpatient clinic within 13 weeks of being referred to a specialist by their GP
- The Charter also states that patients can expect to be given a specific appointment time, and to be seen in the outpatient clinic within 30 minutes of that time.

The charter was an extension of the citizen's charter and having been presented with all these rights the patients expected that they would be enacted. This fuelled 'patient expectation' which could not be fulfilled.

By 1997 Chris Ham, initially a supporter of the reforms, wrote[4]:

> "….notwithstanding the benefits that have resulted from the NHS reforms the long term underfunding of the NHS continues to present a major challenge to policy makers. The additional funding …to assist the implementations of the reforms undoubtedly helped to ease the funding pressures in the early 1990s…the much lower levels of expenditure experienced in the mid 1990s coupled with increased demands, caused these pressures to return."

Most of the doctors looking back at the reforms during the Thatcher era would agree that some change was necessary. Unfortunately change was piled on change with no time for assessment. If modern practices such as quality assurance and audit needed to be introduced this should not have been done at the expense of the service to the patients….it was surely intended that they would improve the service.

Many of the advances would have occurred anyway without the need for an ever-increasing bureaucracy. The internal market resulted in unnecessary and wasteful duplication of services. This occurred because a Trust would not like to send patients out to more expensive facilities elsewhere. They therefore duplicated the facilities at their own base and kept it "in-house". Previously doctors had been able to send patients to a recognized specialist in another hospital with no financial penalty. After the reforms this was not the case. Moreover previous to the reforms the medical profession could prescribe whatever their patient needed. After the reforms it depended on whether or not the money was available and this frequently depended on where you lived. Perversely in our own Oncology Centre, for example, a patient from outside our own Trust's area may well receive the necessary drugs, such as Herceptin, but from inside the area it would not be permitted. The very real worries which I had expressed before we had taken Trust status had turned out to be completely correct. Medical services were being refused on the ground of cost and it did depend on where you lived. The postcode prescribing scandal, which still continues today, made a complete mockery of the idea of a **national** health service. The ability of Trusts to ignore national pay structures for staff also banged a further nail into the coffin of the NHS.

Care in the Community

All the lonely people, where do they all come from? All the lonely people, where do they all belong?
John Lennon and Paul McCartney (Eleanor Rigby)

With all its attendant officialdom and management structure the managed market was vastly more expensive than the old self-governed health-worker led system. It became obvious later that the only way in which the extremely expensive shift had been at all financially viable was by 'selling off the family silver'. This involved closing down and selling for development, local cottage hospitals and the larger psychiatric units with their huge grounds where the patients had traditionally worked on the farms. This was done under the guise of "care in the community". Unfortunately the care in the community was also lacking and many of the institutionalized mentally ill ended up living rough and

104

begging on our streets. The long stay elderly patients who had stayed in the cottage hospitals were now dependant on local authorities rather than on the NHS. If they had sufficient funds they could find a place in a care home for the elderly. With only a small proportion of the fees paid by the local authority, the elderly found that they had to use up nearly all of their savings and, if they had been living alone, they even had to sell their homes to pay for their long stay care.

The weakest and least able, the mentally ill and the elderly, were no longer being looked after sufficiently by the NHS and were barely attended to by the Welfare State. For the elderly this was a particularly bitter blow. They were the people who had come through the Second World War and voted for the Labour Government in order to put the Welfare State in place. All their lives they had paid via the National Insurance Stamp and Income Tax and now, when they needed help, they had to use their own funds.......which were the savings from already-taxed income.

Under Major the concept of selling off the family silver gathered steam. In addition the idea of Private Finance Initiatives (PFIs) was developed. The private sector would be invited to own and run hospitals for the NHS. This idea was brought in under the misguided belief that the private hospitals could be run more efficiently than NHS hospitals. When examined against the knowledge that the NHS was the cheapest effective healthcare system in the developed world, the instigation of competition, increased management, PFIs etc. never made financial sense. They basically did not add up but that did not stop them from happening....under the next government.

These were some of the problems that were in the public domain during the build up to the election of 1997.

New Labour, same old problems (but worse)

Dictators ride to and fro on tigers which they dare not dismount. And the tigers are getting hungry.
Winston Churchill (1874-1965) (While England Slept)

When Blair's government took over in 1997 there were many people who expected that the new boys and girls in charge would immediately support the NHS with increased funds. They thought that Blair would roll back many of the changes that Thatcher and Major had put in place. They had good reason for thinking this. When in opposition the Labour party had made it clear that they did not agree with the policies. The 1995 Labour policy document *Renewing the NHS* denounced Private Finance Initiative (PFI) and expressed strong disapproval of Conservative attempts to dragoon hospitals and health authorities into long-term PFI contracts. PFI was regarded as inconsistent with Labour's concept of a 'unified public service'.

This was not to be the case. Once they were in power the New Labour government acted in a manner which was more right wing than Major had ever been. They immediately bought new missiles and presided over the sales of more of the " family silver".

105

The Chancellor of the Exchequer made it clear that he was going to keep to Major's spending plans. In fact I believe that he put *less* money into health care than Major had planned. Whereas the percentage of GNP had been 7% in 1996 it fell to around 6.7% in 97 and 6.8% and 6.9% in the following two years.

The Patient's Charter was abolished as part of changes to the NHS implemented in the year 2000 under the 10-year "NHS plan"[8] and appears to have been replaced by Your Guide to the NHS.

In 2000, Blair's direct control over the NHS was strengthened by appointing Nigel Crisp to the combined posts of NHS Chief Executive *and* Permanent Secretary. The new post replaced the two former posts of Chief Executive for the NHS and Permanent Secretary for the Department of Health.

2002 was a busy year. The United Kingdom Central Council (UKCC) and English National Board were replaced in April 2002 with a New Nursing and Midwifery Council (NMC) Also from April 2002 the primary care trusts (PCTs) were established to replace district health authorities and GP fundholders. 304 PCTs covered the entire English population.

In October 2002 the Department of Health published **Reforming NHS financial flows: introducing payment by results.** This told us that National tariffs would be introduced for almost every non-emergency procedure and weighted to take into account higher costs in the London area. PCTs would pay hospitals on the basis of the number of cases at a national tariff rate. The system of national tariffs would not apply to commissioning of NHS care from the private sector, which would set its own prices. The government also made it clear that they soon expected at least 15% of NHS work to be undertaken under the auspices of the private sector in some form or other.

The national health services union UNISON commented

> "The problem is that fee-for-service creates opposing incentives among commissioners and providers - one seeking cost containment, the other income maximisation through competition, careful selection of patients, and cost shifting to patients."

Neither of which do anything good for the patients. Cost cutting and caring only for the easiest patients is not a good recipe for a comprehensive health service.

It was also announced that management contracts for 'failing' hospitals would be instigated. Three of the eight acute NHS hospitals that failed to achieve any 'stars' in the government's review of hospital performance in July 2002 were to be taken out of normal NHS management and run under three-year management contracts. The Royal United Hospital in Bath, United Bristol Healthcare, and the Good Hope Hospital in Birmingham would be the first hospitals to be franchised out, under a scheme announced by Alan

Milburn for approved NHS hospitals and private sector corporations to take over 'failing' NHS hospital.

I published a letter in the Daily Telegraph at this time pointing out that the Government's own figures showed that the star rating system was inversely proportional to clinical results. I will discuss this fully in a later chapter.

The Department of Health's **Guide to NHS Foundation Trusts** was published in December 2002. These detailed the following[9].

Earned autonomy freedoms for three-star and two-star hospitals
Freedom 1   Direct allocation of additional capital
Freedom 2   Higher delegated limits for the approval of capital investments
Freedom 3   Retention of more of the proceeds of local land sales for reinvestment in local services
Freedom 4   Additional funds from the 2003/04 Local Capital Modernisation Fund
Freedom 5   Opportunity to shape national policy
Freedom 6   Less frequent monitoring from the centre
Freedom 7   Removal of management cost limits
Freedom 8   Fewer and better co-ordinated inspections
Freedom 9   Automatic entry on to the NHS Franchising Register of Expertise
Freedom 10   Direct access to 'fair shares' of 2003/04 central budgets without the need to bid
Freedom 11   Additional freedom when establishing 'spin-out' companies
Freedom 12   Additional funding for sabbaticals to support the Trust in contributing to the work of the Department of Health and the Modernisation Agency
Freedom 13   Eligibility to apply for NHS Foundation Trust status

The hospitals to be offered these freedoms were the very ones which were doing the worst clinical work but keeping within their budgets…. Those with a two or three star rating.

We had certainly come along way from the original concept of the NHS. The patients and doctors now had little influence. Blair was being advised on targets by an anthropologist or two. A cadre of arts graduate or nurse managers were in charge and fiscal health was more important than health care.

It certainly felt as if the NHS was in a mess but was this really the case. Were there any objective measures by which we could compare the NHS with other health services? Did other countries even have a comprehensive health service and, if so, how were they faring?

Chapter 8
How does the NHS compare with the Health Services in other Countries?

It has been the proud boast from many British politicians over the years that the NHS is the best health service in the World.

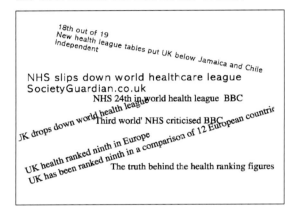

This comment is not heard so often these days, probably because it is just not true. It is possible, or even probable, that it was true in the first few years after its inception but independent analysis over the past decade or so has shown that on nearly all ratings the UK's health service ranks low compared with other developed nations. The league tables are based on a number of factors but perhaps the most basic of them is life expectancy at birth.

Table 1 (life expectancy) at the end of this section was extracted from United Nations' data[1,2]. The original chart contains all 195 countries. I have included most of the European and major industrialised nations and the points around the world average.

Top is Japan at 82.6 years, followed closely by Hong Kong at 82.2. Uzbekistan is at the world average of 67.2 years with Swaziland bottom 40% below world average.

The results do not appear to be directly due to geographic or racial characteristics. Sweden enters at 7th with Denmark, racially identical and very closely related geographically at 36th. Iceland, mainly of Danish extract, is the first European country at third.

Hong Kong, as described above, is second on the chart but China is 82nd at 73 years.

Australia, with a population containing a large number of descendants of British origin, is a very creditable 5th whilst the United Kingdom does not reach the top 20, coming in below the majority of Western European countries at 22nd.

Spain (6th) and Italy (12th) do well but Greece (19th) and Cyprus (28th) not so well. The Mediterranean Nations, contrary to some statements, do not appear to have a universal elixir of youth.

Table 1 Life Expectancy at Birth from UN data 2006 [1,2]

Rank	Country/Territory	Overall	Male	Female
	World Average(WA)	67.2	65.0	69.5
1	Japan	82.6	79.0	86.1
2	Hong Kong	82.2	79.4	85.1
3	Iceland	81.8	80.2	83.3
4	Switzerland	81.7	79.0	84.2
5	Australia	81.2	78.9	83.6
6	Spain	80.9	77.7	84.2
7	Sweden	80.9	78.7	83.0
8	Israel	80.7	78.5	82.8
9	Macau	80.7	78.5	82.8
10	France	80.7	77.1	84.1
11	Canada	80.7	78.3	82.9
12	Italy (20% above WA)	80.5	77.5	83.5
13	New Zealand	80.2	78.2	82.2
14	Norway	80.2	77.8	82.5
15	Singapore	80.0	78.0	81.9
16	Austria	79.8	76.9	82.6
17	Netherlands	79.8	77.5	81.9
18	Martinique	79.5	76.5	82.3
19	Greece	79.5	77.1	81.9
20	Belgium	79.4	76.5	82.3
22	United Kingdom	79.4	77.2	81.6
23	Germany	79.4	76.5	82.1
28	Cyprus	79.0	76.5	81.6
29	Republic of Ireland	78.9	76.5	81.3
32	Luxembourg	78.7	75.7	81.6
36	Denmark	78.3	76.0	80.6
37	Cuba	78.3	76.2	80.4
38	United States	78.2	75.6	80.8
39	Portugal	78.1	75.0	81.2
44	Czech Republic	76.5	73.4	79.5
56	Poland	75.6	71.3	79.8
65	Vietnam	74.2	72.3	76.2
78	Hungary	73.3	69.2	77.4
82	China (mainland)	73.0	71.3	74.8
98	Turkey	71.8	69.4	74.3
126	Uzbekistan (World Av.)	67.2	64.0	70.4
137	Russia	65.5	59.0	72.6
139	India	64.7	63.2	66.4
182	Nigeria (30% below WA)	46.9	46.4	47.3
189	Zimbabwe	43.5	44.1	42.6
195	Swaziland(40% below WA)	39.6	39.8	39.4

Clearly the causes are multi-factorial. The world average is pulled down by the Acquired Immune Deficiency Syndrome (AIDS) epidemic in Africa. All the sub-Saharan African countries have very low life expectancy due to AIDS. In addition high infant mortality rate will pull down the life expectancy at birth so countries with higher than average infant mortality will have a low life expectancy (see also table 2).

Table 2

Infant Mortality Rates ref. 6

Albania	20.0	Japan	3.2
Angola	184.4	Kenya	57.4
Australia	4.6	Korea, South	6.1
Austria	4.5	Mexico	19.6
Bangladesh	59.1	Mozambique	109.9
Brazil	27.6	New Zealand	5.7
Canada	4.6	Nigeria	95.5
Chile	8.4	Norway	3.6
China	22.1	Pakistan	68.5
Costa Rica	9.5	Panama	16.0
Cyprus	6.9	Peru	30.0
Czech Republic	3.9	Poland	7.1
Denmark	4.5	Portugal	4.9
Ecuador	22.1	Russia	11.1
Egypt	30.1	Slovakia	7.1
Finland	3.5	South Africa	59.4
France	4.2	Spain	4.3
Germany	4.1	Sri Lanka	19.5
Greece	5.3	Sweden	2.8
Guatemala	29.8	Switzerland	4.3
Hungary	8.2	Syria	27.7
India	34.6	United Kingdom	5.0
Iran	38.1	United States	6.4
Ireland	5.2	Venezuela	20.9
Israel	6.8	Zimbabwe	51.1
Italy	5.7		

Infant deaths per 1,000 live births.

Source: U.S. Census Bureau, International Database

Overall, as expected, the countries that are the most developed and with the most expenditure on healthcare do have better life expectancy than the lesser developed. But life expectancy is not directly related to healthcare expenditure. The United States (38th) spends the most on healthcare but is just beaten by Cuba in the table. Germany, another big spender, is well beaten by Spain.

Other factors will include diet, smoking habits, alcohol ingestion and extremely importantly public health measures such as sanitation and clean water supplies.

So although the life expectancy figures are very important they are not a satisfactory sole measure of the efficacy of a health service.

Recently several assessments of the UK's National Health Service have been made. In 2001 a paper based on WHO data placed the NHS 24th out of 191 countries. The UK came above Germany and Switzerland in the rankings but was below Italy, France, Jamaica, Morocco and Chile. The US came even lower, at 72nd[3,4].

Research from the London School of Hygiene and Tropical Medicine in 2003 ranked the

UK as 18th out of 19 industrialised nations (Table 3) with Sweden top and the UK only able to beat Portugal. Research from Sweden (Table 4) comparing 12 European countries' healthcare systems also ranked the UK's healthcare system very low. The analysis took into account 20 indicators in five areas - patients' rights and information, waiting times for common treatments, care outcomes, customer friendliness and access to medication[5]. The UK came top for information but fared very badly in all other fields receiving a score of 36 out of a potential 60.

Whilst these tables differ in detail they do agree in overall content. Countries such as Sweden and France do well but the UK fares badly amongst the larger industrialized nations. The USA generally does very badly.

So the most objective measures we have do show that the NHS is not doing well when compared with other European nations.

Now is the time to look at a number of different healthcare systems around the world and then we shall return to a further debate as to where and why the NHS is failing and what, if anything, can be done about it. The countries have been chosen because they represent different types of healthcare systems with varying degrees of succes.

Table 3	Table 4
Ranking of Health Services of 19 industrialised nations [7]	Ranking of Healthcare in Europe [5]
1. Sweden	Netherlands - 48/60
2. Norway	Switzerland - 47
3. Australia	Germany - 46
4. Canada	Sweden - 40
5. France	Belgium - 40
6. Germany	Estonia - 40
7. Spain	France - 39
8. Finland	Spain - 37
9. Italy	UK - 36
10. Denmark	Hungary - 35
11. Netherlands	Italy 29
12. Greece	Poland – 25
13. Japan	
14. Austria	Countries ranked out of a possible total of 60
15. New Zealand	
16. United States	
17. Ireland	
18. United Kingdom	
19. Portugal	

Verdict: The Best

Sweden

Sweden provides a healthcare system which is ideologically similar to that of the United Kingdom's NHS. While patients have to pay for public health care, fees are nominal, limited to a ceiling of £60 a year. Cancer survival rates, infant mortality and life expectancy figures all outstrip many of its European neighbours. The Swedish results are now considerably better than the UK's, so why is that the case?

The simple answer, according to Nick Triggle[8], is that they have consistently spent more money on health. A lot more money. Triggle states 'In the early 1980s, the country was splashing out 9.2% of its GDP on health care - the highest in Europe and over 3% more than the NHS got at the time. Two decades on it may still be spending the same proportion, but many countries, including the UK, are still playing catch up.

The result is that Sweden has more doctors per head than most - 3.3 per 1,000 compared to two per 1,000 in the UK - allowing patients to have direct access to everyone from hospital consultant down'.

In addition the Swedes have reorganized healthcare such that more is done in the community than previously. This has been successful because it has been adequately funded compared with similar policies in the UK that have not been well funded.

Verdict: Highest Life Expectancy

Japan

In Japan, healthcare services are provided by national and local governments. Payment for personal medical services is offered through a universal health care insurance system that provides relative equality of access, with fees set by a government committee. People without insurance through employers can participate in a national health insurance program administered by local governments. Since 1973, all elderly persons have been covered by government-sponsored insurance. Patients are free to select physicians or facilities of their choice and because Japanese health insurance systems are universal, there is no distinction between public and private hospitals from the view point of the user. In fact, users are free to choose any medical service providers without constraint in terms of hospital type, location or other   factors such as having referral or not.[9,10,11]

France

On 1 January 2002 the euro replaced the old national currencies in twelve of the EU countries (Germany, France, Italy, Spain, Portugal, Belgium, Luxembourg, the Netherlands, Austria, Finland, Greece and Ireland).

The French healthcare system in the last ten years or so has frequently been rated above that of the UK and the life expectancy in France is greater than in the UK. Everybody in France who is employed or spouse/child of someone employed is covered by a national health insurance plan, known as *securite sociale*. Since 2000 France has provided a   healthcare system for all people with legal residence status, interpreted to mean uninterrupted residence for at least three months. This is based on the CMU (*couverture maladie universelle*) plan, which provides health insurance to which all residents not otherwise covered by *securite sociale* are obligated by law to enroll. This plan is free for households with taxable revenue less than 6,609 euros per year.[12,13,14,15,16]

Unfortunately the high cost of healthcare as a proportion of GDP has meant that it has come under the scrutiny of the new President of France, Nicolas Sarkozy. He was elected on a right wing ticket including cuts in taxes and is intending to cut free services to those under 60. This may include services to British citizens living in France. The British Government appealed for Britons living in France to be exempted from the new, strict regulations. This will have knock-on effects on reciprocal arrangements which had become one of the successes of modern medical management.

France urged to keep free health care for expats

Daily Telegraph Nov 16th 2007

France: Historical Anecdote
The Touch-piece Story, continued

Earlier in the book in several places, we followed the story of touch-pieces, starting with the Roman Emperor Vespasian, taken up again by Edward the Confessor and continuing, with a few gaps, until Queen Anne. But this is not the whole story. Touching for the King's Evil (Scrofula) was also a tradition in France. Laurentius[17] stated that this was started by Clovis, the King of the Franks, around 481AD. Clovis had defeated the Roman Syagrius and could have taken on a Roman tradition. Louis I (814) continued the practice and the kings of France touched for Scrofula, giving the patient a gold coin, until the time of the French Revolution and the execution of the King on 21st January 1793. Interestingly from

1688 to 1717 there were two royal touch-piece traditions in France since the exiled James II continued his Scrofula work by touching for the condition and giving the patient a silver amulet or touch-piece similar to his previous gold pieces. This was continued by his son, who styled himself James III. In 1717 James III had moved from France to Rome as the result of British pressure on the French. Bonnie Prince Charlie, James III's son and also known as the young pretender, touched for Scrofula when his father was still alive and continued as Charles III when his father died. His brother Henry, a catholic cardinal, carried on touching after the death of the young pretender. On his touch-pieces Henry used the title Henry IX[18]. Henry died in 1807.

In 1793 the old touch-piece tradition effectively died with the death of the French king but a new superstition was started and attached to a specific coin. Augustus Dupré, had designed a new gold coin which had on its design a guardian angel. Dupre´claimed to have been saved from the guillotine by the lucky Angel coin in his pocket. According to legend, Dupré said a quick prayer as he knelt beneath the deadly blade. Suddenly, a bolt of lightning struck nearby, igniting a panic that halted his execution. Within six months Dupré was a free man, believing forever after that he was saved from certain death by the protective powers of his guardian gold Angel. In 1871, the design was resurrected by the Third Republic for the French gold 20-franc coin[19].

The French 'Angel' 1877 Gold 20 francs

These coins became good luck charms and amulets. They have also been forged and copied. Fake gold Angel coins are widely available today to be kept 'for their luck'.

Verdict: Good Value for Money :-   Cuba

Ernesto (Che) Guevara on a Cuban banknote

The Cuban Government runs a national health service for its citizens. No private healthcare is permitted[20]. The Cuban economy is in a bad way, mainly due to trade embargos and blockades by the USA and the loss of support from the USSR since the Soviet Union collapsed.

However the health system is a priority and about three-quarters of Cuban citizens are positive about their country's education and healthcare systems[21] . The World Health Organization has reported that Cuba provides a doctor for every 170 residents[22] and has the second highest doctor to patient ratio in the world after Italy. The health system costs just £125 per head, about one tenth of the UK's cost per person. There is little money for research but they still undertake valuable work, for example Cuban researchers recently reported that inactivated (killed) polio vaccine **is** effective in tropical countries. Cuba has been free of polio since 1963, but continues with mass immunization campaigns.

Fidel Castro came to power in the revolution of January 1st 1959 and until very recently was still the President. Due to illness he has passed the Presidency to his brother, Raúl Modesto Castro Ruz. Che Guevara, see illustration, was an Argentinian who studied medicine in Buenos Aires. He was one of the leaders amongst the Cuban rebels who overthrew Batista. Che Guevara gained a reputation for bravery and military prowess but he was also feared for his ruthlessness, having personally executed people considered as traitors. He became finance minister and President of the National Bank of Cuba and was considered to be second in power only to Castro. Guevara tried to organize revolutions in South America and Africa without much success and was finally executed in Bolivia on the 9th October 1967. He was a man driven by revolutionary zeal to a murderous extent but who would look after the medical needs of wounded soldiers of either side[23].

Verdict: Patchy

Healthcare in the USA

For he that hath, to him shall be given: and he that hath not, from him shall be taken even that which he hath
(Mark 4.25 King James, Authorised Version of the Bible)

The United States of America is unusual amongst the nations of the developed world in that it does not provide a universal back-up health service for the uninsured or provide a nationally run compulsory insurance linked to employment. They share the distinction with South Africa of being the only two industrialized nations that do not provide universal health coverage by some means. When I first visited the USA a quarter of a century ago (1983) I visited thirteen different hospitals and as many cities. I was very impressed by a system that seemed to include nearly everybody without the government, either State or Federal, having to organise everything. The majority of the healthcare work was provided privately. Surprisingly the US government was spending as much per head of population on healthcare as we were in the UK but the money was mostly spent in University or Veteran's Hospitals and these establishments were undertaking very advanced medical research. The hospitals were better made, staffed and equipped than our UK hospitals and the poorer people seemed to be looked after well. I spoke to a number of patients who were being provided with a free service and were even able to obtain multiple free consultations and second opinions. Perhaps many of the people were eligible for free care because it was immediately after the Vietnam war and they were either veterans or members of veteran's families and thus covered by the Veteran's Administration. Government insurance programs such as Medicare and Medicaid covered many individuals who were not protected by private insurance.

Since that time the healthcare situation in the USA has considerably worsened. The U.S. spends more on health care, both as a proportion of gross domestic product (GDP) and on a per-capita basis, than any other nation in the world. Current estimates put U.S. healthcare spending at approximately 15% of GDP, the world's highest.[24]

However, the number of uninsured people in the USA increased by nearly 7 million between 2000 and 2005. Nearly 16 percent of non-elderly Americans, 47 million people, were without health insurance coverage in 2005, nearly one in six of the population in the richest nation on Earth. About one third of the population spend part of the year uninsured. Partly this is due to the considerable reduction in employment-related health insurance. This has plummeted from70 percent in 1987 to 59 percent in 2004[25]. About 25% of the uninsured are eligible for government health care programs but have not enrolled. This is not necessarily easy to achieve since reimbursement rates are poor, the administration is expensive and the number of doctors accepting Medicaid cases has dropped.

As would be expected the uninsured receive less healthcare than the insured, (about half) and it is reckoned that 18,000 unnecessary deaths occur in the USA per annum due to this lack of care. The US government is still spending huge sums on medical research and the American medical scientists definitely lead the world in their number of publications and in the quality of their work. In fact they are always surprised that we, in the UK, manage to do any research at all given that the NHS seems to them to be working at the level of a third world country. My response has always been that we do get value for money from our own medical scientists since they are often obliged to provide their own research funds and to do much of their work outside the normal working hours unpaid.

This does not, however, take away from the fact that the Americans are failing their own people. One example that shows this failure is the infant mortality rate. A recent report in the New Scientist[26] poses the question 'Why do so many infants born in the richest country on earth die before they reach their first birthday? The answer seems to be poverty and the concomitant lack of healthcare. Sweden, Japan and Singapore lose fewer than 3 infants per thousand live births, the UK rate is 5 per thousand and the USA 6.4. But this is not the whole story. In Mississippi and nearby US States the death rate is rising. In 2005 it rose from 9.7 to 11.4 per thousand live births.

There are also problems in other areas of the USA. The percentage of severely poor people is increasing and across the whole of the USA the black infant mortality rate is twice that of white infants . President Bush meanwhile has vetoed extension of a national health insurance programme for children.

There are other health problems in the USA. Perhaps the most obvious when visiting the United States is the number of morbidly obese people. Again this is a problem that is mostly affecting the poorer members of society and will lead to an increased incidence of diabetes, cardiovascular problems and cancer. This is a problem that we, in the UK, seem to be copying.

So what do we make of this?

There is no doubt that healthcare in the USA can be very good, possibly the very best in the world, for those who are insured. Moreover the rest of the world should be grateful for the superb medical research that is undertaken. But the rich get richer and the poor get poorer. It is an interesting debate as to whether government money is better spent on providing a standard level of care for the poor or on advanced research from which only the rich will benefit. The overall health of the nation will not improve if the majority of the population receive no health education and no healthcare. In many ways this lack of care for the poor is a disgrace.

USA: good luck coins and 'touch-pieces'

Don't want a silver dollar, rabbit's foot on a string
The happiness in your warm caress, no rabbit's foot can bring.
From the song *Good luck charm*
Elvis Presley 1962 (Aaron Schroeder / Wally Gold)

Despite the amazing scientific prowess of the USA many of the people are superstitious. Witness to this is the number of objects that are considered as good luck charms with the ability to ward off bad luck and ill health. These include several coins with perhaps the most famous being a silver dollar as eluded too, but discarded, in the song by Elvis Presley. These have some similarity with the tradition of 'touch pieces' described in earlier chapters. Other 'lucky' coins include the Mercury dime and the Indian Head cent

Silver 'Peace' Dollar

First minted in 1921, Peace silver dollars were created to commemorate the end of World War One. Coins made from silver are considered to be lucky and a silver dollar was carried for good luck. 'The Peace dollar remains a symbol of unwavering American optimism and resilience during the best and worst of times'.[27]

American silver 'Mercury' dimes, especially with a leap year date, are considered to be especially lucky. Gamblers' charms are often these dimes, Mercury being the

'Mercury' Dime 1944   **Indian Head One Cent 1902**

Roman god who ruled the crossroads, games of chance, etc. A silver dime worn at the throat will supposedly turn black if someone tries to poison your food or drink. American 'Indian Head' cents are worn by some people as amulets to ward off evil or negative spirits. This appears to hark back to Shamanic ideas.[28] The Indian Head one-cent coin is also known as an Indian Penny and was produced by the United States Mint from 1859 to 1909. It depicts a Native American wearing a feather headdress as an allegorical Liberty.[29]

USA: St Michael and the Dragon

There is an even more direct link with the 'touch-pieces' distributed by the monarchs of England and France. This is seen in the coins, medallions and badges featuring the Archangel St Michael. These are sold to protect the **police** from bad luck since it appears that, in Catholicism, St Michael is now the patron saint of the police. The range and prices of these modern day 'touch pieces' which are on display at just one website [30] (of many) show that this continues to be good business. It is often possible to slip into a feeling of superiority with regard to the gullibility of patients in the past who wished to be cured by the touch of the king. This continuance of the tradition should dispel our hubris but not our scepticism. Many other medallions for an enormous number of saints and angels are also available and the most common 'amulet' is a crucifix.

Coin-like medallion

Medallion shaped like a Police Badge

Both of these amulets feature St Michael and the Dragon and the images are very similar to those on the Angel coinweight of Charles I and the touch-piece of James II (both featured in Chapter 3). They are also surprisingly similar to the design of a soldier spearing a fallen horseman on the Romano-British Coin (end of chapter 1). It seems possible that the Romano-British coins, which were copied unofficially after the Romans left, could have been used as amulets by the Anglo-Saxons when coins were rare thus making a continuity in design from around 337AD to the present day. A total of 1670 years !

USA: Therapeutic Touch (TT)

Therapeutic Touch (TT) was conceived in the early 1970s by Dolores Krieger, Ph.D., R.N., a faculty member at New York University's Division of Nursing. It is propagated as a method of healing based on the idea of a human energy field. This, they believe, is abundant and flows in balanced patterns in health but is depleted and/or unbalanced in illness or injury. Practitioners believe they can restore health by sensing and adjusting such fields. Unfortunately there is no evidence that this works in any way other than as a placebo and psychological boost. Experiments show that the TT practitioner cannot detect the presence of a person's hands near theirs if they cannot see them and at no time has science shown an all-pervasive energy field around human beings[31,32,33,34,].

Therapeutic Touch does, however, follow in the tradition of the 'laying-on of hands' by royalty and by priests and is fervently believed by many people.

Verdict: Very Worrying

Healthcare in the USSR, Russian Federation and Post-Soviet States

Commemorative One Rouble Coins of the USSR

1)   2)
1) 1967: 50th Anniversary of the Russian Revolution, (Lenin standing)
2) 1985: 175th Anniversary of the birth of Friedrich Engels

Before the Second World War there were many admirers of the Soviet Healthcare system. The principle of providing healthcare for all, free at the point of use, was borrowed to set up the United Kingdom's NHS. But the Soviet healthcare system certainly had problems. Medical staff were not accorded the respect or anywhere near the salaries that they had in the Western nations. Doctors were distrusted by the party leaders because they were considered as effete intellectuals. Some doctors, such as psychiatrists, had a dubious reputation with the public since political dissidents were likely to be sent to so-called psychiatric hospitals for 'correction' of their dissident behaviour. Sometimes this suspicion was justified and sometimes not.

Throughout Stalin's long period in power, despite having a national heath service, it cannot be argued that the health of the nation was a primary concern for the Soviet Government. Stalin's murderous purges killed countless millions of his own people but overseas visitors were shown a sanitised version of communism and were kept unaware of the real state of affairs.

The Doctors' Plot and the Death of Stalin₃₅

On January 13th 1953 nine distinguished physicians were arrested and apparently confessed to the murder of Zhadnov, a prominent Politburo member and of Alexander Shcherbakov, Chief of the main political administration of the Army. Officials denounced the physicians as agents of American Intelligence and stated that the doctors' aim had been to liquidate Marshals and Generals and other public figures thus undermining the Soviet defences.

On March 5th, 1953 it was announced that Stalin had died from a massive brain haemorrhage having been under the care of 'the best medical personnel'. A collective leadership emerged with Molotov as the front-runner. All personnel who had been present at Stalin's death were comprehensively purged including Tretiakov, the Health Minister, who had treated Stalin and Vasily, Stalin's son. In April 1953 it was announced that the charges against the physicians had been fabricated, that the confessions had been obtained by torture and that the doctors were exonerated. Only seven of the nine had survived. Much manoeuvring later, the leadership was assumed by Nikita Khrushchev.

Khrushchev to Gorbachev

On October 14th 1964 the leadership of the USSR passed from Khrushchev to Brezhnev who remained in power until November 1982 when he was followed in turn by a succession of two elderly politicians who each lasted only a short time as supreme ruler. Andropov was leader for 15 months until 1984 and Chernenko just over a year until he died and was replaced by Mikhail Gorbachev on March 11th 1985

The Soviet Health System at the start of this period had, at its best, been fairly level with other national healthcare systems. There were good hospitals for party members and in some areas, such as orthopaedic surgery, they had excelled. Over the subsequent 30 years or so the USSR healthcare system slipped backwards compared with the West. This was partly because of the overall financial problems; it is clear now that the Cold War was very draining on Soviet resources. It was also partly ideological; they did not accept many of the pharmaceutical agents developed in the West simply because they had been produced by Capitalist businesses.

In 1986 a series of errors when testing a nuclear power plant led to the catastrophic fire and explosion at Chernobyl (Ukraine) with widespread radioactive contamination. This has undoubtedly led to an enormous increase in incidence of neoplasia (cancer) and in particular Thyroid Carcinoma. The lack of the power plant also led to serious power shortages. Gorbachev, in 1987, launched a policy of *perestroika*, (reform) and *glasnost*, (openness)[36].

Wishing to improve the economic condition of the USSR he also strongly discouraged drunkenness by a form of prohibition. This may have had little effect on the economy, which continued to be a problem, but it certainly improved the health of the nation

Chernobyl volunteer's medal

with life expectancy noticeably improving for men. Gorbachev also reduced the Red Army by 10% which was a contributory factor leading to a coup by Army hardliners in August 1991. The coup failed, partly due to heroism on the part of the Moscow mayor, Boris

The author (third from right) in the Ukraine with officers of the 43rd Rocket Army and personnel from the Japanese government and the British Crown Agents

Yeltsin. Yeltsin became the Russian President and the role of Gorbachev faded away as the USSR broke up on Christmas Day 1991, leaving a much smaller Russian Federation and numerous free countries, some allied with Russia as a Commonwealth.

1994 Ukraine

In 1994 I was invited by the British Crown Agents to visit the Ukraine as the medical lead in an eight million dollar aid mission. This was aimed at improving the medical services of the personnel breaking up nuclear weapons under a SALT agreement and had been funded by the Japanese Government.[37]

This gave me a chance to see the medical services in a former Soviet bloc country and many things fascinated me. We studied four military hospitals, which had been amongst the better funded compared with the civilian hospitals. In particular I noted that:

- Diagnostic services were, or had been, generally very good with access to modern radiological equipment, such as computed tomography, and machinery for biochemical analysis. Due to the break-up of the Soviet regime and the Warsaw Pact, access to spare parts for the machinery had become very difficult since it had mostly been made in East Germany or Poland. It was clear, however, that knowledge of physics and technology was of a high standard.
- The therapeutic side was much more eclectic. There was evidence of a high standard of surgery, particularly orthopaedic. The physicians, however, did not really believe in Western medicines. Some of them were under the impression that antibiotics, diuretics and even simple analgesics were an unnecessary product of the capitalist pharmaceutical industry. When I told them about the benefits of these drugs they really did not want to know. They treated infections with radiotherapy, laser light and electromagnetism. (Radiotherapy does work but has the inherent hazards of radiation including causing malignancies such as leukaemia. Laser light might be useful as a placebo but is almost certainly completely ineffective otherwise. Electromagnetism may have some small action but the results are debatable). Major advances in therapy had completely passed them by. They had large numbers of patients with peptic ulceration. I told them that most ulcers are caused by an infection with the bacterium, *Helicobacter pylori*, and can be cured in about two weeks with antibiotics. They found this almost impossible to believe.
- Their medical sciences had diverged from ours in 1917. Political control of medicine meant that some advances were acceptable, such as highly technical equipment, and some were not (antibiotics, for example). Their isolation from the rest of the world had, not surprisingly, resulted in a peculiar attitude to Western medical science. They were still using herbal medicines with no real knowledge of their constituent chemistry and practises, such as radiotherapy for infection, which had been banned in the West due to their dangers.
- On the plus side their surgery, such as leg lengthening, had developed in ways that had not been explored in the rest of the world and their infection control throughout the hospitals was excellent. I noted that every patient had fresh clean bed linen (which I thought happened throughout the British NHS but certainly is not always the case now). In addition between each patient the mattress was thoroughly sterilized.

The break-up of the USSR had led to major problems. Although they were now embracing a form of capitalism it was not clear where the money was going to come from to keep their health service, or the country as a whole, running. It was clear that this was a much more

121

expensive proposition under the new competitive system. There were major logistic problems such as fuel shortages and power cuts.

They were all keen on drinking vodka for breakfast, lunch and supper.

The Health Crisis in the Russian Federation

Health in the Russian Federation is a major problem today. Russian men now have what a recent World Bank report called 'short brutal lives'. The life expectancy of men has plummeted from 68 years to a low of 58 years due to an epidemic of alcoholism. The only old people are old women. Of the seven million deaths in the last decade 34% were due to alcohol[38].

The World Bank report states;

> 'If current low fertility and high mortality trends continue, the Russian Federation will lose approximately 18 million people by 2025. As a result, Russia will go from being the 6th-most-populous country in the world to being the 17th.
> Russian working-age men are particularly at risk. If current ill health and disability are considered, the healthy life expectancy of Russian males will fall to 53 years.'[39]

The advent of capitalist politics with its emphasis on competition has allowed greater freedom in the states other than Russia that were previously controlled by the USSR. In Russia itself the impact on health has been dire. In particular several areas within the Federation have a worse health record than the average for Russia. The post-conflict area of Chechnya is one of the worst with limited access to specialist care. The United Nations recently said with regard to Chechnya and to a lesser extent in Ingushetia and Dagesta:

> 'Patients in need of specialized health care need to seek specialized services outside the republic, but the majority of the population cannot afford the high costs of outside medical treatment. In the first six months of 2006, over 4,450 people were referred to other regions of the Russian Federation mostly for oncology, abdominal and cardiovascular surgery, urology, ophthalmology, and haemodialysis treatment'[40].

Verdict: The Worst

34 of the 35 countries with the worst life expectancy are to be found in Sub-Saharan Africa. Much of their mortality is due to the AIDS epidemic but in addition Malaria and Tuberculosis are still big killers. Some African countries with a previously good healthcare record are now in severe trouble. Examples include Kenya (life-expectancy 20% below world average) and Nigeria (30% below). We shall look at Kenya.

Kenya (Africa)

The first president of Kenya, Jomo Kenyatta

Kenya has had a democratic system of government having gained independence in 1963. As I write the country is in turmoil as a result of a disputed presidential election.

For the first 10 years of independence the economy was buoyant with GDP growing at an average of 6.6% per annum. After this the economy declined severely.

According to some sources average life expectancy in Kenya has decreased by 10 years compared with 20 years ago.

In addition to the AIDS epidemic much of this decline is said to be due to the worsening of the economic situation. This in turn can be put down to:
1) Government mismanagement of the economy
2) Interference by the International Monetary Fund (IMF) and International Financial Institutions (IFI)

Inflation hits the people with money and the lenders of such money do not like this. The anti-inflationary policies of the IMF and the World Bank particularly affect the poor adversely.

Soren Ambrose[41] states that 'Kenya's health care system was hit hard by the "structural adjustment" policies imposed by the IMF and World Bank as conditions on loans and as prerequisites for getting IFI approval of the country's economic policies. Those policies were introduced in the 1980s, and have left a lasting mark on Kenya's health. As usual with such programs, the emphasis was on cutting budget expenditures. As a result, local health clinics and dispensaries had fewer supplies and medicines, and user fees became more common. The public hospitals saw their standard of care deteriorate'.

The hospitals cannot employ staff because of the IMF and IFI policies even though the Kenyan Minister for Health would like to do so[42]. AIDS in particular affects the working age group. Thus the worsening of the healthcare situation will, in turn, affect the economy adversely creating a negative feedback situation.

Swaziland (Africa)

The worst healthcare results derive from the poorest countries or nations which are at war. The very worst life expectancy is to be found in Swaziland. This is an extremely poor country adjacent to South Africa and ruled by an absolute monarch. The article in Wikipedia states 'Despite calls for international solidarity against the oppressive royal regime, Swaziland's human rights record remains largely ignored by the international community, and cases of human rights violations are rife'.[43]

Afghanistan

Afghanistan is the odd one out amongst the 35 countries with the worst life expectancy in that it is not in Sub-Saharan Africa. Its average life expectancy stands at 43.8 years placing it at 188th out of 195.

According to Deborah MacKenzie[44] constant fighting after the Soviet Union invasion of 1979 left the country's already rudimentary healthcare system in ruins. In 2001 there were 3 million cases of malaria, 50 times as many as in the 1970s. Women fared worse under the Taliban with 65 out of every 1000 mothers dying in childbirth, the highest rates ever recorded.

Since the US and NATO defeated the Taliban in 2001 the situation has improved but the continued fighting has caused some setbacks. Achievements include bringing 77% of the population within range of a clinic, immunising 16 million children for measles in 2004 and giving two thirds of the children 'vaccination' for polio in 2005. Lack of security is a problem and the USA policy of promising aid only to people who cooperate with American troops has backfired: insurgents are now targeting aid workers. Funding of healthcare remains a problem.

Supranational Health Services

In the past sixty years whilst the British NHS has been in existence there has been a further trend in the delivery, management and political control of healthcare. This is the development of supranational health services. The United Nations claim that the World Health Organisation is not a supranational health organization and, insomuch that it does not usually deliver the healthcare itself, it is right. But in other ways the WHO does fit the bill. Its concerns are not limited by the boundaries of a single nation, it collects data about healthcare worldwide and publishes that data internationally. Its resolutions are moral commitments in the main part but it is a global health authority and it is exercising its right to develop legally binding protocols and treaties. These include promotion of the WHO Protocol on Water and Health, the Framework Convention on Tobacco Control and revision of the International Health Regulations[45]. The stated aim of the WHO is "the attainment by all peoples of the highest possible level of health."[46] The WHO combats disease and promotes health worldwide. It is particularly active in promoting the use of vaccines having announced the eradication of smallpox in 1979. They are developing immunization against malaria and schistosomiasis and hope to eradicate polio soon. WHO is funded by member states and from donations and works in collaboration with the pharmaceutical industry and with large charitable foundations.

Go anywhere in the EU for free health treatment, says Brussels

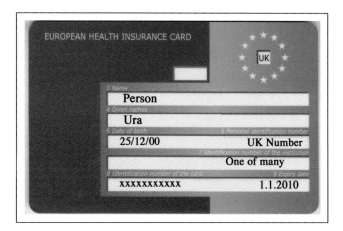

As a Supranational Health Service the WHO does not have the field to itself. The European Union (EU) is intending that healthcare should be provided free to EU residents anywhere in the EU. The radical new laws being drawn up in Brussels will mean that British patients will be able to travel anywhere in the EU to receive treatment and they will only have to pay for their travel and accommodation. The NHS will foot the bill.

This arrangement is a welcome one but does seem to fly in the face of the French proposition to cut free healthcare. It appears to extend the rights that are obtainable by possessing a European Health Insurance Card which is, in itself, an improvement on the E111. When travelling in Europe, if you are usually a UK resident there are reciprocal arrangements for healthcare. You are entitled to medical treatment that becomes necessary, at reduced cost or sometimes free, when temporarily visiting a European Union (EU) country, Iceland, Liechtenstein, Norway or Switzerland. Possession of an EHI card confirms that you are entitled to this service. Only treatment provided under the state scheme is covered[48]. It also covers pre-existing conditions.

International laws relating to healthcare are becoming progressively more important and more complex due to general globalization. Nearly all the significant pharmaceutical companies and medical manufacturing companies are multinational corporations working internationally. For these companies to work efficiently and ethically there has to be some agreement on standards and international patent law. Moreover health and safety at work, mainly a preventative subject, is no longer purely a national concern but in Europe is under the control of the European Agency for Safety and Health at Work[49].

The International Organization for Standardization (ISO) is a network of national standard institutes. It has members from 157 different countries and is funded from subscriptions paid by the national members. The standards set by this organization now supersede the standards set by national committees (unless the national standards are more stringent, which is becoming rare). The standards not only apply to a large range of equipment and machinery but are also being developed for project management. They have considerable significance with regard to medical technology[50]. The ISO involvement in Health Care Technology include standards in the following areas:

- Medical sciences and health care facilities in general (Including quality and environmental management in health care technology and IT application in health care technology)
- Medical equipment
- Dentistry
- Sterilization and disinfection
- Laboratory medicine
- Pharmaceutics
- Hospital equipment (Including hospital beds, surgical tables, medical garments, medical gloves, containers for sharp disposal, etc.)
- First aid (Including kits, equipment, facilities and medical transport for first aid)
- Aids for disabled or handicapped persons (Including aids for elderly people)
- Birth control. Mechanical contraceptives
- Veterinary medicine (Including equipment specific to veterinary medicine)

Growing numbers of UK patients are opting to go abroad for healthcare. This is not surprising considering the poor rating of the UK's National Health Service, the high cost of our private sector and the improved standards of some hospitals elsewhere. It is estimated that more than 70,000 Britons will have had treatment abroad in 2007 rising to 200,000 by 2010[51]. There are, of course, many people who travel **to** the UK to gain the benefit of our healthcare system.

Comment

The UK's health service would probably be placed as slightly better than that of Cuba's for work performed but, having at one time been excellent, is now nowhere near as good value for money. I would therefore place it just above that of the USA in the patchy category. This is corroborated by the numerous surveys that show the NHS low down in the charts.

It is to be noted that the USA policy is to only provide assistance to the people who pay for it (in the USA) or support them politically (outside the USA). Examples of places where health care is suffering because of the policies of the USA are seen in both Cuba and Afghanistan. This is having a deleterious effect on the world's opinion of the USA. General Sir Rupert Smith, one of Britain's most distinguished soldiers,[52,53] would consider this to be very bad policy since it is "preaching only to the converted" and more in keeping with Industrial War than the modern war amongst the people. The USA should get the people on their side by offering medical support to their opponents. This is a policy that was understood by Saladin more than 800 years ago when he sent his physician, Maimonides, to the aid of his sick opponent Richard the Lionheart, thus boosting Saladin's reputation among the Christians for generosity and chivalry. Unfortunately at the moment, although the USA is the richest nation they do not seem to be able to even provide fair medical services for their own people.

In many places in the world unproven alternative medical practice has increased in the last few years. Perhaps many of the poor being unable to afford medical services are turning to other sources for their hope. The rise in the belief in amulets may also be put down to the same cause but another possibility is loss of belief in scientific medicine due to its apparent inability to deal with latter day 'plagues' such as cancer, AIDS and dementia. By questioning religious friends and relatives I have discovered that the 'laying-on of hands' as a healing ceremony has become very widespread in the Christian church. This is certainly a change over the last thirty years or so, particularly in the Church of England where such practices would previously have been frowned on as dangerous quackery. It is also interesting to consider that it used to be the prerogative of Royalty.

Mostly on the positive side is the growth of Supranational Health Services. The World Health Organization was the first amongst a growing number of international organizations involved in the regulation and provision of healthcare. Due to general globalization, healthcare has become supranational. This has brought considerable benefits to the healthcare tourist who in Europe, for example, may be covered for free or low cost treatment in a large number of countries. International standards set by the ISO are generally improving manufacturing standards around the world and this impinges directly on healthcare technology.

Not so beneficial is the high cost of pharmaceuticals. These are kept high when there is strict adherence to patent law and there is a growing debate about the harmful effects on the poorer countries such as those in sub-Saharan Africa. These countries are suffering a pandemic of AIDS and are not able to afford the expensive drugs that can combat the condition.

Chapter 9
Successes in the present day NHS but also ethical dilemmas in a rationed health service.

Still glides the stream and shall for ever glide; The form remains, the function never dies.
William Wordsworth 1770-1850 (The River Duddon)

The range of activities of the United Kingdom's National Health Service is vast. It treats millions of people every year but in addition provides an enormous educational and research role. On the treatment front almost every type of medical, surgical and diagnostic service is provided somewhere. The main worry is that it is not evenly provided around the UK or amongst age and socio-economic groups and that in some places provision may include elective plastic surgery and fertility treatment but in other areas they cannot afford (or refuse) to give patients the required radiotherapy for cancer palliation or the necessary cancer drugs. Some old people do not receive good treatment and many hospitals are worrying because they are filthy. It is, however, wrong to believe the pessimistic idea that the NHS no longer works at all. The function of the NHS continues and in the majority of cases this function is good.

In 1976 the Department of Health and Social Security published a booklet entitled *Prevention and health: everybody's business*[1]. In this they trumpeted some of the success stories of medicine in the UK. They pointed out the great success in eliminating cholera, typhoid and paratyphoid by insuring safe water supplies, the virtual elimination of the fatal childhood illnesses diphtheria and whooping cough by immunisation and the potential of measles vaccines to do the same for measles. Tuberculosis was becoming rare and poliomyelitis vaccines had been extremely successful. There were, however, worries with regard to the polio vaccination programme because 'Public memory is short......one child in three is now not being taken for vaccination'.

Maternal mortality had dropped and deaths of live-born infants had fallen.

These programmes continue to be successful although the worries about polio vaccination now extend to the measles, whooping cough, mumps and diphtheria immunisation schedules. The parents who do not take their children for immunisation are relying on the general 'herd immunity'. When this goes below a critical level epidemics become a real worry.

In writing this book I wished to present the reader with examples of good care in our present-day health service and to counter the otherwise negative information that I obtained from my own experiences, from colleagues and from the media.

Thus, in order to provide more evidence on the recent successes of the NHS, I wrote to the Secretary of State for Health as follows.

To: The Rt. Hon. Alan Johnson   26.11.07
Secretary of State for Health
79 Richmond House,
Whitehall,
London
SW1A 2NS

Dear Mr. Johnson

I am in the process of writing a book on the history of health services of the world. Naturally the NHS plays an important part in this book. I am keen that the book should have a balanced approach but have found that most of the press coverage about the NHS has recently been very critical. As a retired medical consultant from the NHS, I know that our National Health Service is still undertaking an enormous amount of good work and I am keen to include a chapter pointing this out. I believe that we would be far worse off as a nation if we did not have the NHS and I am of the belief that our type of health service provides the best value for money. Do you have any evidence that would help me to back this premise? What present-day achievements of the NHS are Whitehall most proud of? What good news is on the horizon for the NHS?

I am hoping to complete the book soon for publishing in Spring next year, the 60th anniversary of the NHS. An early reply would therefore be particularly welcome.

Thank you for your assistance.

Kind regards

Prof. Paul Goddard

Here is the reply from the Department of Health reproduced exactly as sent to me:

Our ref: TO00000259032

Richmond House
79 Whitehall
London
SW1A 2NS

Tel: 020 7210 4850

27 December 2007

Dear Professor Goddard,

Thank you for your letter of 26 November to Alan Johnson about the NHS. Due to the large amount of correspondence Mr Johnson receives, he is unable to respond directly to each individual letter. I have therefore been asked to reply on his behalf.

To aid you in the process of writing your book on the history of health services in the world, I have enclosed several lines the Department responds with when answering to criticism of the NHS.

At the centre of the Department's policy is the fact that the core principles of the NHS will continue to be the provision of quality care that is free at the point of need whilst meeting the needs of all patients based on their clinical requirements and not their ability to pay. However, the Department is aware that there is a need for improvements to cope with the demands of the 21st century. The NHS is changing the way it works to make sure patients always come first, and there is now an unprecedented level of public involvement.

Department-sponsored surveys have shown that nine out of ten people rate the inpatient care they receive as excellent, very good or good and most patients and service users rate their experience of NHS services as 'excellent' or 'very good', whilst only a small minority have serious complaints about their care. Unfortunately, as you say, the media tend to concentrate on areas of concern rather than reporting good news, of which there is a great deal.

For instance, the death rates from what used to be the major killer illnesses – heart disease and cancer – have fallen significantly in the past few years. Medical advances, together with significantly increased investment, mean that more people, from very premature babies to much older people, are now living longer and more healthy lives.

Overall, more patients are being treated than ever before, and waiting times and waiting lists have both reduced greatly. At the end of February 2007, there were 119 outpatients in England waiting over 13 weeks for a first appointment with a consultant, a fall of 121,789 (99.9 per cent) since December 2003. In 1997, patients waited up to 18 months for treatment after a GP referral, after seeing a consultant, and after diagnostic tests. When the *NHS Improvement Plan* has been delivered in 2008, the 1997 maximum wait of 18 months for only part of the patient journey will have been reduced to 18 weeks for the whole course of treatment.

The Department has embarked upon a programme of change to improve efficiency and cut bureaucracy in the management of the NHS and in the Department itself. The objective is to reduce the burden on the frontline and free up more resources for the delivery of frontline services to patients and users. This wider programme is to ensure that the increased annual investment in the NHS (over £90billion) is accompanied by modernisation and efficiency savings.

Between 75 and 80 per cent of funds are now allocated direct to the Primary Care Trusts (PCTs), whose job it is to purchase healthcare for the patients in their local area. PCT allocations are therefore used to pay for the clinical and medical treatment given to local people – patient care. In addition, part of the remaining percentage is used for special care or tertiary services, with only a very small amount now being spent on central administration by Whitehall.

The *Making a Difference* reports published jointly by the Cabinet Office and the Department have provided a number of specific outcomes dedicated to reducing the burden on clinicians and other health professionals and NHS staff and are available to view on the Department's website at www.dh.gov.uk by typing 'making a difference: reducing burdens in hospitals' into the search bar. These reports have led to over 100 changes, all recommended by frontline staff. For example, GPs no longer have to sign passports or issue sickness certificates for less than seven days absence and prescribing responsibilities have been extended to nurses and community pharmacists – not only giving health professionals opportunities to learn new skills but also freeing up more time for health professionals and clinicians to spend with patients.

There has also been major investment in the NHS workforce. In September 2006, over 1.33 million people were employed in the NHS in England, an increase of over 280,000 or 27 per cent since 1997. Between September 1997 and September 2006, the number of doctors employed in the NHS in England increased by 36,632 and the number of nurses employed in the NHS increased by 79,479.

It is important to recognise the huge strides and real, quantified improvements that have been made in the past few years, thanks to the hard work of dedicated NHS staff. In the past, many people waited up to two years for routine operations, and some waited even longer. Fewer people survived major illnesses, and access to public health information and services such as smoking cessation, dietary advice and immunisation was not always easily available.

In addition to this, the Government is demonstrating its commitment to engaging with the public about the NHS, and to this end, Lord Darzi has been asked by the Secretary of State to conduct a wide-ranging review of the NHS, and the Department has been welcoming input from both NHS staff and members of the public on how NHS services can be improved. Further information about the Next Stage Review

can be found on the *Our NHS* website, at www.ournhs.nhs.uk. The website also contains details of upcoming events across the country.

More information on the achievements of the NHS is available on the website at www.nhs.uk. The Department believes that the NHS, the largest organisation in Europe and recognised as one of the best health services in the world by the World Health Organisation, has much to be proud of.

Yours sincerely,

James Butler
Customer Service Centre
Department of Health

So in précis the Department is most proud of

1) Provision of quality care free at the point of need
2) Their own surveys show 90% of in-patients rate their care as excellent, very good or good
3) Death rates from cancer and heart disease have fallen
4) People are living longer and healthier lives
5) More patients are being treated
6) Waiting times are down
7) The Department is improving efficiency and reducing bureaucracy
8) 36,632 more doctors and 79,479 more nurses employed in 2006 compared with 1997
9) Lord Darzi has been asked to review the NHS and the public and NHS staff will be invited to comment.
10) The NHS is the largest organisation in Europe and is recognised as one of the best health services in the world by the WHO

All of these points are important although I would perhaps have thought more detail would have been in order about the range of treatment offered to patients, the preventative measures undertaken and the latest diagnostic facilities provided. Later in this chapter I will detail my attempts to find out more about these clinical aspects of the NHS. I shall be using the websites mentioned in the letter.

But first I would like to look at some aspects of the 10 points that I have précised from the letter.

Regarding point 1

Unfortunately the letter was written on the same day (December 27th 2007) that the following headline appeared in the Daily Telegraph.

NHS to cut free care for cancer mother

By Daily Telegraph Reporter   in that argument. You can now

It appears that the mother in question had raised £36,000 for additional cancer treatment, the drug Avastin, which was not made available on the NHS. But because she is now taking the drug as a course of private treatment, the NHS will not allow her to have for free the other drugs she was previously receiving.

The Department's comment, quoted in the paper, was " It is a fundamental principle of the NHS that treatment should be free at the point of need. Co-payments would undermine this principle as they involve an element of subsidy of private treatment by the taxpayer".

That is one way of looking at it. But since the treatment may be available in some hospitals and not in others it really looks as if the patient's fund-raising was taking a burden off the NHS rather than the other way round and that it was simply levelling up rather than levelling down. I realise that there may be other considerations such as extra follow-up and investigations that are required when the extra drug is taken and that it would make sense if these were also covered by the fund-raising. But if all extra costs are covered it would be my opinion that the mantra of " free at the point of need" is being used in this case to ration the service and make the poor unfortunate cancer sufferer pay for all her treatment. Or she can, if she wishes, take the free treatment without the additional drug.

It has been put to me that you cannot have people sitting together in clinics receiving different treatments depending on their ability to pay. It would be too unfair.

But this is happening anyway due to post-code prescribing, which will be discussed in a later chapter and it is typical for patients in a dental surgery to share the same waiting room and to receive different treatment depending on their ability to pay even if they are all NHS patients. It most certainly is unfair, however it also seems unfair that some people pay the most tax and therefore the most for their healthcare and do not get free prescriptions, or free dentistry, or free spectacles whilst the patients who pay the least tax do get these things.

Avastin had been evaluated by the National Institute for Health and Clinical Excellence. They had decided that it was not value for money and left the decision regarding funding up to local Trusts. But value for money for the NHS is not the same as value for money for an individual. If the drug *is* effective but expensive should our National Health Service be able to prevent patients from receiving it even if they are happy to pay for it themselves? Clearly this is what they are doing when they say that co-payments are not permitted. The cost of all the care could run into hundreds of thousands of pounds when the expense of operations, radiotherapy and other drugs are totalled. Few patients could raise enough money for all this and nor should they be expected to do so.

The NHS does provide a service that is mostly (but not entirely) free at the point of need. But the quality is sometimes lacking and there are aspects of care that the NHS appears to have forgotten.

There are indications that patients may be allowed to "top up" their treatment. Many people would welcome this. The NHS does provide a service that is mostly (but not entirely) free at the point of need but the quality is sometimes lacking and there are aspects of care that the NHS appears to have forgotten.

Point 2. So even in their own surveys 10% of inpatients do not rate their care as good. The latest You Gov poll (Daily Telegraph 30.6.08) shows that 81% of patients are satisfied with their NHS treatment compared with 91% in 1998 and 92% in 1948.

Points 3 and 4. It is true that death rates from cancer and heart disease have fallen and that life expectancy has increased but these changes have not been as marked as in other developed nations and do constitute some cause for concern.

5 and 6. More patients are being treated and waiting lists are down. This is good.

7. Is the Department really improving efficiency and reducing bureaucracy? Evidence seems to point in the opposite direction.

8. In 2006 the number of nurses and doctors was certainly high. In 2007 large numbers seem to have been made redundant or have simply not been found posts when their present training jobs finished.

9. Lord Darzi has now reported. He believes the NHS has improved in the last ten years. I shall certainly send him a copy of this book.

Point number 10 in our list: Unfortunately the last chapter has shown that is not completely fair. Yes, the NHS is the largest organisation in Europe (the Red Army used to take this position) but this is not necessarily something to be proud of. As to being one of the best health services in the world, it really depends on which other countries you compare us with. We are certainly better than the developing nations and the previous Soviet bloc. The last chapter has shown us that we are not rated highly in Europe, which is where we really have to compare ourselves. Value for money is still good but the quality has dropped in comparison with countries such as Sweden or France and there does appear to be rationing in the NHS although this is not expressed directly.

In 2000, the start of the new millennium, I wrote an article jointly with Richard Ashcroft, who was then working at the Centre for Ethics in Medicine of Bristol University. Entitled 'Ethical dilemmas in a Rationed Health Service', the article appeared in a radiological newspaper called Rad. It summarised the problems of the health service at that time and made at least some impression since I saw photocopies of the piece on various notice boards in my own hospital and other local hospitals. One radiologist from a nearby hospital told me that she had copied the article and posted it up since it was the most sensible article she had read in years. I take the liberty of reproducing the article in its entirety since I consider the points we made to be entirely relevant today and it acts as an introduction to themes I shall be expanding in the second part of the book.

Ethical dilemmas in a Rationed Health Service₂

One of the most famous ethical problems is that immortalized by Shaw in The Doctor's Dilemma. How do you decide who should be treated when the resources are limited? Do you treat your friend or the world famous poet, the old man who has spent a lifetime working or the young child with a lifetime ahead of her?

This dilemma was perhaps mostly theoretical when George Bernard Shaw was writing his play but has become all the more real in our modern world. Medicine has become a victim of its own success... as we become able to efficaciously treat more patients and more diseases the cost of treatment spirals. Why are there such problems and who should make the decisions? Should the problem of rationing be left to a manager? Is the problem due to inefficiency or lazy, corrupt doctors? ...

Inefficiency

There is some inefficiency in the British National Health Service as there is in any large or small organisation. This is a relatively minor problem but it is sometimes presented as a smokescreen to incorrectly explain the lack of money. In fact the NHS is the cheapest provider of Health Care per head of population in the Western world. It is likely that there is considerably greater inefficiency in the health care systems of other countries.

If efficiency is considered to mean a situation in which the personnel and buildings are utilised 100% of the time it could be dangerous to be totally efficient. The requirements for medical care cannot be predicted with great certainty since the outbreak of epidemics of infectious diseases; the vagaries of the weather and attendant complications and the occurrence of accidents in the home and on transport are chaotic events. Thus a degree of 'inefficiency' or 'slack' must be built into the system to allow for these events. At times our system has been too 'efficient' and had not been able to cope with flu epidemics, for instance.

Corrupt lazy doctors and poorly trained staff

Much has been written recently about doctors needing better training, about their arrogance and corruption and about general laziness.

The ratio of doctors to patients in the UK is one third that of some European countries and their income about a fifth. The same applies for other staff such as nurses and radiographers. Surveys have shown that rather than being lazy the NHS staff are actually working longer hours than other comparable personnel and that they are seeing many more patients in that time. The training of staff

135

in the UK is still reckoned to be of an excellent standard and many medical personnel from around the world still travel to the UK for training.

Whilst occasional staff may be lazy or arrogant, overall it is clear that the NHS staff from porters to doctors are hard working and dedicated. It is important to ensure that they are not over-worked and exploited. There is no evidence of significant corruption amongst medical staff.

Medical Inflation

Medical Inflation, the cost of investigating and treating patients, has for many years outstripped that of general inflation of the retail price index.

This is partly due to the increased sophistication of new treatments… the more complex a treatment be it surgery, drugs or whatever, the more expensive it will be. The cost of developing a new pharmaceutical is vast and the techniques now involved, such as genetic engineering, are considerably more time-consuming and technically more difficult than previously.

International standards and regulations have become progressively tougher which has certainly improved safety but has also increased the cost of newer techniques and treatment.

The Beveridge Myth

When the NHS was first set up it was thought that the provision of health care to all would lead to improved health of the Nation and that the cost of health care would then fall. This has never been the case. Severely ill patients who may otherwise have died have been saved to fall ill another time (and perhaps another and another) before eventually succumbing to a final illness. Minor ailments that would have been ignored are now considered more significant. Overall the expectation of the public has changed.

The funding of the service has not kept match with this expectation. This is partly a political matter and partly due to the way in which the service was organised. It is possible to maintain the health service but improvements are not built into the formula. Thus the advance in one area may well be funded by removing the finance from another area…..Health service innovation works by robbing Peter to pay Paul. Who 'Peter' and 'Paul' are is very often determined not by need or rational argument, but by the ability of particular specialities, geographical locations or medical conditions to catch the public or politicians' attention.

Rationing

It is clear that rationing is occurring in the NHS. How else can we describe the fact that certain drugs will not be available in certain Trusts because they do not have the finance to pay for them? Or that there are enormously long waiting lists effectively cutting down the opportunity to have routine operations?

The rationing occurs both directly because of lack of finance and because of staff shortages. The latter usually also occur due to lack of finance but this is over a longer period and involves poor recruitment to training programmes, inadequate provision of such programmes and an overall low wage structure and poor working conditions.

If an investigation or treatment is not available in a particular Trust but is available in another this should be made clear to patients. If the doctors have to explain this to patients it puts a considerable strain on the patient-doctor relationship. Even worse is the situation where a doctor is not permitted to explain to the patient about rationing.

Most people would agree that the doctor should provide the very best care that is available for that patient. The doctor should be the patient's champion in a similar way to a barrister acting as a defendant's advocate. In this scenario there would be no place for the doctor acting as a gatekeeper for his own patients.

But if the medical staff are allowed to provide whatever treatment they desire for their patients there is a widely held belief amongst administration and management that the cost will spiral. Presently the medical profession are being persistently and repeatedly told by the managers to make savings wherever they can. The managers themselves are being put under considerable duress with bonuses only paid if Trusts are within budget and there are legal requirements for the Trusts to remain solvent. Hence there is a major level of stress amongst managers and much of this is also being transmitted to the medical staff. Frequently medical directorates are asked to work on a reducing budget but to increase throughput, whilst providing a service more cheerfully!

When is it ethical to ration the service?

It is clearly ethical to ration a service only if:

- The rationing is done openly and honestly and the causes of the rationing are known
- All methods of avoiding rationing have been considered
- The staff are not abused by being overworked and/or underpaid.
- Mutually exclusive targets are not set staff by their superiors, be they politicians, managers, consultants or whoever.

Until we in the NHS are satisfied that these conditions are met, we must be suspicious of the drive to 'realism' in debates about rationing. The economists may well be right to insist that resources are scarce by their very nature. But much of the 'scarcity' in the NHS today is due to politics, not economics.

It is unethical to introduce rationing secretly, to target the weak, to suspend staff when they complain and to put managers and staff under stress in order to save money.

Since this article was published there has been a considerable increase in the spending on health care. Unfortunately the extra finance was put in with considerable ties and further reorganisation as discussed earlier in the book and the main effect was to add numerous useless managerial staff watching what the doctors and nurses are doing and to turn more of these doctors and nurses into non-productive managers. The government cannot seem to understand that too tight control of health care by managers will in itself lead to inefficiency. Thus the NHS is more inefficient now than it was when the article was written. This is discussed later in the book.

An example of excessive 'efficiency' occurred recently with influenza immunisation. More patients turned up at the GP surgeries for their annual 'flu jab' than would have normally been expected. This was partly because of the publicity over bird flu but in addition the government had included carers and other groups as 'at risk' groups who should be immunised. The GPs had efficiently ordered the same number of 'jabs' as the previous year plus a prudent extra 10%. This however proved to be woefully inadequate and it was reported that there were queues of disappointed patients when the supply ran out. The orders had been supplied efficiently but the tight budgetary control meant that only the required amount was made and some people missed out. The government immediately blamed the doctors saying that they must have immunised people who were not in the risk groups. This was hotly denied by the GPs who said that they were very careful to keep to the guidelines. It was, in fact, the result of a mostly unpredictable increase in demand and if any body was at fault it was the government. Of interest here is that there have been reports that the 'at risk' groups set by the government are not the best ones to immunise against influenza anyway. Some people argue that the elderly do not mount a sufficient immune response to the influenza immunisation. If that is the case it is better to immunise people who can respond significantly and cut the incidence of influenza in the population thereby helping reduce the infection rate in everyone including the previously identified 'at risk' groups.

Advances and Achievements in British State Medicine

Looking at the websites suggested in the letter from the Department of Health I had great difficulty in identifying anything resembling an advance or recent achievement. Certainly the websites themselves represented an educational advance from which patients may benefit but I very much doubt whether many children would bother to look at the sites ….perhaps the content aimed at them is there to assist their parents.

I searched as suggested on the www.dh.gov.uk site by typing in the words 'making a difference'. The results were disappointing…..a few initiatives from 2000 and 2001 which should have been effective by now if they were to be any use.

To discover whether there *were* any recent medical advances in the UK, I put the words 'recent medical advance' into Google. I was relieved to discover that the Medical Research Council, which was set up in 1913 using National Insurance money, is still going strong. What is more, much of their research does appear to meet the original primary aim of improving the nation's health. According to their website (www.mrc.ac.uk) the MRC's current priority areas include:

- Clinical and public health research
- Infections and vaccine research
- Global health
- Biomarkers
- Ageing-related research
- Sustaining capability in areas of strategic importance

Recent achievements over the past seven years cover a broad range of research. I have selected the following excerpts from the MRC site since they show considerable potential benefit for mankind.

138

Safer pregnancy for mother and child

MRC research has shown that the injection of a simple and affordable anti-convulsive drug could halve the risk of a major pregnancy complication that is responsible for 15 per cent of maternal deaths in the UK, and kills over 50,000 mothers and unborn babies a year worldwide[3].

Screening men for abdominal aneurysms can reduce mortality

Results from the MRC-funded Multi-centre Aneurysm Screening Study suggest that a national ultrasound screening programme for men over 65 could prevent more than 2,000 deaths from abdominal aortic aneurysms each year[4].

1918 flu virus - riddle solved

Scientists from the MRC's National Institute for Medical Research (NIMR) have solved an 85-year-old mystery by revealing the modus operandi of the world's most lethal influenza outbreak[5].

Reducing health inequalities

Since 1985, the Whitehall II study has tracked the effects of stress, job security, work-life balance and a range of lifestyle factors on the health of more than 10,000 civil servants working in central London, with the aim of reducing health inequalities in society. In 2004/2005, the MRC-funded University College London scientists reported a wide range of results. Stress at work and home increased the risk of heart disease, while a good work-life balance was linked to better mental health[6].

Pneumococcus vaccine could save a million young lives

Vaccinating infants against pneumococcus – a bacterium that causes pneumonia, meningitis and bloodstream infections – could prevent up to a million deaths every year among children in developing countries. In a joint study by MRC researchers and scientists from the London School of Hygiene and Tropical Medicine, 17,000 infants in The Gambia were vaccinated against pneumococcus and tracked for four years. The results showed a 17 per cent drop in the number of deaths and a 37per cent decrease in cases of pneumonia[7].

Stemming the effects of heart attack and stroke

Heart attacks and strokes cause around half of all deaths in developed countries. They strike when the blood supply to the heart or brain is cut off. Scientists led by Professor Mark Pepys at University College London have previously shown that stroke and heart attack damage is compounded by a molecule known as C-reactive protein. It is produced and circulates through the blood stream in response to the injury. Now, Professor Pepys's team has designed a new agent that is bound by C-reactive protein and stops it from doing damage. " If it is approved for use, it should reduce the severity of heart attacks and strokes, leading to improved survival," said Professor Pepys. The next step is to develop the compound as a drug for regulatory approval and clinical use[8].

Whilst the MRC is not the same as the NHS it is important to point out that it *is* funded by the Government and that it therefore represents one aspect of State Medicine. Much of the MRC clinical research is carried out in NHS hospitals. If research projects listed above are put into full clinical use the results could profoundly improve the health of the nation.

Are there other aspects of State Medicine that can be considered to have advanced in the last ten years?

There has certainly been a major investment in hospital buildings and equipment, diagnostic and treatment centres and health centres. Unfortunately most of this investment has been undertaken as Private Finance Initiatives (PFIs). The problems with these are discussed elsewhere but looking on the bright side it is important to point out that the developments mean that many areas of the UK do now have new facilities.

In my own field of radiology it is noticeable that many hospitals now have new complex equipment such as digital radiography, computed tomography, magnetic resonance imaging and even PET-CT scanners.

Picture Archiving and Communication System
(Courtesy of Agfa HealthCare UK Limited)

The resulting images from these machines are stored in Picture Archiving and Communication Systems (PACS). These systems in turn link with other hospitals and to on-call doctors by teleradiology. This type of equipment is revolutionizing the reporting of radiological investigations and is significantly influencing the clinical management of patients.

Picture Archiving and Communication Systems are a successful example of technology developed by private enterprise rather than by the government. The government-led patient information computer programs have been very slow to succeed (some would say they have been an unmitigated disaster) whilst the same type of problem has been independently solved in radiology by a number of different firms.

Has it all gone wrong?

As stated at the start of this chapter, despite pessimistic pronouncements it would not be true to say that it has all gone wrong. An enormous amount of good work has been and is being done by staff in the NHS. However it is true to say that there is a general feeling of gloom and despair in the NHS and that more and more the government is trying to get away from the simple concept of state supplied medical services on a national basis. That is to say that, despite denials and cries to the contrary, they are turning their back on the basic initial concepts of the National Health Service.

Each area of the NHS has its own particular problems and its own background of complications and failure leading to the present situation. In this section, part II of the book, we shall examine a number of the major health professions in turn. By looking at the problems in the development of their service in the NHS we may be able to understand where things started to go wrong and how they might be put right, since that, after all, is the entire point in the writing of this book. We shall start with the doctors.

Chapter 10
The Medical profession and the NHS: what went wrong?

Doctors and the early NHS

Something has gone drastically wrong with the medical profession over the past two decades or probably even longer. Searching Google on the Internet for the phrase 'complaints about doctors' elicited 4.4 million hits! The reasons are myriad and we will need to look back into the recent history of the medical profession.

As we have seen in the earlier chapters the evolution of the medical profession took millennia. Concomitant with the development of medical science came the development of medical ethics. The debate as to whether or not doctors should be inspired by the profit motive has been argued throughout the ages but whatever way the doctors were reimbursed the higher ethical principles demanded that they did their best for each patient. This required that the doctors should individually practice as a professional answerable to the profession as a whole, always acting on behalf of their patients and in their patients' best interests.

"Whatever houses I may visit, I will come for the benefit of the sick, remaining free of all intentional injustice, of all mischief"......"Primum non nocere" — *"First, do no harm"...**Hippocrates**[1]*

and from the (General Medical Council) GMC[2]

"Patients must be able to trust doctors with their lives and well-being. To justify that trust, we as a profession have a duty to maintain a good standard of practice and care and to show respect for human life. In particular as a doctor you must:

- *make the care of your patient your first concern;*
- *treat every patient politely and considerately;*
- *respect patients' dignity and privacy;*
- *listen to patients and respect their views;*
- *give patients information in a way they can understand;*
- *respect the rights of patients to be fully involved in decisions about their care;*
- *keep your professional knowledge and skills up to date;*
- *recognise the limits of your professional competence;*
- *be honest and trustworthy;*
- *respect and protect confidential information;*
- *make sure that your personal beliefs do not prejudice your patients' care;*
- *act quickly to protect patients from risk if you have good reason to believe that you or a colleague may not be fit to practise;*
- *avoid abusing your position as a doctor; and*
- *work with colleagues in the ways that best serve patients' interests".*

I believe that many changes in the structure of the NHS have led to conflicts with these ethics. In particular the increasing control wielded by the politicians via the managers creates dilemmas for the discerning doctor. You cannot put the patient first if you are told, time and again, that your main objective is decreasing the waiting list or reducing trolley waits. Targets set by government are frequently not in the individual patient's interests and may be in the interests of no patients. They have often been set by spin-doctors rather than "real" doctors.

How have we come to this situation and have the doctors, an admittedly powerful group of intelligent individuals, not been able to prevent it?

Some of the reasons may lie in the compromises which were necessary at the inception of the National Health Service.

At the inception of the NHS one thorny problem needed to be solved. How could you get the doctors on board? Although some doctors were in favour of a health service, many feared that it would interfere with both the clinical and financial freedom they had traditionally enjoyed. The general practitioners (GPs) were independent and could go straight into practice as soon as they qualified. The consultants worked for free in the charity hospitals but earned high fees privately. The junior hospital doctors worked long hours for experience, often for next to no pay but with the knowledge that they would be wealthy once they also became Consultants.

I quote from the Medical Annual of 1947[3].

'The act (National Health Service Act) is to come into force on April 1st, 1948.
Whereas the Coalition Government, before drafting a Bill, called representatives of the professions into consultation, the present Minister of Health has not done so at any stage. This, and the autocratic position given to the Minister have aroused considerable resentment in a large section of the medical profession, and strong objection has been expressed to the appropriation of the property of hospitals, and to the modified "direction" of general practitioners resulting form the power of excluding applicants from "adequately doctored" areas.'

How could the Labour Government get the doctors 'on board'? If the doctors refused to take part the National Health Service would be stillborn.
The answer lay with the British Medical Association (BMA) and was hinted at by a statement in the next passage in the same Medical Annual[3].

'The Government and associations of local authorities and the Trade Union Congress, recognize the B.M.A. as the negotiating body for the medical profession....'

The labour Government persuaded the BMA to back the scheme by promising that they would have sole negotiating rights for doctors in perpetuity. As long as the NHS existed the BMA would be the only organisation permitted to represent the medical profession nationally when negotiating pay, conditions and service.

The general practitioners were allowed to continue an independent existence, owning their own surgeries and supported by generous grants.

All consultants would be well paid, they would be given the right to practice private medicine within the health service and the mantra of "clinical freedom" meant that they would be able to provide their NHS patients with the standard of medical care that they needed without interference from the government but with the necessary financial support. In addition the consultant could act as an independent agent whilst at the same time receiving the benefits of state salary and pension.

The more experienced and prestigious consultants would receive extra rewards known as Merit Awards. These would be awarded by a committee of peers (consultant colleagues) with input from management and the various medical Royal Colleges and the BMA.

The presidents of the Royal Colleges would continue to be invited into the elite establishment by the giving of medals and well-placed knighthoods (and occasional Dames!)

All of these interventions helped to ensure that the doctors would not speak out against the inception of the NHS. Unfortunately it also meant that their voices would be stifled when detrimental changes in the service were later made.

I have many times heard people say that they were worried about being vocal because of their forthcoming assessment for a merit award and I have even heard presidents of colleges state that they felt it 'best to keep their head down'. Many consultants would not like to be 'too bolshie' in case it interfered with their private practice and would not speak out loudly against a chief executive for fear of negative input when being assessed for discretionary points . They would certainly not consider it to be wise to confront a senior consultant colleague whose work was not up to the highest standards or argue with a colleague undertaking a dubious management role since the consultant in question would almost certainly sit on committees awarding merit awards or be a potential referrer of private patients or both!

These responses are not surprising when it has been possible to double your salary by private practice with maybe only 25% more time taken or to nearly double your salary with an A+ merit award with no extra work at all! I would like to state that these words have not been written because of jealousy on my part of more fortunate colleagues. I was a lucky recipient of both a substantial private practice and a significant merit award. However I was well aware of the effect that these ways of increasing the salary had on myself and other consultants.

That is not to say that private practice and merit awards have had a completely negative influence. In many ways they have been both individually beneficial and helpful to the overall health care situation.

Private practice has many benefits.

- It provides patients with a choice whilst the NHS has traditionally not done so (although this is supposedly changing with the 'patient choice' being a new mantra for our present government).
- Better relationships with patients. I greatly enjoyed private work because it allowed me to directly relate to the patients and practice medicine at a reasonable pace, which the NHS frequently did not. In my experience, the doctors who were the best at communication, the politest to patients, the most reliable, most obtainable and the most innovative also had the largest private practices. Surprisingly these good attributes were also apparent in their NHS practice. I was never sure whether treating private patients taught the doctors to improve their manners (etc.) or whether the most personable consultants naturally did well in private practice but it is probably a combination of the two.
- Private practice within the NHS greatly supported the organisation financially before 1975 as discussed elsewhere in the book. Since 1975 it has taken some load (approximately 15%) off the NHS.
- The NHS has never been able to afford the market rate for the highest performing doctors. If they had not been able to earn so well privately there would have been a considerably greater 'brain drain' of top consultants to the USA, Canada, Australia and other high paying destinations. In fact the UK has managed to attract a significant number of top doctors from abroad

The merit award system certainly encouraged some consultants to write research papers, sit on committees and generally improve their CVs. The potential reward of a merit award or discretionary points definitely motivated many consultants as shown by the example of a colleague who, on being told that only articles with a high citation rating published in highly regarded journals would assist on his CV questionnaire, replied that there was therefore no point in finishing the review articles he had been writing for minor medical journals. If they were not of value on his CV for merit awards he could not see why he should do the work. Clearly the hope of a merit award was motivating him more then the desire to teach or enlighten.

Nevertheless the private practice and merit award systems have been deeply unfair and deeply divisive. Some specialties (such as paediatrics) support almost no private practice and for many years the University posts forbade private work. Some specialties historically have a very high percentage of the awards and some a very low percentage. There have also been unsolved merit award discrepancies with regard to gender and race.

With these ulterior motives, hidden agendas and differing expectations, trying to get a group of consultants to agree on any course of action has been unfavourably compared with attempting to herd cats. When this action might involve disagreement with the Department of Health, the government of the day, be it Socialist, Conservative or New Labour, has always been very adept at divide and rule. The government has frequently succeeded in setting the GPs off against the hospital doctors, the juniors against the consultants and the consultants against each other.

Are there more problems with doctors now?

Despite the problems experienced in getting the doctors to agree to the formation of the NHS, once it had started they were its greatest supporters. It is the doctors of the NHS who have been the backbone of the service throughout the years that the NHS has functioned. If the public were asked who worked the hardest in the NHS they would probably answer 'the nurses'. In reality most nurses work a standard week of 37.5 hours, do little overtime and no unpaid work. When they work antisocial hours, they do so as shift work, are well paid and have time off in lieu. In comparison the average doctor has worked longer than the contracted hours and put in many hours of extra work on a voluntary, unpaid basis. The doctors have far too frequently missed lunch breaks and too often started early and finished late. They have often worked day and night dealing with emergencies to the detriment of their own well-being. As a junior hospital doctor I truthfully worked three times as many hours as the nurses. Many of the junior doctors in particular still work 50% longer than the nurses and the new consultant contract is for a standard 44 or 48 hour week and many consultants work longer than this. The average is now just over 50 hours, slightly down from previously after implementation of the new contract (this had surprised the government who thought they would get more work out of consultants by pinning them down to exact hours).

However there have always been problems with doctors. Although enormously respected by the community they have also been accused of being arrogant and poor communicators. In addition they have been troubled souls with a history of excess alcohol intake, a high level of drug dependence and an above average rate of suicide[4,5,6,7].

However, despite all this most doctors enjoyed their job and it was difficult to get them to retire even though they knew that retiring at 60 gave them an extra 5 years on their life compared with those who retired at 65.

This has changed. In the hospital service I hardly know a single doctor who does not say that he or she wishes to retire early. Recent reports on 1001 doctors stated that 77 percent intended planned early retirement from the NHS.

Many of them, including myself, have done just that.

Forty years ago, when I was considering applying for a place at medical school, the places were amongst the most sort after in all the universities. There are now difficulties in recruiting the right level of candidate for medical school and the dropout rate during training has vastly increased . Newly qualified doctors are said to have a dropout rate of 25%. In my own year I believe there may have been at the most a one or two percent dropout overall, so the change is vast.

Why has there been a change for the worse?

There are several factors at work here and I will try to untangle the various influences.

Doctors used to be very highly respected and highly paid. They had high self-regard because they felt that what they were doing was worthwhile, that they could do a good and satisfying job and that they were appreciated. As consultants or general practitioners they worked long hours but had a comfortable life style, able to afford whatever luxuries they desired and able to send their children to the schools they wished without worrying about the cost.

The most junior of the hospital doctors, the house officers and senior house officers, were badly paid and worked long hours. There was, however, considerable camaraderie amongst the doctors who lived a military-like mess existence.

When I was a houseman the ancillary staff at least had respect for the junior doctors. I had a cup of tea brought to my room when I awoke, all my meals were made for me and served to me (silver service!) in the doctors' mess and the food was free. Our laundry was done for us and our beds changed and rooms cleaned, all for free. Moreover we could look forward to a better existence when the wages would markedly improve, the hours decrease and our position in society would be assured.

(Unfortunately I was also amongst the first batch of housemen to carry bleeps (pagers) and to be on call for emergencies such as cardiac arrests. The hospital staff had previously called the housemen only occasionally overnight but now they started calling us at any time as if we were the night staff rather than working almost continuously night and day. See the junior doctors' dispute in Part I of this book).

Surveys show that the doctors are still highly regarded by the general population but that is not necessarily how we perceive the situation. Patients very frequently abuse medical staff but even more often we are abused by the media and the politicians.

A number of very high publicity medical scandals have rocked our assurance that we are doing a good job. The politicians and managers have hammered home the message that we are constantly making mistakes. Medical litigation rocketed from a few cases a year at a cost of tens of thousands of pounds in the 1950s to around three billion pounds a year in 2000.

As a response to some of these changes the government and their managers tried to control medical practice more and more closely. They introduced quality assurance, compulsory continuing medical education, medical audit, clinical governance, assessment, annual appraisal and revalidation. In my own experience, all of these non-clinical activities were introduced into the working week without taking anything out.

In addition we were now expected to work in large teams and to attend long-winded multi-disciplinary meetings where the most straightforward cases were discussed *ad-nauseum* and the difficult cases ignored. Most of these meetings took the place of lunch breaks, which, in any case, could no longer be taken in the doctors' dining room because that was closed down several years ago.

The few medical diehards had taken to eating in the dining area of the post-graduate centre but the post-grad centre then decamped to a splendid new academic centre open to all but *not* including a dining room.

Meanwhile the social club of the hospital had been closed down to make way for a new children's hospital and the main staff dining room also closed. We were finally left with a very small bistro serving staff, visitors and the occasional patient in unbelievably cramped conditions. Similar changes have occurred all over the country.

Meanwhile the pressure of clinical work had markedly increased. We were expected to increase throughput but asked to do this whilst making savings. Lip service was given to research and teaching but no supporting finance and no allocated time.

As regards to the financial situation it is rather interesting. The salaries of doctors are not bad and compared with the population average they would be considered as relatively good. But in the past GPs and consultants had strikingly better incomes than the vast proportion of their patients. They could afford the large houses and good schools without difficulty. Now they cannot do so. Moreover we are regaled all the time with stories of the vast sums of money made by financial advisers in the city or by footballers. So the young doctors drop out to become financial advisers (they already had better grades at A-level maths than their friends who went on to business school).

In addition to the amount of work, the stress of the work has also vastly increased. With regard to the hospital service I believe that one of the reasons for this is because the doctors are progressively being turned into middle management.

When I started in the health service a consultant was as close to a demigod as one could get. The hospital administrators were afraid of the consultant's wrath and everyone else lived in awe of him (or occasionally her). The only equal figure was the Matron who was rarely seen but greatly feared and admired.

Nowadays the consultant has a line manager above him or her. This is the clinical director, often also a doctor. In addition in each directorate there is a non-medical general manager who has considerable control over the consultants working day. The consultant is being progressively moved away from his previous position of ownership of a specialty headship in the hospital. Locally the GPs are instructed to send surgical referrals to the manager or the directorate rather than to a specific surgeon. The GP is therefore no longer permitted to request a named surgeon. The operating lists are not organised by the surgical team but by the managers since they wish to make sure that the waiting lists are being dealt with "efficiently".

In X-ray departments if requests for examinations would exceed the specified waiting period they are not shown to the radiologists and therefore do not enter on to the official waiting lists. The fact that urgent cases do not necessarily receive priority for surgery or for investigation and that inevitably patients will suffer and die from this is ignored by management and pushed down into their subconscious by the doctors.

The line manager has a manager above him or her and so on up to the level of the chief executive. The Trust chief executive answers to the Trust Board and to the Dept of Health. Often the consultant has only one or two junior staff to assist him or her and much of the time none at all. The nursing staff, radiographers, physiotherapists, technicians, catering staff and cleaners are all under parallel lines of command and certainly do not consider that a doctor can instruct them in what to do. (request-may be, hope-frequently and order-never).

As a result of the working time directive the junior staff do far shorter hours. So the consultant, who of course spent many years as a junior doing slave-like long hours, has to fill in doing a junior's work during the day and often also at night.

What is more the medical post is no longer secure. Almost no doctors were ever sacked when I first started in the NHS. To do so required the intervention of the Secretary of State for Health, so it was a job for life. Now many are suspended, struck-off, sacked and even made redundant.

So from a position of respect, wealth, security and power the consultants have been turned into fairly lowly middle managers or 'pit face workers'. Their jobs may be changed at the whim of a line manager, they are over-worked and unable to afford the house and children's schools they would like. At school they were the hardest working and most successful of the pupils. Forty years later they are being treated as idiots by a bunch of under-educated political toadies. Worried about their own error rate which may be exposed at any time in a major media witch hunt, he or she is clearly being made into the scapegoat for the inevitable failure of the NHS.

Coupled with the fact that the consultants are very bright and can see what is going wrong whilst the managers frequently cannot, it all leads to enormous frustration and a desperate attempt to succeed by working harder and harder

So why have the sixty year olds not all retired already? (Or even all those over fifty-five when you can first pick up an inflation-linked pension).

Many have. But the reasons so many stay on despite the fact that they would love to retire include:

- **Nothing else to do**:

The consultant has spent so many hours a week and so many weeks in a year thinking about, slaving at and generally being a doctor that he (rather than she) does not know what else to do. He knows he'll die at 66 if he keeps working till 65 but what else is there in life?

- **They can't afford to**

The 'generous' pension is not as generous as it seems: I have seen many reports in the media about the great generosity of the NHS and civil service pensions. It is true that the scheme, being based on final salary, is a good one. Many doctors do want to stay on to get a good pension.

There are differences between the NHS pension scheme and the (genuinely generous) civil service scheme. The civil service pension is non-contributory whilst in the NHS pension scheme the contributions must balance the outgoings. Our pension is based on 40 years service but theirs on 30.

Very few consultants even if they reach 65 will be eligible for the full pension of 50%. The pension has been based on years of full time practice in the NHS, each year being worth one eightieth of the final pensionable salary. The youngest it is possible to qualify as a doctor is twenty three after a 5 year course, with no gap year. Many, such as myself, will have undertaken an additional 'intercalated' degree lengthening the course to 6 years so that I was nearly 25 by the time I qualified. Although my early house jobs were 120 hours per week the extra hours counted as nothing but the gaps, say of six weeks unpaid, between jobs simply because they did not start at regular times certainly counted against me. Having worked three times as many hours as a normal employee, such as a nurse, at the end of the year I had less pensionable right.
Couple this with the fact that so many doctors die young and the pension does not seem so generous.

Many have large mortgages or loans to pay for their children's schooling and university costs. The pension would not be sufficient.

- **Most consultants undertake private work**

If this exceeded 10% of their NHS income they had to drop one session from their NHS pay whilst doing the same hours as before. This has also come off their salary so not only have they worked the same hours but they have been penalised on pay and pension. The years spent as a part-time consultant meant that I and many other consultants would not reach the forty years even if we worked to sixty-five. When consultants are in their fifties and start looking at their pension entitlement they are frequently shocked at how much less it is than they had fondly imagined.

- **Loss of private work**

It would be possible to retire and work privately. Many try to do this but they usually find that their income from private work diminishes very rapidly when they are no longer working in close proximity to their referrers in the NHS. This is one factor that is likely to change under the new outsourcing arrangements of Blair (and now Brown). It does not

149

really represent retiring and if the managers of the private hospitals have their way it would be no better than working in the NHS.

- **Private pensions have performed badly**

I bought a private pension and just like yourself my profits have been removed by bad management on the part of the pension companies and windfall taxes by Gordon Brown.

- **Loss of status**

There are factors affecting all people mitigating against early retirement such as loss of status and lack of contact with colleagues and loss of companionship

So doctors certainly are a problem. Many of the older hospital doctors either want to work but hate the conditions they are working in or they want to retire but are unable to do so. Or both. Many younger doctors are filled with resentment and act in a manner, which would have been considered as very unprofessional only a few years ago. They wish, with as little commitment as possible, to get out of the system as much as they possibly can.

In the next two chapters I shall address, in much greater depth, two topics I have started discussing above.

The first is error and medical negligence in the brave new world of human rights. Why is there so much error in medicine and why have the doctors not spoken up about it before?

The second aspect could be classed as the political aspects of medicine. Many doctors have privately voiced their opinion that the changes in healthcare have been wrong. They object to management control of clinical practice but they do not speak up in public against the political interference. I shall be exploring this and give my opinions as to why they have, in the most part, remained a silent majority against the changes.

Chapter 11
Medical Error and Negligence,
The Witch-hunt and Suspension.

NHS staff 'cover up blunders'

Doctors and nurses are covering up the scale of infections and mistakes that patients
suffer because of bad hospital treatment, the national audit office says in a report published today.
Staff who report errors worry that they will be disciplined by the trust, and a culture of covering up
incidents has grown up in the NHS, says Parliament's financial watchdog

David Hencke , Wednesday September 17, 2003, The Guardian

The above quote is one example of the recent reports highlighting error in medicine. There
have been numerous headlines and newspaper stories about the problems of error and
negligence in the medical profession and the vast majority, apart from those in the medical
press, have assumed that the fault lay with the doctors.

Error in medical practice is inevitable. That is not to say that all error is inevitable since
some can be avoided but it is important that the patients, the politicians, the managers, the
tax-paying public and the doctors themselves acknowledge the fact that there are both
avoidable and unavoidable errors. There is a growing tendency in our society to need a
scapegoat whenever something is perceived as having gone wrong. However, whilst it is
important to search out causes of error it is also important not to blame people for mistakes
when they are inevitable.

Litigation over medical error and successful prosecution of medical negligence has
increased almost exponentially which may lead one to believe that medical errors are also
increasing dramatically. This is not necessarily the case. What has happened is more
complex and is more to do with the awareness of error and the 'sophistication' of the public
than with true error rates.

I will write mainly about investigation and diagnosis since this is the area of my greatest
expertise but the same principles apply whether we are discussing investigation or
treatment.

Firstly, is it true that there is a lot of error in medicine?

I am sorry to say that the national audit office report, as quoted above in the Guardian, is
correct. There are numerous errors as there are in all human endeavours. Sonderegga Iseli
et al in a paper in the Lancet in 2000 [1] compared the accuracy of clinical diagnosis in
unselected patients who died in hospital in three different medical eras. The post mortem
was taken as the gold standard and errors were classified as major or minor. (Major
diagnostic error is that which affects treatment, prognosis and outcome whilst minor error
is a definite mistake but one which does not affect the outcome).

Diagnostic errors in three medical eras Ref. 1		
Year	Classification of error	
	Major	Minor
1972	30%	23%
1982	18%	32%
1992	14%	46%

These figures are very interesting. The initial response is one of great alarm. Is it really true that in 1972 nearly a third of patients dying in hospitals had suffered a major diagnostic error? Yes it is and there are many papers to back up this sort of error level in medical diagnosis[2-11]. More worrying still, the number of errors has gone up, overall, from 53% in 1972 to 60% in 1992.

Further analysis is a little more reassuring. Whilst the minor error has gone up, which we might have expected with the increase in litigation, the major diagnostic error rate has gone down, which is not what we may have been led to believe. Over the period of twenty years in question the serious errors halved but the less important errors have doubled.

Why should this be the case? The twenty years in question saw the introduction of major new diagnostic tests. A short (and very incomplete) table of radiological investigations will illustrate this.

Approximate date of introduction into clinical practice	Technique
1975	Computed Tomography (CT, CAT or EMI scan)
1978	Double contrast barium enema
1980	Real time ultrasound (US)
1985	Magnetic Resonance Imaging (MRI)

With these tests it has been possible to drastically reduce the need for explorative surgery such as laparotomy for abdominal problems or burr holes into the head for brain-related abnormalities. The new techniques do not get the result absolutely right always and will result in minor errors but they do considerably assist in avoidance of major errors. In the past undertaking the exploratory surgery in a very sick patient was, in itself, a cause of mortality. The newer techniques have an almost infinitesimal mortality risk. So the major errors go down and the minor errors go up.

This is not the whole reason for the change in error. The problems are multi-factorial. For example management policies may affect error in several unexpected ways. Whilst the introduction of scientific advance is lowering the error rate, decreased staffing levels may be raising it. The improved science would be masking the adverse effects of the staff cuts. Audit controls may clamp down on major error but the time taken to do the audit may result in increased minor error. In an imperfect world the politically driven management might insist, against advice, on bringing in overseas staff who have not been tried and tested by the usual methods of interview and membership of Royal Colleges. This could lead to increased error. Or they might find it politically necessary to meet some imposed target. To do this they could, for example, insist that mobile diagnostic units are put onto hospital sites whilst the hospital facilities are standing empty. This also could lead to error. But it wouldn't happen in our well-run NHS, would it?

Hospital Doctor 19th May 2005

A catalogue of procedural errors and surgeons' suspensions emerged during an investigation of 18 adverse incidents. The British Orthopaedic Association (BOA) assessed the incidents which occurred when foreign teams were doing 'general supplementary work' for the NHS in the private sector. The BOA requested a formal DoH investigation.

RADIOLOGY
Radiology solution doesn't scan

Hospital Doctor 5 August 2004 p2

Frenchay Hospital, Bristol, forced to use an Alliance Medical privately owned mobile scanner whilst the radiology department in the hospital has its own lying unused due to staff shortages. Rather than spend the money on staff they were obliged by management under government guidance, to spend vastly more on the Alliance Medical machine.

Can the errors be completely eliminated?

The answer to this question is definitely no but we must try as much as possible. To understand why it is not possible to remove error completely from a test, I include here a few simplified graphs.

The Perfect Test

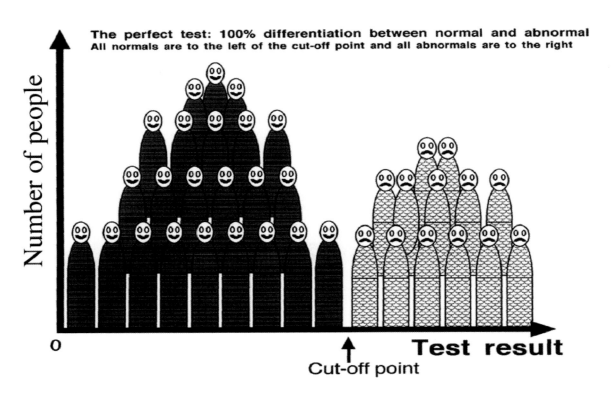

The perfect test: 100% differentiation between normal and abnormal
All normals are to the left of the cut-off point and all abnormals are to the right

Number of people

Test result

0

Cut-off point

With a perfect test there is no overlap between the normal and abnormal populations. Thus it is easy when reading the test to decide whether the patient has the disease or not by knowledge of the cut-off point.

Unfortunately this almost never happens. Nearly all diagnostic tests involve overlapping normal and abnormal populations. The populations may be equal or, as is more commonly the case, the diseased population may be considerably smaller than the normal population.

154

The Usual Type of Test: A seriously imperfect one

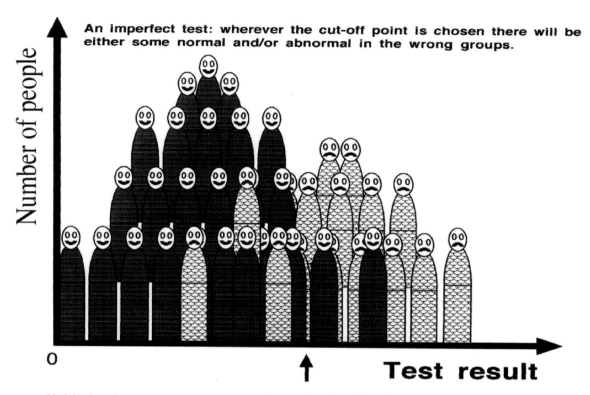

An imperfect test: wherever the cut-off point is chosen there will be either some normal and/or abnormal in the wrong groups.

If this is chosen as a compromise cut-off point there are normal people included in the abnormal . These are false positive results
There are abnormals in the normal group (false negative).

Most tests, if not all, are imperfect and there is no single cut-off point between those people who are normal and those who are ill. This is what one would expect since early in a disease the abnormality will not be very marked and so would not show up. Conversely there are always a few less fortunate people who are not ill but look as if they are. Some tests are very imperfect and do not distinguish a proportion of patients from the normal population even if they are very ill.

Since there is no definite cut-off point between normality and abnormality the way in which the test is interpreted depends on how it is being used and the knowledge of the tester. For example if it is a screening test or a preliminary test for someone presenting with symptoms it may be important to include all the patients with an abnormality. This would mean that a negative test in which the person was diagnosed as normal (i.e. not having the disease) would be highly accurate. Unfortunately by setting the cut off point in this way many normal patients would be included in the positive result. Eliminating

155

some of the normal patients in this way may be very useful if there was a further test to be performed which was more accurate but perhaps more risky or highly expensive. Eventually by a series of tests the error rate could be reduced. In the next graph the test result has been interpreted with a low threshold.

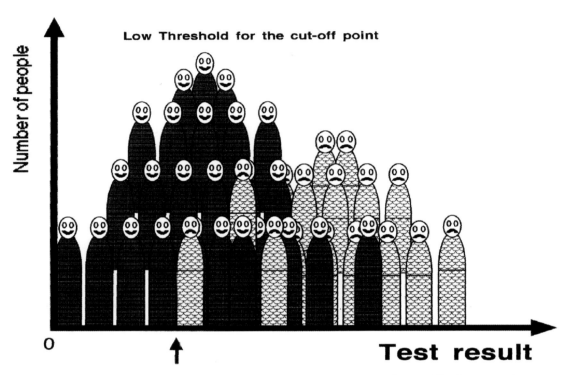

Low Threshold for the cut-off point

Number of people

0

Test result

If this is chosen as a cut-off point the threshold is low. All abnormal people have been picked up but many normal people are included in the abnormal group. There are no false negatives but there are many false positive results.

In the example the low threshold has picked up all the sick patients (the abnormal population) but to do so has included a large proportion of normal patients. It is reassuring for those who have a negative result since they are highly likely to be normal but those with a positive result have about a fifty/fifty chance of having the particular illness tested for.

If it was important to make sure that nobody is diagnosed as abnormal when they might in fact be normal the cut-off point or threshold would have to be set far to the right of the graph as shown on the next page.

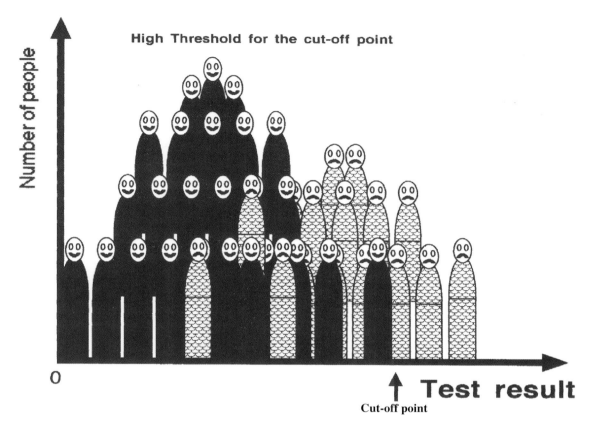

Choosing a high threshold will mean that no normal patients (or very, very few) will be included in the abnormal group. In the test above the patients to the right of the cut-off point are all abnormal but to the left there is a mixture of normal and abnormal patients.

It could be important to use a high threshold if the treatment was particularly toxic or dangerous. It may be safer to treat only those who are definitely ill and wait for further developments in the others. Or perhaps do a series of different tests.

These are examples of inevitable errors occurring in a test because of the inherent characteristics of the populations being studied. It is important that medical staff are not castigated for making this sort of inevitable error since it will prevent them from admitting the case when they make errors which are avoidable

Inevitable errors can only be avoided by changing the type of investigation or treatment to one that does not have such a high level of error. Getting the diagnosis right is fundamental. If you cannot be certain of the diagnosis it is, of course, difficult to be sure of the required treatment. Indeed similar graphs could be drawn for treatment for once again some error cannot be avoided. Some complications will occur however good the service provided by the surgeon or physician.

It is a different matter when the error is avoidable.

Avoidable errors

We have left undone those things which we ought to have done and done those things which we ought not to have done: and there is no health in us,
A general confession, **The Book of Common Prayer**.

Avoidable errors can occur due to many causes. They can be classified as errors of omission and commission. The former is not doing what one should have done and the latter is doing or saying something one should not have done. In addition in radiology, my subject before retirement, there are errors of perception or interpretation.

Errors of perception occur when an abnormality is missed despite being visible on a test (error of omission) or reported as present when it is not there (commission). When the abnormality is noted an error of interpretation may mean that the wrong connotation is given to the finding.

There are many reasons for errors of perception or interpretation including:
- Lack of knowledge (poor training, trained in a different field, hasn't kept up with continuing medical education)
- Less than perfect investigation (old or faulty technology, inadequate technicians, wrong choice of investigation)
- Poor viewing conditions (poor ambient conditions, noisy, interrupted, poor eyesight)[12]
- Working too fast (overworked, tired)
- Serendipity (by chance the abnormality may be spotted or missed.)

There are well-tried ways of decreasing error in radiological investigation but it is first important to believe that the errors do exist. This may be a bigger stumbling block than one would at first imagine and is one of the reasons that doctors do not speak out with regard to problems.

In my own research on radiology error I have found that the overall error rate is between 2% and 30% depending on a combination of the inherent accuracy of the technique and the competence of the investigator. When I have reported these error rates to colleagues at medical meetings I have been greeted with incredulity. One colleague stated that if he had even as much as a two percent error rate his clinical colleagues would have picked this up years ago and would have enjoyed ramming the mistakes down his throat. I asked him whether he had joint clinical and radiological meetings with his colleagues (which have all been hijacked now and renamed multi-disciplinary meetings). He replied that of course he did. I asked whether he had ever had the experience of finding more information on a radiological film at the meeting compared with the initial report he had made. Yes, all the time, he agreed, since that was the entire purpose of the meetings. I then pointed out to him that if the information was on the films but he had not noted it on the initial report his first reporting was in error. He had substantiated for me that in his reporting there were significant discrepancies, which were picked up at subsequent meetings. I am sorry to say that my colleague was still not convinced that the error rates I was discussing were at all realistic even though he had not seriously studied his own errors in any scientific way.

Unlike some barristers that I have met, I do not believe that most doctors most of the time purposely and consciously cover up errors. I think it is more likely that the process of *being* a doctor encourages them to believe in their own infallibility. There are several factors involved in this.

I am now going to produce some amateur psychology (not my area but we all have opinions on it). I believe that many, if not most, doctors suffer from stress-induced anxiety when they are practising medicine. The stress is brought about by numerous factors and has become worse over the past ten years leading to many, including myself, feeling that it is not worth continuing.

The stress for a traditionally trained doctor such as myself probably started on the first day at medical school. We were thrust into a huge room full of naked, foul smelling corpses. With very little instruction we were told to dissect them (cut them up!) This we did over a period of a year or eighteen months accompanied by fortnightly anatomy exams, which we were obliged to pass. Just seeing all the dead bodies for most people nowadays would be considered as a major shock let alone cutting them to pieces. But doctors are supposed to be different from the normal population and this we accepted, ending up laughing about death and discussing diarrhoea at suppertime like all our peers. If members of the public see one dead body these days there is a call for counselling to prevent post-traumatic stress. The medical students have to hide their post-traumatic stress from day one onwards and they do so, eventually not even realising that it was there.

The next shock is the realisation of the enormity of the subject. At school it was perfectly possible for an assiduous student to study the entire syllabus on each of the subjects at O level (now GCSE) and at A level. The required level of knowledge was understandable and hard work meant that it could all be covered. Not so with medicine. The subject is so vast that it is not even possible to know all the titles of all the books on medicine or even of one small specialty within medical science.

Then there is the lack of knowledge. Whilst the information on medicine is definitely huge it is also true that there are vast areas about which we know little or nothing. There are conditions and diseases that have resisted all attempts to find a cause or a treatment. Often when treatment does work we do not know exactly why and when a patient dies we may never know the reason since we do not usually obtain a post mortem (see also in this book the section on Body Parts).

It would be hoped that the stress would diminish as a qualified doctor. But the enormously long hours, the huge amount of work and the novelty of each case mean that the junior doctor can never get on top of his subject. I have detailed elsewhere the ways in which the consultant's job has worsened as he has become a middle manager or lowly worker and has been set mutually exclusive targets.

The simple response to all this is denial. A medical student confronted with the realities of clinical medicine develops a veneer of omniscience. Pretending to the world that they understand and know everything and that they are totally confident, internally they know this is a lie. To live with this they are the most excessive drinkers and get up to the most outrageous behaviour in the students' union. The medical students are notorious.

As doctors some of the graduates gradually begin to believe their own lies, aided and abetted by people who also want to believe in them. In the end admitting any weakness or any lack of knowledge becomes unacceptable. Throughout my time in medicine I have been amazed by the way in which doctors avoid looking facts up in books. I was able to develop a reputation by doing just that .....when others were flummoxed I looked up the answer in a book and latterly I was able to do the same and better on the Internet.

Such a doctor, believing in his own hubris, can inspire confidence in a patient or, when the pride is seen for the sham it really is, can lead to hatred of his arrogance. In some ways we may consider that the doctor is not really at fault in this scenario. His training, overwork, lack of time and necessity have led him to this situation.

In addition to knowledge, training and preparation, enormous confidence is required if you are, for example, to operate on someone's beating heart or open their skull to operate on their brain. It is important that the confidence is not misplaced and that the arrogance does not hide ignorance. If the confidence was well-placed but excessive criticism has removed that confidence, it is inevitable that he or she will not be able to continue in their previous role. Thus we are always on the horns of a dilemma.

Finally it must be realised that all men (and women) are mortal. If the aim of medicine is to keep people alive it must eventually fail since every patient will eventually die. Even the very best doctors will witness this failure many times over. They can only continue to work if they do not ascribe this failure as being their own.

If the doctor does not believe he makes mistakes he will not want to check for error. When complications of his practice occur, as they inevitably will, he will not wish to confront them and will certainly not want to apologise to patients for mistakes he has made. If he is confronted directly and irrefutably with these errors he may find that he is unable to function as a doctor.

On some relatively rare occasions a doctor may know that he has made a mistake but will try to cover it up. This is likely to be due to fear of reprisal; by disapproval of his colleagues, litigation on the part of the patient, suspension or dismissal by his employing authority or being struck off by the General Medical Council. There have been moves to encourage reporting of errors such as the introduction of critical incident reporting and error meetings. Some clinical departments that I have known flatly refused to hold error meetings " because they are too dangerous". Unfortunately too many doctors see critical incident reporting and error (or 'discrepancy') meetings as methods the managers can use to gain information that may be used against them. Unfortunately too many managers also see critical incident reporting and error meetings in exactly the same way and use them to the disadvantage of the medical staff.

Can errors be reduced?

There are nearly always means by which error can be reduced. The most effective way is by changing systems rather than people. If a technique or investigation has an inevitable built in error, consideration should be given to changing to another technique. If the error is not inevitable then error can be reduced by improving knowledge, skills and working conditions.

Litigation and negligence
A little neglect may breed mischief: Benjamin Franklin 1706-1790

So is error the explanation for the massive litigation problems?

Yes and no.

There is a deep well of error running through medicine but doctors do not go out each day saying to themselves " Today I'm not going to bother about my patients at all. I'm going to be negligent". In fact they do exactly the opposite. The vast majority of them try their hardest to get things right. I had some considerable experience of medico-legal cases and I found that the mistakes that led to litigation usually occurred due to a series of errors. One mistake was compounded by another.....something that was wrong but should have been picked up by another routine check was again missed leading to detriment on the part of the patient. Only occasionally was an individual doctor, nurse or technician the sole person to blame and even then it was usually debatable as to whether or not that person had been negligent.

Most cases brought against doctors fail. In some cases there is no doubt that the patient has suffered hugely due to medical error or complication but that there was no negligence, just bad luck. I feel very sorry for patients in such a category and believe, like many, that there should be a workable no-faults system of compensation for iatrogenic disaster.

Other cases have been frivolously brought by patients and they are simply chasing the money. It is nearly always stated that they are only bringing the case to "stop it happening to someone else". But if they win enormous damages they never seem to donate it to medical education which might, indeed, succeed in their espoused aim.

It can be difficult to determine what negligence is and it is all bound up with the nature of the doctor-patient relationship. On this point Professor R.K. Nayak[13] states that

"In the area of patient-doctor relationship two important models dominate viz. one is based on paternalism and other is founded on the doctrine of informed consent. According to Dworkin's standard definition of paternalism means "interference with a person's liberty of action justified by reasons referring exclusively to the welfare, good, happiness, needs, interests or values of

161

person coerced". Such definition may serve the needs of patients but it does not serve the whole concept of welfare of the patients. Feinberg advocates a division in the definition of paternalism, one that preaches how to prevent harm and the other how to ensure the patient's good. Feinberg divided paternalism into "weak" and "strong".

In Britain, the paternalistic model of the physician-patient relationship has been a dominant feature in the medical profession since its inception. This has been well emphasized in the modern English law through the famous Bolam principle, which states that a doctor is not liable in negligence when he acted "in accordance with a practice accepted as proper by a responsible body of medical men, skilled in the particular art". In the United States, the doctor-patient relationship is based on the doctrine of informed consent. As per the doctrine of informed consent, a patient must be supplied with all the necessary information about the nature of treatment, risks involved and the feasible alternatives, so as to enable him/her to make a rational and intelligent choice whether to proceed with treatment or surgery or not. In case informed consent of the patient concerned is not obtained, then the physician would face tortuous liability. In Roe v. Minister of Health,[14] Lord Denning aptly said:

'It is so easy to be wise after the event and to condemn as negligence that which was only a misadventure. We ought always to be on our guard against it, especially in cases against the hospital and the doctor. Medical science has conferred great benefits on mankind, but these benefits are attended by considerable risks. We cannot take the benefits without taking risks. Every advance in technology is attended by the risks. Doctors, like the rest of us, have to learn by experience, and experience often teaches in a hard way. Something goes wrong and shows up a weakness and then it is put right'."

This is the historic view of negligence as viewed by the courts in the United Kingdom. Over the past five years or more the importance of informed consent has been reiterated and the Human Rights Act (1998) has been brought into force.

This act includes a right to life and if, under the act, a claim was brought for inadequate treatment the focus may no longer be on whether the doctor acted in an appropriate manner but whether the treatment was adequate to meet the rights of the patient. Since all patients eventually die their rights will inevitably be violated.

Abnegation of responsibility : why have the doctors not spoken out before now?

Some of the doctors **have** been vocal about the changes occurring in the National Health Service. You only have to look at the books written by Allyson Pollock (NHS plc, the Privatisation of Our Health Care) and Raymond Tallis (Hippocratic Oaths: Medicine and Its Discontents) to realise that we have not all remained silent. Unfortunately our voices have not been listened to. The targets for the NHS are not set for the government by the medical profession but by anthropologists such as Professor Paul Bate of University College.

It is difficult to understand why government should train people to be proficient in a subject and then refuse to listen to their wisdom on that same discipline. Several reasons spring to mind including the desire on the part of ministers that they should not be bogged down with detail, the thought that doctors may not 'see the wood for the trees' and that doctors may be too partisan.

However, I do not believe that these are the main reason at all. It is interesting to me that, as quoted earlier in this book, the author in the Medical Annual of 1947 stated that 'Whereas the Coalition Government, before drafting a Bill, called representatives of the professions into consultation, the present Minister of Health has not done so at any stage'. The medical profession are not well received by Socialist governments. Apparently this is also the case under New Labour. I believe that this is the result of one of the old sins of Albion: class warfare. The doctors are perceived by the Labour party, new or old, as being bumped up arrogant upper middle class toffs (which some of us are). If they can avoid dealing with us they will.

If the majority of the medical profession were to speak up all the time the politicians would have to listen. This is not going to happen for many reasons including the fact that most doctors are too busy, the specific problems of merit awards (now called clinical excellence awards) and private practice, referred to in an earlier section and the general problem of lethargy.

The witch-hunt and suspension of doctors
For my part, I have believed and do now know, that there are witches.
Sir Tomas Browne 1605-1682 Religio Medici I.30

Surgeon suspended after taking extra croutons

Doctor in the soup over lunch

Evening Post Tuesday March 23rd 2004 and BBC News Wed 24th March 2004
Neurosurgeon Terence Hope of Queen's Medical Centre in Nottingham was suspended on 17th March for alleged theft after taking an extra helping of croutons. Mr Hope vehemently denied the ludicrous charge and it was later dropped.
He was reinstated by the Friday of the same week but surgery on three patients was cancelled.

Many doctors are understandably afraid of 'the witch-hunt'.

We are all familiar with the historical concept of the witch-hunt. An unpopular old woman, usually a spinster living alone, is accused of witchcraft. Usually the accusation is made by one or more of the female neighbours and acted on by 'men in authority'. Unless a large number of people speak up against the accusation a trial takes place. To tell whether the woman is a witch or not she is dunked in the river. If she survives she must be a witch and is burnt at the stake. If she drowns she is declared 'not a witch' and given a proper Christian burial. Either way unless the process is stopped at the beginning the poor unfortunate woman is doomed. Modern estimates suggest that there were perhaps 100,000 trials between 1450 and 1750, with something between 40,000 and 50,000 executions, of which 20 to 25 per cent were men[15,16]. Witch-hunts of this nature still occur in the world, particularly in sub-Saharan Africa.

It is not that type of witch-hunt to which I am referring. It only takes a few minutes reflection to realize that there are many other types of witch-hunt going on in the modern world. Consider the McCarthy era and the so-called communists, the social workers accusing parents of child abuse (and devil worship!) or the present day pathologists and their denouncement as body-snatchers (which will be discussed later).

Only a few factors are required to set off a witch-hunt:

1) People who are willing to denounce their neighbour or colleague as a witch (communist, body snatcher etc.) on the basis of gossip or rumour.
2) An accusation which is often so ridiculous it is difficult to refute.
3) A general level of fear so that although the accusations may be absurd the colleagues or neighbours dare not speak out in case they are also accused of being a witch.
4) A form of trial which does not permit a fair hearing.

These factors exist in the present climate of doctor-bashing. If a doctor is too vocal it is easy for the management to suspend him or her. If the doctor is not immediately supported by colleagues and especially if there are colleagues willing to 'put the boot in' the witch-hunt begins. Against all rules of fair play the doctor will not be told why he (or she) is being suspended, he will be told to leave the hospital immediately and that he is not allowed to speak to anyone. His office will be immediately sealed and his documents and computers removed by management. Colleagues may speak up against the suspension but will be told that if they persist they will also be put on disciplinary proceedings.

There will then follow a period during which the consultant will begin to realize that he is not being treated fairly and will get in touch with his medical defence organization, trade union or solicitor. The management will refuse to explain why the suspension has occurred. New phrases may be made up on the spot to explain away the suspension such as "He has not been suspended, he has only been excluded".

Eventually to find out why he has been suspended and to get a fair hearing the poor consultant will probably have to hire a lawyer and put an injunction on the hospital management. At this point they will panic and look for an excuse.

Majority of suspended staff eventually cleared

Trivial complaints cost NHS millions

Evening Post Tuesday October 28th 2003
Reader's Digest investigators reported £50 million cost of suspending doctors. Many suspensions were to punish whistle blowers. "They are suspended at once and managers start to look into their clinical records in the hope of finding a real reason for suspension" said a BMA representative.

The real reason for the suspension will be that the person has been too argumentative with management and/or colleagues, usually on behalf of the service (such as speaking out about postcode prescribing, disagreeing with poor practice or generally complaining about the detrimental effects of targets onhealth care). They will certainly not cite these reasons. Colleagues who have denounced the doctor will usually have other reasons for disliking him since they would otherwise have a sneaky admiration for his stand against the management. Their reasons will be envy or rivalry over position, pay (including merit awards) or private practice.

Having been put in the position that they must have a reason for the disciplinary proceedings they will search through the records of his recent patients to try to find errors. Inevitably they will find some. Or they will try to find staff, such as secretaries, who will agree that he has been harassing them. If the staff do not agree that he has been doing this the management will get angry and denounce them as 'also being involved'. The fact that the management are harassing the very staff they are ostensibly trying to protect never seems to worry them.

Having collected the errors the management will arrange the disciplinary hearing. They will try to circumvent the involvement of the trade union or solicitor by arranging hearings on days when the representative is not available. By doing so they will be breaking all the rules which they themselves have carefully laid out in writing to the consultant.

The consultant's errors may be sent out by the management to an expert for examination. He or she will be given much more information than the consultant had at the time of the investigation or procedure and will usually want to show how clever he is by agreeing that they are errors he would never make in a month of Sundays.

Unless at some point in these proceedings the absurdity of it all is not pointed out the doctor will attend the hearing. In fact the system will grind on with management stating that 'once a complaint has been made the case must be heard' although many complaints about management are made without the case ever being heard!

At a minimum the doctor will be told to shut up for six months or a year and at the worst he (or she) will be sacked. In the majority of cases the doctor is allowed back to work although he may be made to 'retrain'. The average length of time this witch-hunt takes is 18 months. Recently the average time a doctor is actually suspended has dropped to 47 weeks but is still far longer than other clinical staff who average 19 weeks (see next page). Whilst he is suspended the doctor will be paid the NHS salary but will frequently also be suspended from local private hospitals, such as BUPA, although there has not been a judgement of guilt by any court or hearing and the suspension from these other places of work infringes the doctors right to work. He will receive little or no payment for private work during this time of suspension.

Audit body sets rules for a fairer future...

SUSPENDED DOCTORS
NATIONAL AUDIT OFFICE STUDY

Hospital Doctor 27 Nov 2003 pp 24-27
National Audit Office (NAO) study "The Management of Suspensions of Clinical Staff in NHS Hospital and Ambulance Trusts in England" showed that Trusts were aware of best practice but actively ignored it. Doctors' suspensions lasted on average for 47 weeks compared with 19 weeks for other clinical staff.
60% of doctors do not return to work. Less than half of suspensions are die to concerns about clinical competence. The NAO produced recommendations to improve the situation.
Every year 40 consultants leave the NHS after being wrongly suspended.
Time limits have been suggested by NAO but previous similar proposals in 1992,1995,1998 and 2001 have been ignored. Only 2 cases out of 300 observed them. The NHS has repeatedly failed to enforce its own rules on suspensions and this will get worse with the independent Foundation Hospitals.

If the findings show that the suspension was unnecessary the doctor will receive no compensation. If he believes he has been unfairly picked on he will probably have to finance a court action to receive any redress and the action would be very one-sided with his own limited resource on one side against the unlimited resources of the government on the other. Moreover there is always some rule or law that can be found to bash anybody with if the government wishes but about which we may not have been made aware.

PAPER MOUNTAINS

Too many laws to tell us about

Too many laws to tell us about
The Sunday Telegraph February 23rd 2003
Lord Stoddart of Swindon asked the Government how many regulations, immediately binding diktats, Brussels had issued since Britain joined the EU in 1973. Lady Symons replied 101,811. Asked if they could be listed she replied "It would incur disproportionate cost". In addition there are directives which must be put into law by statutory instruments. They cannot even be listed but we still have to obey them.

It is no surprise that there is an increased risk of heart attacks, depression, alcoholism and suicide amongst suspended doctors. It is also not surprising that the other doctors do not wish to go through the same procedure. In fact the whole procedure is so unfair that I question whether or not disciplinary hearings should *ever* take place. I had a long conversation with a medical colleague who had joined the management team and was now the medical director of a large hospital. His view was that I was being irrational in my objections to such procedures. Without them, he opined, how would modern management ever work. My considered opinion is that it does not work and the disciplinary 'Sword of Damocles' is one of the reasons.

How fair is a system that can, without notice, exclude a person from work who has made complaints to management, tell that person that he must speak to no-one at all about his exclusion, hunt through past records to try to find a *different* reason for the exclusion because the real reason will not be considered sufficient and then tell the person that they are obliged to attend a 'disciplinary hearing'? The name itself predisposes guilt.

166

It is not an enquiry into the problems but is a hearing to decide the level of discipline to be exacted. And the people who will decide the punishment? The very same management that suspended the staff member in the first place. If the staff member appeals it is the management who will once again hear the appeal. At no time will they bother to address the problem that made the whistle blower upset in the first place. This is not justice it is dictatorial management control.

How surprising is this, though, when the European Union (which is now the ruling power in the land) acts in a similar manner?

Consider the case of Marta Andreasan. She was the commission's chief accountant when she warned officials of the wide risk of fraud and corruption in the EU. Nothing was done so she told the press in 2002...... and was instantly dismissed from her job for disloyalty. The EU's civil service tribunal has recently upheld the decision to dismiss her and agreed that she was disloyal. They did nothing to look at the substance of her concerns about potential fraud or her protestations that she had told officials and that she had a wider duty to the public. Meanwhile the European court of auditors has refused to sign off the EU's 2006 accounts for the 13th year in a row so it appears highly likely that Andreasan was right. Private Eye[13] states that the commission has launched an action plan to fix things but that in the meantime, in the words of Jules Muis (former head of the commission's own internal audit service) the commission's accounts will remain 'chronically sordid'.

Chapter 12
Why do some doctors find it hard to work in the present political climate?

No man can serve two masters: for either he will hate the one, and love the other; or else he will hold to the one and despise the other. (Matthew 6: 24 AV Bible)

Some proverbs are cultural statements of universal truths......Different cultures express this idea in their own distinctive ways. For example, the Kipsigis say, "Magibeeljindos kirokwek oeng" ("Two walking sticks cannot be burned together"); the Bukusu of Kenya, "He who wants to start a new home must destroy the old"; and certain Zaireans, "Can a woman marry two husbands?" Each of these proverbs conveys the same truth by using different analogies
Learning Through Indigenous Proverbs and Myths[1]

I have posed the question above as to why some doctors find it hard to work in the present political climate. I believe the answer is simple but the solution is not. We have been finding it hard because we are trying to do our very best for the patients but are being told to do something quite different by the politicians and managers.

The doctors who are having the most trouble with the micro-management control of medicine are exactly those doctors that most patients would like to be treated by. They are the doctors who really care about their work and take their duties to the patients really seriously. They are also the brightest of the bunch and are able to see that the targets set by politicians for political reasons are not necessarily in the best interests of the patients. They are the doctors who were trained traditionally to look after patients as their main priority regardless of the cost and regardless of the consequences to themselves. They take seriously the GMC code of practice and the Hippocratic oath but they are constantly being forced to compromise.

The Sun p22 Tuesday November 15th 2005
A patient with aggressive HER-2 form of breast cancer had double mastectomy, radiotherapy and chemotherapy but was still at 50%risk of recurrence. Originally denied Herceptin, which would have doubled her chance of survival. Following a newspaper campaign and thousands of letters to Health Secretary, Patricia Hewitt, Lewisham PCT finally agreed to treat her with the drug.

Although having no apparent choice but to obey the management the hospital doctors may tell their patients what is happening. For example an oncologist treating a patient with cancer may point out that there are drugs, which the hospital will not allow the doctors to prescribe, that would help the patient's condition. To admit this to the patient is very difficult for the doctor because it interferes with the doctor/patient relationship. It is highly likely to upset the patient. It reveals the doctor's inability to treat the patient optimally and the patient may accuse the doctor of trying to boost his or her private work. In addition, by bringing the problem out into the open the doctor runs a considerable risk of annoying the management, including the clinical director and medical director. These two are now very powerful figures in a hospital doctor's life acting, as they do, as line managers for the consultant. Previously consultants could ignore the diktat of administrators with impunity as long as they were acting in the patients or the services best interests. Not any more. The line managers have the power to suspend hospital consultants and more and more frequently do so.

So perhaps the doctor decides not to tell the patient. The doctor is no longer acting in the patient's best interest, no longer obeying the GMC code of practice but keeping the management happy. The patient will suffer for the lack of the correct medication and the doctor will be unhappy every time he thinks about the patient. The patient may find out about the drug he or she is missing and indeed this is becoming more and more easy to do, because of the access to information on the Internet. So into the hospital he comes with a printout from his computer and a very worried expression......and the doctor/patient relationship is in an even worse state.

We have detailed earlier the briefest outlines of the rules set up by the General Medical Council. Whilst the good judge presiding over the Shipman enquiry may consider the GMC to be an old pals' club (see headline below) I can assure you that most of the doctors do not at all. Moreover if the GMC does decide you are not guilty there is now following the formation of The Council for Healthcare Regulatory Excellence in 2003, the possibility of double jeopardy. Medical scandals and double jeopardy will be discussed later in this section.

Daily Telegraph Friday December 10th 2004 p 8

The Shipman Enquiry led by Dame Janet Smith, high court judge, gave a damning indictment of GMC procedures.
Her central recommendations 'would emasculate the GMC'. GMC accused of being a cosy club for doctors.

Maybe the doctor will decide that the only way the patient has a chance of getting the drugs is to go on a trial. Free drugs are frequently given to hospitals for use in trials of a controlled or uncontrolled nature. Many of these trials are set up under strict ethical control (with permission from the Hospital Ethical Committee, which is not easy to obtain), with randomised, double-blind cross-over techniques. They may be funded by a research grant from an organisation such as the Medical Research Council or directly by a pharmaceutical company. Whichever way they are set up they will involve the patient having the chance of taking the drug that is known to work or another competing new drug and maybe a third possibility of a placebo, which is known to work only by psychological effects. The doctor will recruit the patient into the trial with the knowledge that:
1) The patient would have a known response rate to the established drug
2) The competing drug's efficacy is probably unknown, as are its side effects or they would not be trialling it in this way
3) The placebo will not have a direct effect

4) There are financial benefits to the doctor's own department, the hospital, the university and maybe the doctor himself if the patient goes on the trial.

Is this a fair choice for the patient in a system that promised cradle to grave security and to which he has contributed all his life? By offering a trial the doctor is now trying to serve three masters rather than the original impossible two. Once on the trial the patient will also be dictated to by the trial protocol and may have to turn up for extra investigations. These will include invasive procedures such as biopsies and techniques involving harmful ionising radiation such as computed tomography. When definitely required for the usual management of the patient these techniques are excellent. When they are only being performed in order to conform to a protocol, which is in turn being followed purely to give the patient a *chance* of getting a known efficacious drug the whole procedure becomes very unsound ethically. It is particularly unethical when they would otherwise have had that drug if it were not for a rationing of the service and even more galling when the same hospital is happy to dish out the effective pills to patients who come from a different postal area.

So the doctor may offer the drugs privately. To make matters worse even if the patient has private medical insurance he may well find that the treatment he needs is expressly excluded.

So in the short passage above we have a well-worked example of a dilemma facing a hospital doctor such as an oncologist. Very similar conflicts of interest are set up in the hospital doctors' working lives every day. Another example: some patients on the waiting list are easy and quick to deal with but not at all clinically urgent, whilst others are urgent but difficult and time-consuming. To reduce the waiting lists in order to meet targets it is the non-urgent cases that must receive priority thus going against the clinical necessity.

The present government seems to thrive on setting up these situations and likes to wash its hands of the consequences. It will tell a Trust to reduce waiting lists but when this inevitably costs more money, penalise the Trust. Or insist on offering a choice to the patient as to where they can be treated when in fact no such choice exists.

When their meddlesome targets, European directives and government diktats make the hospitals overspend they will answer the criticism by putting in still more unproductive highly paid managers or even more highly paid "trouble shooters" and "management consultants".

The Chief Executive of the Trust will usually have no qualms or divided conscience in the way that the doctors will. Having been chosen from a non-medical background he or she will have no ethical hang-ups about serving patients. Nor will he have any worries about ruthlessly bullying the medical staff who are unfortunate or ambitious enough to hold medical management posts. These doctors, who continue to spend a major proportion of their lives working as clinical doctors, are told that they are now managers rather than clinicians and that they must act in the best interests of the Trust by ordering the doctors under them to keep to the management rules......which are nearly all about saving money and/or keeping to government targets. The managerial doctors may put up a fight but this will not last long because they will simply be relieved of their management roles. Many will argue that it is better to go along with the management rather than fight them and attend directors' meetings because "at least they will know what is happening". But once again they are trying to serve two masters.

Medical staff in management and doctors involved in medical politics frequently use this excuse for staying on committees even though they fundamentally disagree with their purpose and direction.

Unfortunately they lend legitimacy and give verisimilitude to these meetings and committees by their very presence. A complete boycott of many of these politically inspired meetings would make a strong message but the desire for power and influence is difficult to resist.

The NHS Consultants' contract

In October 2002 66% of the consultants voting in England were against the new contract offered to them. I was asked by the Financial Times why this was the case considering that the BMA were heavily in favour[2]. I was quoted as saying that 'We like to treat patients for their benefit, not to meet targets set by the government'. Targets were already having a dire effect on clinical results and I considered that concern for our patients was a major reason for voting against the contract even though it provided a boost in salary. I also considered that the contract was unfair to junior consultants and the concomitant increase in contracted hours was not family-friendly. It was also my opinion that the contract would not prove to be in the interests of the health service since although the contracted hours would increase the number of hours actually undertaken might well fall. Many consultants were working extra hours for free, something which the management and politicians found very hard to believe.

After some minor changes, mostly to the benefit of the more junior colleagues, the contract was finally accepted by the consultant body and now the majority of consultants have signed up to it. Amongst the management controls agreed in the contract is the ability of the managers to determine where the consultant works. The manager can insist that the consultant works in a different hospital or even in a private hospital on their NHS salary. The contracted hours are now 44 with an additional four to be offered to the NHS before the consultant may do private work in his own time. Unfortunately that means that he or she will have undertaken 48 hours before taking on more work. In view of the 48 hour directive from the EU, if problems do arise in the consultant's work he or she will find it hard to justify the extra work.......thus all consultants working in the independent sector in addition to the NHS are in great danger of being sued if they make mistakes or are perceived to be doing so. This was, of course, apparent to the government negotiators who would like to keep the consultants solely working in the NHS.

171

The right of consultants to take a session off to do private work has been lost in the new contract. This 'right" had not been the drain on the NHS that managers and politicians assumed since the consultants in question had to do the work at some other time and they had to take a part-time contract with reduced salary and pension rights. Consultants had requested that the loss in salary for doing private work should be removed. This had occurred in the new contract but unfortunately the price had been an increase in the sessions to be worked, whilst also increasing the length of sessions to four hours each

There are many other problems with the new contract and perhaps the most obvious is that the consultant's job plan has to be agreed with the management. Many of the previously acceptable and time-consuming roles have not being given validity by managers. In particular the training roles are not popular with the Trusts because their benefit is long term and not necessarily related to that Trust. Thus the roles of tutor and programme director are discouraged. These can take many sessions but the poor doctor is permitted to only include one session if he is lucky.

On the positive side, the new contract is supposed to pay for all the hours that the consultants work. This is one of the reasons that it was finally accepted since the majority of consultants were fed up with the open-ended nature of the old contract and the bad press they were receiving despite working so hard. Some Hospital Trusts have negotiated extra sessions to cover work beyond the usual 11 or 12 sessions. Some have refused to accept that such work is being done and have persuaded the consultant staff to continue doing it on a 'voluntary' basis. Other Trusts, having negotiated the extra sessions have reneged on their promises and refused to pay. These Trusts are likely to end up with expensive court action unless they 'mend their ways'.

The contract has inevitably cost the government much more money than they had bargained for. In 1975 they underestimated the number of hours that juniors were working and in 2003/4 they seriously underestimated the voluntary and salaried work that consultants were putting into the NHS. A report in the Daily Telegraph[3] recently stated that hospital consultants' pay had soared although they were seeing fewer patients. Apparently the average pay had risen from £86,746 in 2003 to £109,974 in 2005. The Department of Health had also over-estimated the productivity gains from the new contract, believing it would rise by 1.5% per year. In fact it fell and the average consultants' work fell from 51.6 to 50.2 hours a week. All of this was inevitable when you accept that much of the consultants' work was previously unrecorded and unpaid. The reduction in hours was to be expected when the maximum was set at 48 hours. Either the politicians purposely misled the public or did not believe the medical profession when the latter said they were over-working.

Whilst this negotiation was going on a new contract was offered to the GPs. In return for handing over some management control to the government the GPs had their 24 hour on-call commitment removed.

Meanwhile the juniors were having **their** hours slashed by the EU working time directive.

Daily Telegraph November 15th 2005 p1
The NHS faces its biggest deficit because the official figures show the cost of bureaucracy leapt by £1.3 billion between 2000 and 2004

As I write this section the NHS has just stated that it is now 'on budget' having been wildly overspent just a year ago. Some of the overspend was due to extra management costs but a fair proportion was due to salary increases and to locum fees. The PCTs are finding that the cost of providing GP cover is enormous. So how come they are now balancing the budget? Partly they have done this by making large numbers of staff redundant and partly by hiding the previous overspend with loans.

The GPs and some of the juniors could not believe the improvement in their lifestyle. The consultants are presently suffering because of the increased workload due to the decrease in assistance from the juniors but it is unlikely that they will continue to do extra hours for free.

The government has realised there is a problem too late in the day. There answer is to try to make the GPs work too late in the day! The Prime Minister, Gordon Brown, is determined that GP surgeries will stay open later with the ultimate goal of opening hours of 8.00am to 8.00pm. If they do not agree to this the GPs will receive a pay cut in real terms for the third year in a row.

Meanwhile although there is a shortage of doctors employed to do the work there is also a shortage of posts for doctors. There have been well-publicised problems with the new postgraduate training programmes for doctors. These have included ridiculous computer application forms, scoring of PhDs as less than the computer driving licence, complete lack of privacy of the doctors' data and an enormous bottleneck of juniors trying to enter the registrar training programmes.

With regard to the present training debacle the problems were entirely predictable. As a programme director for radiology in the South West of England, I attended a SW Deanery meeting early in 2003 when the new training schemes and their implementation were muted. I voiced the opinion that the schemes would not work because the training period was too short and that the manpower planning numbers did not add up. I was also sceptical about the proposed computerised application forms. I was told that it was " not the forum for discussion on this matter".....so I left (and never returned).

So where was the forum for discussion?

Unfortunately there is no forum for discussion. If you are not fully in agreement with all the absurd Departmental proposals you are not welcomed in the company of the managers.

The management really do believe that doctors who disagree with them are wreckers of the management (and politicians') dream of a completely efficient NHS, so they are deemed to warrant punishment.

No jobs for 4,000 UK junior doctors

Almost 4000 UK medics have not got training posts in the disastrous junior doctors recruitment system.
Daily Telegraph 1.11.07

There is now a major bottleneck at the registrar level due to the new training programmes and due to lack of money for employing doctors in that grade. Thus we have the peculiar situation of an excess of qualified doctors applying for posts but a deficiency of medical manpower working in the NHS. Already many of the unemployed doctors will either be leaving the profession and/or leaving the country.

Academic medicine

It has, for some years, been difficult to recruit suitable candidates into academic medical posts. Why should this be the case when they are supposed to be the posts with the greatest prestige?

Before the reorganisations in the 70s and 80s the great teaching hospitals of the UK were exempt from many of the administrative controls of the NHS. They answered via their Boards of Governors directly to the Secretary of State rather than via the Regional or Area Health Authorities. The reorganisations changed this.

In particular the Resource Allocation Working Party formula was used to reduce funding in hospitals considered too expensive. Then Thatcher introduced an annual charge of 6% on capital assets, including buildings.

So hospitals in expensive areas, from being a blessing, suddenly became a liability. The inner city hospitals were the worst affected and the teaching hospitals were an obvious example.

In order to stay within their all-important budget they started using non-recurring funds, such as endowments, to pay the increased running costs. These endowments would have previously been used to provide research and social facilities for staff. Both areas were badly affected.

In addition the Teaching Hospital title was removed from its pedestal and widely distributed to a large number of District General Hospitals that had a variable input on clinical teaching.

174

Meanwhile in the universities of the UK the Research Assessment Exercise (RAE) had become a vitally important source of funding. "The Research Assessment Exercise is a peer review exercise to evaluate the quality of research in UK higher education institutions. This assessment informs the selective distribution of funds by the UK higher education funding bodies"[4]

To the management of the universities these funds are all consuming in their significance. The RAE looks at the presentations from the university departments and judges their rating on a 1 to 5* score. All universities strive to reach the higher scores because these will guarantee future funding. The assessors look at the research output of selected staff. This assessment will not include clinical, editorial or teaching work[5]. The research output must usually be available in the public domain and mostly consists of research papers in academic journals. These are assessed on their citation rating, which in turn is based on the number of citations the journal receives in a period of eighteen months.

This has led to the grading of university staff based on the likely grade their research output would achieve. Some are listed as research active and others denoted as research inactive. Those who are listed as active are expected to have their research published in journals with a high citation rating. Those who are judged as research inactive are considered as second-class citizens.

Unfortunately some subjects are almost never covered in the journals with high citation indices. Perhaps part of this is due to the method of creating the index. The half-life of citations for a medical subject such as AIDS is said to be around eighteen months, the period used for assessment. In comparison the half-life for citations of radiology articles is ten years. So the radiology articles go on being cited for many years but the journals are given low citation ratings. For other very specialist subjects there are few researchers in the field although the area of study may be of considerable importance. In this situation so few people would be available to cite the articles in their own research papers that, although seminal to the field, they would receive few citations. If a radiologist managed to get an article on a scientific aspect of radiology published in a highly cited journal such as Nature it is highly unlikely that any other radiologist would read it. The radiologists can only just about keep up with the literature which is constantly being published in their own field although given a low citation rating.

In times previous to these Research Assessment Exercises the Medical School clinical professors were usually very interested in teaching students, clinical work and editing the medical journals of their specialty. They did relatively little highly cited research; this was left to their clinical fellows and to the pre-clinical professors. The Professor of Medicine or the Professor of Surgery was expected to be a well-established clinician who could teach by example in his established clinical practice.

**Hospital Doctor
30th March 2006 p2**

Consultants at the Royal
Free Hospital, London,
have been told to cut 200
programmed activities in
the next planning review
but that it should not
result in reduced clinical
services The Medical
Director announced
plans for 480 job cuts.

FUNDING CRISIS

Consultants told to cut their activities

The Teaching Hospital consultants were also an esteemed group of doctors who were looked upon by the rest of the profession as a step above the District Hospital consultants. They were commensurately expected to keep up to date more extensively than District Hospital consultants and to have a particular clinical interest in which they were an authority.

The Professors and the Teaching Hospital consultants received numerous referrals from the District Hospitals, acting as secondary and tertiary referral centres.

This has all changed. Due to the "managed market" of the NHS the District Hospitals are not keen to refer patients since it costs them much needed money and due to the Research Assessment Exercises the clinical professors no longer have time to be clinical or even to teach. The spending cuts in the major teaching hospitals such as the Royal Free Hospital in London (as described above) have resulted in the old teaching hospitals turning into places where research and tuition by the NHS consultants is progressively squeezed out of the schedule. How else can one maintain services whilst reducing programmed activities?

So the academic base of medicine has enormously changed over the last twenty years. Only people with a deep interest in research which can be published in highly-cited journals can expect to make it to a professor's post. Once there the pressure to publish is enormous and they are expected to bring in grants greatly in excess of their own salaries. Teaching and other academic roles have been downgraded in significance and clinical work is actively discouraged by the universities because they see it as interfering with the time the academic staff have for churning out yet more papers.

The Teaching Hospital consultant appointment no longer has any cachet and academia, both teaching and research, may be seen by NHS management as getting in the way of the clinical work. The only research the management will encourage will be that which brings in significant funds from large grant giving bodies and this will leave no scope for innovation on the part of the clinical researcher.

Doctors interested in a mixture of clinical work and academia are finding it very hard to find a niche in this environment. Having at one time been the very pinnacle of the medical profession the clinical academic is now seen as an unwanted anachronism. As time given to academic work in the NHS is slowly squeezed out of existence the very lifeblood of the NHS is being drained away. In the system that prevails, the new merit award system gives much greater credence to management roles and to achievement of management targets and the way in which the doctor has helped these politically motivated goals.

Private medicine has, for a long time, been more available to consultants in District Hospitals than it is to those in the old Teaching Hospitals. Private work was also, until very recently, forbidden to university appointees unless they gave all the money into the university.

I remember a very senior teaching hospital colleague of mine who applied for a professor's post in Wales. The colleague's curriculum vitae (CV) was very impressive and on paper he was the strongest candidate. He may have felt quite confident until the Provost leant across the table at the interview and accusingly said " I see that you have been indulging in private medicine".

A very good friend of mine was the Professor of Surgery at Bristol University. He was a clinical professor in the traditional sense with a major clinical role, huge teaching load and impressive editorial and academic output. He worked from early in the morning until late at night every day of the week and most of the weekend but even this was not good enough for the university. He died of massive myocardial infarction attending the meeting at which the university was attempting to axe his department and downgrade his position. It is not at all surprising that recruitment of candidates into medical academic posts is very difficult

Patient Advocate

There has been a recent move to employ patient advocates in the NHS. Our large local teaching hospital has just one such employee.

His role is to speak up on behalf of patients and put the patients point of view first. This is considered necessary since all the other staff are working for the NHS and cannot be expected or trusted to put the patient first.

This idea is extraordinary in several ways.

Firstly: The idea that just one person can act as patient advocate for all of the patients in a very busy hospital is risible. The advocate would not have enough time to look after a whole ward let alone a whole hospital.

Secondly: It has always been the duty of the doctor to put the patient first. This is clearly stated by the General Medical Council in their advice to doctors as discussed earlier in the book and is drummed into medical students throughout their training. The patient's advocate is first and foremost their doctor. If this is not the case then any semblance of a patient-doctor relationship is lost.

Thirdly and sadly: The people who have insisted on patient advocates being employed may be right. The pressure on doctors to obey the managers, forget the days of clinical freedom and jump to the political whim of the target touts is so great that they may well have forgotten their role as the one true advocate of the patient. The medical practitioner may have forgotten that working for the benefit of the individual patient being seen at the time is the doctor's primary duty. Or, acting in the patient's best interest, they may need someone to back them up when they fight against management on behalf of a patient. Or a nurse or a member of 'other professions allied to medicine' may need assistance in fighting against a doctor when they consider the medical staff are not working for the patient's benefit.

Unfortunately the advocates I have seen have only been a sop to patients and their support bodies. The advocate can mouth platitudes but has no power.

I cite an example that, I was reliably informed, had occurred in a large hospital trust about five years ago. The one 'patient's advocate' in the whole trust had come to the consultant's department to deliver a short talk explaining her role. She was asked by a consultant whether she could help in cases where a patient's confidentiality and privacy was being compromised.
" Certainly", she replied, " that is exactly my role".
" Well", he continued, " in my department there are constant complaints from the patients that they cannot change in privacy and that their examinations can be overheard and seen by others."
" Is this a space problem?" she asked.
" In many ways it is," replied the consultant, " certainly with more space we could overcome the difficulties".
" Then there is nothing I can do", said the advocate, " the allocation of space and anything to do with it is outside my remit".

Stymied immediately! There was to be no help for the consultant on that particular case even though he was speaking up entirely for the benefit of his patients.

As the management controls bite deeper into clinical freedom the role of a patient advocate must become more and more important. I believe that the doctors should still take that role. It may be necessary to employ medical staff just to undertake such a position but if they are employed by the NHS there is no doubt that they will also be compromised by management bullying.

Medical Scandals

If thou beholdeth thy brother in the agonies of a slow death is it not mercy to put a period to his life? And is it not also death to be his murderer? The Oeconomy of Human Life, translated from an Indian Manuscript, written by an ancient Bramin, Publishers John Donaldson, London MDCCLXXV (1775) page 119

There have recently been several widely publicised medical scandals. They are relevant in our understanding of the position medicine finds itself in at the beginning of the twenty-first century. The disasters which received the most coverage have included the mass-murderer Shipman, the Body Parts scandal and the Bristol Cardiac Surgery scandal. All of these have been thoroughly investigated and I do not intend to go over the same ground except by way of introduction to their effect on the medical profession and the ways in which clinical practice in the NHS has been affected.

By far the most shocking of these was the case of Shipman, a general practitioner, who murdered his patients with lethal opiate injections becoming Britain's most prolific serial killer in the process. It is also the only one of the scandals which would have reached the public's ear if it had occurred thirty years ago.

On the 31st January 2000, Harold Fred Shipman was convicted of murdering 15 of his patients.[6]

Shipman had qualified in 1970 (a friend who trained with him rather unwisely said of Shipman's bar-football prowess "An excellent player, he had a murderous attack"). In 1974 Shipman was a drug addict and was convicted of forgery and fraud having made prescriptions of pethidine to himself. He re-emerged as a GP in Hyde, eventually breaking away from his partners to become a single-handed General Practitioner with his wife as the practice manager.

Over a period of some years Shipman killed numerous patients by injecting them with opiates. At one point in March 1998 another doctor was suspicious and asked the police to investigate but Shipman's reputation as a caring doctor was so high that the investigators got no further than asking him whether he had a problem in his surgery, which, of course, he denied.

His crimes came to light when he forged the will of one of the patients he killed. Estimates of the number of patients he killed vary from hundreds to over a thousand. This was an extreme example of a serial killer and, in view of the fact that he had previously been convicted of drug-related crimes and that he was disciplined by the General Medical Council, an inquiry was held to establish what changes to current systems should be made in order to safeguard patients in the future[7].

The final report was delivered on January 27th 2005. The second report had concluded that if the police investigation in 1998 had been conducted properly three deaths of patients could have been avoided. The final report concluded that the GMC was a cosy club for doctors and needed further reform, presumably agreeing that the Council for Healthcare Regulatory Excellence should be strengthened in its control over doctors[8].

Several points have to be made here. Shipman, whatever his initial motives, falls into the same category as Fred West or other serial killers. Shipman's conduct represent a completely different type of disaster than the Bristol Cardiac problems or the Body Parts scandal. In both the latter two cases there was no deliberate aim to harm anybody….in fact quite the reverse.

All the doctors I have spoken to about the Shipman murders were immensely shocked by them and it leaves the profession feeling very vulnerable. Any doctor who has worked with the terminally ill knows that the dose of opiate, such as morphine or pethidine, required to control pain rises as the illness progresses. Eventually one reaches a dose which could kill the patient and may indeed help the dying patient ease gently away. As long as the intention has been to relieve pain rather than kill the patient, the doctor's conscience is clear......but in the wake of Shipman the doctors, not without cause, are very worried about giving high doses of opiates.

At a recent reunion of our medical school a friend spoke of his own experiences. He had been the GP for a man terminally ill with cancer in his leg and pelvis. The patient was in a hospital oncology unit but he and his family begged the GP to look after his last days at home. The GP agreed even though he knew it would mean an enormous amount of work for himself and his partners. The patient duly went home and the GP and colleagues visited at least twice a day for some weeks. Eventually the patient was so ill and in such pain that the doses of opiate required to treat him were enormous. My friend enquired of the pain relief clinic whether or not there was anything else he could do. He was told that the options were limited and that he should press on with his present policies. About a week later the patient died soon after an injection of opiate given by my friend.

My college friend was immediately arrested for the murder of his patient.

The case went to trial. The family was arraigned against him stating, in a most hateful manner, that the patient was fine until the doctor had killed him. The levels of opiates in the body were assessed at many times the normal dose and the expert witnesses declared that they were easily sufficient to kill the patient. The only factor in the doctor's favour was his phone call to the pain clinic.

The trial progressed until one of the family broke down in the witness box and confessed that they did not think for a moment that the doctor had killed the patient. The family understood all along that the man was going to die and the doctor had discussed with the patient and the family his worry about the high levels of opiates required to control the pain. The patient had not died immediately after the doctor's injection and his death had been a blessing.

So why had they called the police? The relative explained that the family had got together and had thought that they might gain some advantage out of the situation and it had immediately escalated into a murder enquiry.

My colleague had worked day and night looking after the patient, had then been arrested, thrown into jail and suffered through a criminal trial. Of course it was not all over for my friend since the trial proceedings were referred to the GMC, where he was eventually exonerated.

To even be told that you may be referred to the GMC is a very disturbing thing. To be referred is truly shocking and something that most doctors would strive to avoid. It means loss of respect, loss of status, loss of income......and that's if they find you innocent! If they do decide to strike you off you will immediately be removed from any professional employment. Even if you are only reprimanded you may face further sanctions from your employers leading in some cases to loss of your job.

Just the threat of referral to the GMC is very often all that is needed to " keep a doctor in line". Hospital Consultants have been threatened in this manner when they have shouted at the incompetent management once too often. The effect is very worrying….. some decide to retire rather than be threatened by both management and the GMC.

I have spoken at length, written letters in support and acted as expert witness for a number doctors who were attacked in this manner. All have found it to be a totally unpleasant experience.

Of course it does not necessarily end there. Patients and employers have always had the right to take the case to the courts if they felt the GMC had got it wrong and been too lenient. The doctor could do the same if he felt the GMC was too harsh.

However since April 2003 medical professionals also have to worry about The Council for Healthcare Regulatory Excellence (CHRE) (Footnote²). This organization has been set above the regulatory bodies of nine clinical professional groups including the doctors and nurses…..and their remit is to check whether the regulatory bodies have been too lenient and to make the punishment harder if the CHRE considers that they have.

Never the opposite.

If they can make things harsher, can they not also change the decisions if the original judgement was too harsh and make things more lenient…thus creating a balance? Their reply is that this is not in their remit and is in any case unnecessary since the professional can always go to court about it….. a ridiculous reply since the patients could also always do the same.

I now quote from Peter Tomlin in Hospital Doctor 10 March 2005
"Recommendations for regulation of doctors post-Shipman Inquiry threaten to undermine their human rights and access to justice", argues Dr Peter Tomlin.

Shipman Inquiry chairman Dame Janet Smith's report ….. suggests revalidation should be made more rigorous, with possible annual examination of all doctors. The inference is that all doctors are bad and must be tightly controlled.
(But)……………… there is no evidence of widespread professional incompetence - the Society of Clinical Psychiatrists has been tracking this for nearly 17 years. Despite hundreds of doctors being suspended, the number of those found to be incompetent was

---

Footnote: The Council for Healthcare Regulatory Excellence
The Council for Healthcare Regulatory Excellence was set up on 1st April 2003, after the Government accepted a recommendation in the 'Kennedy Report' into events at Bristol Royal Infirmary
The Council for Healthcare Regulatory Excellence is referred to in the National Health Service Reform and Health Care Professions Act 2002 as the Council for the Regulation of Healthcare Professionals.
Over and above GMC, NMC and seven other health professions regulatory bodies "creating double jeopardy for health care professions". They will only intervene to make decisions harsher on the professionals, never more lenient.

less than three a year in a workforce of many thousands. And the burden of proof was the lowly balance of probabilities.

Dame Janet also recommended that the GMC should be appointed by government. In fact, nearly half the GMC is already appointed by government via the recommendations of the Privy Council. These lay persons are without proper medical or legal training but they take part in all the GMC's judicial panels and sometimes form the majority. Magistrates get better training than they do.

Peter Tomlin continues " *Dame Janet also appears to think the GMC is too clubby. In reality, the GMC's performance reassessment tests are extremely draconian and insensitive. Doctors can be ordered to handle, ungloved, tissues to which they are allergic or objects about which they have objections arising out of their personal beliefs. The standard demanded is higher than the relevant college pass.*"

Not everybody would agree with Peter Tomlin's comments but nearly all the doctors I speak to certainly think he is right. It is interesting that Dame Janet's report on the GMC should so contradict Merrison's report of 1975. Footnote[3]

Body Parts

During the enquiry into the Bristol Cardiac scandal a local very esteemed pathologist was asked to give evidence on the fatal cases. He was able to demonstrate, on the retained hearts from Coroner's post mortem, which of the operations were successful and which were not. This allowed the enquiry to determine whether the death was probably the result of surgery or due to other factors around the time of surgery such as anaesthesia or post-surgical care. The esteemed pathologist was commended on his work and told that without his specific evidence the inquiry would not have been able to progress. In the afternoon he was again invited back and this time told how appalling it was that he had retained so many poor dead children's hearts and that the public could not possibly condone such wrong behaviour. His protestations, that without retention of the hearts he would not have been able to provide the morning's evidence and that he had a duty to retain them because he had been instructed to do so by the Coroner (the law!), fell on deaf ears. The esteemed pathologist hearing these contradictory words from the same source decided that the lunatics had taken control of the asylum. He promptly resigned from his post and the South West lost its foremost specialist in paediatric pathology.

3

Footnote
In 1975 the Committee of Inquiry into the Regulation of the Medical Profession,(chairman, AW Merrison, later
Sir Alec) reviewed the regulation of medical education, fitness to practice, professional conduct and the structure and
function of the General Medical Council. Specialist registration by the General Medical Council to be a precondition
for the independent practice of medicine. The committee stated that the Council should be independent and
predominantly professional, financed mainly by the medical profession ref
www.chronology.ndo.co.uk/1975-1984.htm

Just describing the occasion above led me initially to two possible conclusions. The first possibility is that the pathologist is right and the lunatics have taken over and do not know what they are doing. However, a different conclusion could be that they did not *want* the enquiry to progress and that their words in the morning were hollow platitudes.

Recently I have come upon a third possibility. The more likely conclusion is that they meant what they said both in the morning and in the afternoon. It is a peculiarity of the scientifically trained mind that it tries to sort out and remove inconsistencies. That the pathologist should not be both praised and condemned for retaining body parts is obvious to a scientist but not to a layman. Even if the layman is well educated in the arts the obvious and glaring nonsense in condemning and praising at the same time may not worry him or her. Political necessity may require that the pathologist be admonished whilst being praised.

But why this sudden interest in body parts? This came very much to the fore due to the Alder Hey Children's hospital organ retention scandal and the admission by many other large hospitals that the pathologists had also retained human organs for research[9]. The health secretary at the time, Alan Milburn, immediately condemned the practice of organ retention as grotesque and shocking. The public were disgusted and appalled that pathologists had retained body parts. They did not seem to be aware of the fact that the job of a pathologist consisted of doing just that.

There are and have been so many films and medical television programmes from Dr Kildare to Doctor in the House, Dr Finlay's Case book to ER. Some of them, such as Quincy M.E., CSI:NY and Silent Witness have been specifically about forensic pathology. Is it really possible that there is anyone out there in the developed world who did not know that pathologists kept body parts? If the pathologists did not keep body parts they were falling down on their job. Without medical slides and organs in pots they could not answer queries, do research, or teach medical students and future pathologists. The post mortem form always included a section indicating that some parts may be retained and nobody ever complained for years and years and years.

Suddenly there is a new-age sensitivity about body parts. People are crying that they have not buried their loved ones properly and the poor souls cannot rest in peace.

Searches were then conducted all over the NHS looking for body parts (even into my own office.) Small glass slides were confiscated from teaching collections even though there is no reason why anybody should be mourning over a small smear of mucus or a slice of appendix. These so-called body parts were then put into little wooden caskets for burial by re-mourning relatives.

The attitudes are very similar to those in the times of Burke and Hare who, due to the shortage of bodies for dissection, started by robbing graves and went on to murder 14 victims for their bodies. The bodies were sold to Robert Knox, a famous Edinburgh surgeon, who, at the peak of his fame, had 500 students. When caught, Hare confessed, Burke was hanged and Knox moved from Edinburgh due to the public's dislike of him.

Up the close and down the stair,
In the house with Burke and Hare.
Burke's the butcher, Hare's the thief
Knox, the man who buys the beef.

A children's song[10]

In the latest body part scandals, the doctors have been pilloried and forced to resign their posts and move away. The crucial difference is that despite all the tabloid publicity to the contrary nobody was murdered to supply bodies in Bristol, Liverpool or London. The patients died despite the doctors doing the best they could to save them. The retention of the organs was frequently necessary in order to allow later research into the causes of death.

It is my contention that we live in an increasingly superstitious age with the public rejecting conventional religion at the same time that they are turning against scientific principles. The result is an upsurge in illogical action.

There has even been a new act of Parliament relating to this. Entitled the Human Tissue Act 2004 it lays down the appropriate consent required before storing body tissues and came into effect in April 2006[11].

Meanwhile the cost to the National Health Service has been enormous. Pathologists have become completely demoralized and almost nobody applies for the training posts. Already almost no post-mortems are taking place so it is impossible to provide conclusive proof for any medical research project or to find out the cause of death when it is unknown. Very soon there will be no pathology service in the NHS.

The Bristol Cardiac Scandal

Due to ongoing court cases I will not explore this subject in great depth. I will, however, try to provide a perspective from my position as someone working in the hospital where it was all happening. This scandal split the profession like a civil war and the repercussions continue worldwide.

It is a matter of history that the Bristol cardiac team had worse than average results with paediatric cases. Dr John Roylance, formerly the Trust chief executive, and Mr James Wisheart, formerly the chief cardiac surgeon and medical director of the Trust were struck off by the General Medical Council (GMC) and Mr. Dhasmana Janardin, a cardiac surgeon, was reprimanded and forbidden from operating on children.

The United Bristol Hospitals Trust promptly sacked Dhasmana despite the fact that he had previously had the best reputation as an adult cardiac surgeon amongst those employed at the Bristol Royal Infirmary.

The Kennedy report[13] into the tragedy recommended tighter controls over doctors and indeed the GMC now have an overseeing watchdog **The Council for Healthcare Regulatory Excellence**. Their remit is to make things harder for the already beleaguered doctors.

It is the opinion of some observers that Kennedy was anything but an impartial chairman given that his initial position was that clinical freedom of doctors was a bad thing: in his book *The unmasking of medicine*[14,15] he had previously advocated a shift from a professional ethic, based on doing the best for the patient, to one based on the most efficient uses of resources and greater control of doctors. The value of his approach has been much disputed[15,16] but this was, naturally, the conclusion he reached at the end of the inquiry[17,18].

Reporting on results from the statistical experts at the Bristol Inquiry the BBC stated "A detailed look at 100 operations found far more potentially-serious errors in pre-operation and post-operation care than actually during the operation itself"[18]

With hindsight it is easy to say that, whatever the cause, once having established that there was a higher death rate than the national average they should have stopped the surgery until they had found out why this was the case. The problem is that they already intrinsically knew the cause and this was lack of money. When it became a Trust the hospital was strapped for cash and the Department of Health were stressing how important it was to stay within budget. For many years adult cardiac surgery had been undertaken at the BRI but the children's cases were considered too difficult and were sent away. This had now become a costly exercise so the cardiac surgeons were encouraged to stop sending the children's cases up to London. To undertake the paediatric cardiac surgery in Bristol they had argued that ideally they would need to improve facilities within a single site. They required a new operating theatre, new diagnostic services, new surgeon and a new intensive care unit. These were not forthcoming so they went ahead without the desired improvements.

After several years and precious lives lost (and of course a much larger number saved) and after the audits, inquiries, and disciplinary hearings the findings were: "You need a new surgeon, a new operating theatre, new diagnostic services and a new intensive care unit". Only this time the money was miraculously provided. With a completely new team, the results at UBHT for children's cardiac surgery is now amongst the best in the country.

So despite the best of intentions the whole thing was a tragic foul-up that happened because of the Trust system and the internal market. All of the doctors involved acted with what they thought to be the best interest of the service and of the patients. The GMC action protected the GMC. I have heard people say that the surgeons in the case were arrogant murderers. To the contrary, I had always found both surgeons to be softly spoken, kindly people. It must be remembered that all of the fatal cases were children who would have died from their congenital heart disease if they received no surgical treatment.

The definition of a murderer is someone who kills by intent not someone who fails to save the life of another despite trying their very best to help. The people who called out these names at the Bristol doctors were slandering them. Can we really blame the doctors or even the local managers when they were trying their very hardest to help the patients, had limited resources at their disposal and were only doing what they were instructed to do by their 'superiors'? If the line manager system had not been put in place could the doctors and administrators have been persuaded to act in the way that they did?

185

Certainly the politicians, the GMC, the press and the public do think that the doctors should be blamed and as yet have not fully realized the significance of the management system in health care, which was already in place when these tragedies occurred. For the Kennedy report to put the blame on the 'clinical freedom' of doctors and say that we should change from a professional ethic, based on doing the best for the patient, to one based on the most efficient uses of resources is a complete reversal of the truth. If a lesson was to be learnt from the tragedy it should have been that the emphasis on saving resources was harmful to patient care.

That everybody has missed this point and still blames the doctors should be a warning to all the doctors and management who are following the latest fashions and diktats of the politicians. When, because they are following these politically led targets, a disaster occurs it is they, the doctors (and maybe in the future the local managers), who will be blamed. It is particularly those doctors in a management role who are giving the whole system verisimilitude who should take notice of this warning but I suspect that they are the very people who will ignore it.

Working at the Bristol Royal Infirmary turned overnight from a highly respected and envied role to one that invited derision. Meeting new acquaintances became a very worrying chore as they inevitably took the opportunity of sniping at doctors in general and the BRI in particular. I found this particularly hard.

Do the management in Bristol listen to the surgeons now? I am afraid that because the problems were incorrectly diagnosed by Kennedy the same problems remain. As I write the disturbing headline local news is that the excellent children's cardiac surgeon, Ash Pawade, has resigned. He had complained of critical shortages in the perfusion department and these had led to a death during surgery. He was not supported by management and the doctors in management could not understand his angst. The report on the death[19] concluded that there is significant concern that good results are masking a number of problems which if not resolved will impact on patient care.

The children's cardiac scandal had a dire effect on life at the BRI and has had a knock-on effect everywhere. One result is that many surgeons will not operate these days on cases that have a poor chance of an optimal outcome. This means that some patients, who are otherwise bound to die, may not get the slim chance that surgery could offer. With the publication of league tables of surgical mortality, the lesson of careful case selection is spreading widely. It would be comforting to believe that, if the only chance, perhaps a slim one, lay with surgery the surgeons would be prepared to have a go.

In our brave, new world this is probably not the case.

Chapter 13

In which we examine what has gone wrong with dentistry, how problems arose in nursing and why the hospitals are filthy.

What went wrong with dentistry?

For there was never yet philosopher that could endure the toothache patiently.
William Shakespeare Much Ado About Nothing V; 35

It has become impossible for many people to find an NHS dentist in the area in which they live. This has been the case increasingly over the past ten years and was difficult before then but why? Dentistry was included in the NHS so why can't we get what we have been promised.

It is another example of successive governments wanting to get something for nothing.

The first people to notice cuts in the NHS dental system were not the patients but the dentists. The general dental practitioners (GDPs or dentists), despite all beliefs to the opposite, have never been as fortunate as the general practitioners. They have had to pay for their own surgeries without grants and with limited access to a derisory level of loans. But worst of all was their contract. The dentists are now 18 months into a new NHS contract but up until now they have always obtained the majority of their income on a 'fee for item of service' basis. This has always encouraged the dentists to work at a stupendous rate and for very long hours.

At the end of the first year of the NHS it was apparent that the dentists had undertaken vastly more work than had ever been budgeted for. Never mind said the Government, it is the dentist who has to pay! The dentists' contract was only partly related to the work they do. In addition there was a target average annual income: the target net income. If this target income was exceeded the money would be recouped against the next years fees. The harder the dentists worked the less they would get in fees! Of course, if everybody slacked off they would get more in their fees the next year. In reality this never happened.

Year on year the dentists did more and more work and each year a correction was put against their income. Imagine the astonishment on the part of my wife when she first qualified and received an income. Her pay had deductions put against it for exceeding the target income in the previous year when in fact she had been a student receiving no income at all (and no grant either but that is another story entirely).

On enquiry she was told that there was no mistake and they explained the "target net income." ....no, she was told, if you, as an individual, are below the target income you do not receive a boost. The system was a check on the national earnings of dentists and led to a progressive lowering of dental fees in real terms.

So the dentists were on a treadmill. If they slowed down they would go bankrupt since they were always having to pay back the excess they earned in the previous year.

Eventually the NHS fees became so low that, even though the patients were providing the bulk of the fee the total was insufficient to cover costs. Whilst the dentists were tied to a diminishing return per item, the dental technicians, used by the dentists, were not. Laboratory fees exceeded NHS remuneration in areas like crown and bridge work and these could not therefore be supplied without subsidy from the dentist's own pocket. Not surprisingly many dentists if they continued working on the NHS limited the work they would do to the very cheapest materials and easiest cases. Overseas dental graduates, particularly Australians, were tempted at one time to come in, work hard and fast (too fast!) for a year and leave before they were affected by claw-backs. Eventually the fees became too low for even the Australians and we reached the situation we have now with a considerably diminished percentage of the population receiving dental care on the NHS.

The new contract offered by the Government in 2005/6 was not properly formulated and frightened most of the dentists that I know. Many dentists signed up for it but did so adding the words 'in dispute'. The money supplied for seeing children does not appear to be anywhere near sufficient and already the Primary Care Trusts are clawing back money from the dentists saying that they did not do the work on the children that had been predicted. Huge queues form wherever a dentist is prepared to take on new patients on the NHS$_1$. Expect a further massive exodus from the NHS!

At a meeting on 10th January 2006 a local dentist attended the Avon Local Dental Committee meeting. At this meeting of local NHS dentists the new contract was discussed. Some dentists discussed minutiae they had brought up with a PCT representative. They were worried that the assurances they had received were likely to mean nothing since the PCT representative had told the dentists that he would be moving on to another project once the contract was implemented on April 1st. A new person would be brought in to run the contracts and without the clarifications having been put in writing the dentists were sensibly concerned that they might not be honoured.

The main presenter from the GDPC (General Dental Practitioner's Committee) discussed his predictions that the gains made in preventative dental care, loyalty to the practice and other similar aspects would not be carried on with the new contract.

The local dentist was particularly worried about the meeting because it was so late in the day… the new contract was to be implemented in less than three months after the meeting. Even then they were not passing out the final contract for general perusal and the copy in the local dentist's possession was only a draft.

The PCTs are running the contract. They in turn are going through changes and even though the money is said to be 'ring-fenced' for dentistry the PCTs may decide to spend it on something else as they have done locally with money supposedly 'ring-fenced' for care of drug addicts.

The impact of the new contract can be assessed by looking at the next two headlines.

188

NHS dental fees soar by £60m

'The system was meant to simplify dentistry. It has ended in chaos'

Sunday Telegraph Jan 6 2008

The amount paid by NHS dental patients in 2006/7 rose to £60m, a rise of 15%, compared with 2005/6. 266,000 fewer patients saw an NHS dentist and 500 dentists left the NHS in the last 18 months. Only 56% of people now have an NHS dentist.

---

52 The Dentist **January 2008**

`politics`

Continuing squeeze

Expect more frayed tempers in 2008, predicts **Colin Brown**.

Dentists are very aggrieved about the imposed new contract and the government is taking more money off a diminishing number of patients. In the NHS as a whole the squeeze on finances and subsequent cost-cutting has been so severe that the NHS is bizarrely heading for a surplus. Despite this the government are insisting on below inflation pay deals. 91% of dentists in a recent survey said the new contract challenged dentists' ethics.

Meanwhile it is becoming impossible to sign on with a dentist on the NHS. Even if you do you might regret it since the pressure to save money does not bode well for the quality of the work. The latest headline states "Million lose out in NHS dental reforms" (Daily Telegraph 2.7.08). The contract is described as farcical by the British Dental Association.

What has gone wrong with the nurses?

And always keep a hold of Nurse, For fear of finding something worse   Hilaire Belloc 1870-1953

Patients leave hospital half-starved and the NHS is chucking food in the bin. Surely there is a solution

Michele Hanson
Tuesday August 7, 2007
The Guardian

This section may be considered as completely politically incorrect since I intend to criticise the nurses. For some reason to criticise nurses and the standards of nursing care is considered the prerogative of the nurses and only the nurses and my, hasn't the standard dropped! However, my mother was a nurse and I worked as both a hospital porter and as a semi-qualified night nurse before qualifying as a doctor. This is inside criticism.

189

Thousands of patients are being allowed to starve on NHS wards

Daily Telegraph 5.1.2008

Last year 140,000 patients were discharged after being inadequately fed on NHS wards. Last year the health minister, Ivan Lewis, admitted patients were starved on wards. Some had too little food given to them, some had meal trays placed out of reach, some had non-pureed food they could not chew and the food was taken away when the patient had not been able to eat any of it. The nurses were 'rushed off their feet' and some elderly patients did not have a meal all day.

Patients 'at risk as student nurses left alone'
By Nic Fleming, Medical Correspondent
Last Updated: 1:55am BST 18/04/2007
Telegraph.co.uk

Neglect of older patients: a systemic or social problem? Who is really to blame for the fact that the NHS is still failing to treat older patients with decent care and respect?
September 27, 2007 8:22 AM
Guardian.co.uk

It is only too common these days to read reports of filthy hospitals, wards infected with super-bugs and patients left untended by the nurses. Vulnerable patients are underfed and because immobile patients are not turned frequently enough they develop bed-sores.

When I first worked in the NHS any single report such as this would have been a national scandal…..the nurses would not have permitted the wards to be dirty, they considered that feeding patients was a major part of their work and to allow a patient to develop a bed-sore was a disgrace.

The primary dictionary definition$_2$ of a nurse is a person (woman or man) who has the care of the sick or infirm. In this context, care means to look after, to protect and to cherish. Indeed the verb "to nurse" means to tend in sickness or infirmity and to look after carefully.

Back in 1968, when I first worked in the NHS as a theatre porter, the Matron of a hospital was a power in the land. In the community outside the hospital the respect she engendered was enormous. Within the hospital she was basically all-powerful and even the doctors were in awe of her. I have described an example in an earlier chapter demonstrating that she was aware of what was going on (and was definitely in charge) all over the hospital.

On each ward there was a Sister (or the male equivalent, a Charge Nurse) who was immensely experienced, often in her/his fifties, who knew everything that went on in the ward and was in control of the nurses, the cleaners, the patients and, to a large extent, the junior doctors. The porters were in awe of the Sisters and greatly feared and respected the Matron. The Sisters made sure that the wards ran smoothly and their direct command over the nursing and cleaning staff and their personal responsibility for the condition of the wards meant that they were spotlessly clean. Feeding the patients was considered to be an important part of the nursing day and attention was given to patients who were unable to feed themselves. Complex nursing procedures for specific medical and surgical conditions were understood because each ward catered for a specific specialty. There were almost no mixed sex wards except intensive care (where the patients were all unconscious).

On a 'minute to minute' basis wards were run by the Staff Nurses and they did this extremely efficiently. A Staff Nurse was a significant end career post in itself and most Staff Nurses knew that they would not be Sisters, or if they did aspire to be such they would only do so by moving when they were sufficiently experienced.

The relationship between the nurses and the medical staff was very good and this is born out by the fact that a majority of doctors married nurses!

However, not all the nurses were contented with their lot since there was a bottleneck with regard to promotion. Under Sir Keith Joseph a report was commissioned into the nursing structure and hierarchy. This was tabled in 1966 as the Salmon Committee Report and implemented by the Labour Government of Harold Wilson in the mid 70's.

The report basically recommended that a tier of nursing officers should be created with a District Nursing Officer in charge rather than a matron. Between the District Nursing Officer and the ward sister there would be numerous other nursing officers who had an administrative role but no direct patient care.

Initially the experienced ward sisters resisted the change. They did not want to give up the care of patients, which they correctly perceived as the main role of a nurse. But the posts had to be filled and less experienced staff nurses were appointed above the experienced sisters making their role non-viable. So, within a short space of time the ward sisters had moved on to the nursing officer roles, where they were profoundly unhappy, or they had retired early. The replacement nursing sisters were much less experienced and the nursing officers had a tendency to interfere in the running of the wards, operating theatres etc. ....which may have been fine when they were knowledgeable about the particular sphere of practice but too often they were not.

Thus in a short space of time the immense well of nursing wisdom was drained in order to provide a civil service-like career structure.

Coupled with this was the introduction of nursing degrees. Previously it was possible to train to become a State Registered Nurse (SRN) if you had obtained five or more O levels Many did have A levels but this was not considered a necessity. To train as a State Enrolled Nurse (SEN) required no O levels but general knowledge and aptitude.

To train for a degree in nursing required A-levels or other equivalent level of qualification. On the first day at college the nursing students were taught that they were not the handmaidens of the doctors or of the patients but a nursing professional in their own right. Any tendency to help doctors and patients was suppressed by the training.

So when I started on the wards as a doctor in 1974 and 75 I found a profoundly changed situation compared with my time as a porter or even as a night nurse (a role I undertook whilst training as a clinical medical student between 1971 and 1974). Some of the sisters were still from the old school. They were knowledgeable, helpful and wise. Like any sensible junior doctor, I found their help invaluable.

They were, however, already complaining about the interfering nursing officers who knew nothing about the clinical work. I quote below from a 1980 paper on nurses' perception of the nursing officer[3].

 " Nurses' descriptions of relationships with superiors suggested that nursing officer superiors were seen more as 'socio-emotional' whilst sisters and charge nurses were seen as 'instrumental' leaders. Asked to choose a person who had annoyed them at work, nurses chose a nursing officer more frequently than other grades of nurse, particularly in the non-general hospitals. Reasons for annoyance with a nursing officer included unwarranted interference, destructive criticism, and lack of specialized knowledge"

The student nurses doing the degree courses were immensely unhelpful. The fact that I was working one hundred and twenty hours a week (yes 120, see the earlier chapter on the junior doctors dispute) did not seem to register with them and they called me at all hours of night and day, refused to assist when I undertook procedures (which they had often requested) and expected me to clear up any mess that had resulted from such a procedure however busy I was. The general public still continued to believe that the nurses (doing 38.5 hours per week) were the hard-worked angels and that the doctors were lazy and rich. My experience as a married male doctor matches in many ways those of the female doctors. Unmarried male doctors for some unknown reason had a much better relationship with the nurses and found them to be far more helpful.

But still the ward sister would join us on the ward round and we would all meet afterwards in her office for a cup of tea (which I frequently made) and discuss the difficult cases, work out when patients should be discharged, organise the operating lists and, in a convivial atmosphere, solve any ongoing problems.

Next came the "nursing procedure and the nursing reports". The nurses were encouraged to spend the majority of their ward time writing reports, which they passed onto the next team of nurses at the time of hand-over. The number of nurses on the wards appeared to decrease and the nurses were too busy "doing report" to join the ward round. The paperwork increased dramatically and took up to 50% of the nurses' working time. Whereas previously the ward sister and staff nurses would join the consultant and his team this was no longer encouraged. The cup of tea afterwards was expressly forbidden. The communication between the nurses and doctors was irrevocably hampered.

Now the wards no longer have a single medical or surgical specialist interest and may even be mixed sex. The number of nurses on the wards has dropped to dangerous levels and they just cannot cope. I am very sorry for the staff working in these circumstances. It was hard enough when, from previous long experience, one knew about the type of surgery patients had undergone or the medical tests that were being undertaken. The ward today may be full of a variety of disparate patients, some surgical and some medical, others with infections or degenerative conditions, some just in for investigation lying next to dying patients. The idea of running such a ward would fill me with horror. The thought of being a house officer (a very junior doctor) running from ward to ward to see my patients scattered over the entire hospital, is simply a nightmare. The nurses on the wards are now too few in number, spend too much time on administration and many are antagonistic towards medical staff and patients. Instead of feeding the patients the food is too often simply slapped down in front of them and taken away uneaten. Campaigners say that 6 out of 10 older hospital patients run the risk of being starved. The Government plans to stop the hospitalised elderly starving to death by asking for them to be weighed weekly.

Nurses told to weigh their elderly patients

Daily Telegraph 31.10.2007

I have personally overheard nurses moaning that they are fully trained medical scientists and should not be expected to deal with patient needs such as bedpans. I have heard other nurses comment that they have gone into nursing in order to become nursing administrators or managers.

Since 1975 doctors have been bemoaning their loss of influence over the running of medicine but the nurses still seem to believe that they should be fighting against medical control of health care. Professor Iain Graham wrote in 1994[4]

Findings from the study highlighted the dynamic nature of how nurses think and experience nursing. This dynamic nature demonstrates the often vulnerable and stressed position nurses find themselves in today when trying to meet their professional aspirations within a medically dominated, bureaucratic health-care system. The findings suggest that not only is educational reform required, but nurses need skills to enable them to form change strategies so that their paradigm of health care can be established.

It seems that the important factors for the leaders of nurses over the last forty years have been meeting their professional aspirations and fighting against the doctors. Although there are many nurses who do wish to care for patients, the pressure to become managers and delegate, delegate, delegate is overwhelming.

It is no wonder that there are an enormous number of complaints about nursing care. A search on Google results in so many hits that I will not even start to list them…. Just the numbers: (Google   10.4.2005 Results **1** - **10** of about **3,970,000** for complaints about nursing. (**0.20** seconds))

But before any doctors reading this become complacent remember that the complaints about doctors are even greater in number.

Overseas Nurses, Care Assistants, Skill Mix

Many nurses and even some of their leaders may agree with the majority of the criticisms I have made of present day nursing. They may also reply that I have missed the obvious strides that nursing care has made over the last decade or so and in particular I have ignored "Skill Mix" (or " Skills Mix" depending on who writes the paper).
They may also claim that the wards are now well staffed with overseas nurses and care assistants. I will address the latter point first

It is true that there are now many excellent overseas nurses working in our health service. Ever since the drive to recruit overseas staff in the 1950s the NHS has relied on foreign imported labour. This has been greatly to the benefit of the people of the United Kingdom and probably to the detriment of the countries that trained the staff.

I consider it a scandal that we do not train and retain enough staff for our own health service. I also consider it a scandal that the overseas staff have too often been given dead-end jobs with little chance of training and no chance of improvement of their position. This has been the case with posts from the top to the bottom with numerous overseas surgeons stuck in senior house officer posts and even more so for foreign cleaning staff, forced to take lower wages when the cleaning services were " outsourced".

It is not true to say the wards are well staffed. They are almost invariably critically understaffed with far too few nurses and those who would like to do good nursing are not able to do so because they just do not have the time. This has been highlighted recently with regard to paediatric nurses but it applies across all specialities.

Shortage of nurses is putting sick babies at risk

> **Daily Telegraph Dec 19th 2007 p 2**
>
> **A National Audit Office study found "significant shortages" of trained nurses across England and crowded special baby care units.**
> **Death rates among babies in some areas is double that in others. £25million allocated to special baby care units could not be accounted for**

It is true that various care assistant posts can do nursing jobs that the nurses no longer wish to do. I remind the reader, however, that looking after the basic needs of a patient represents the basis of nursing and that nurses who deny this role cannot really be classified as nurses.

So what are they? This is where we come to "skill mix". In 2000 I wrote an article with the help of medical ethicist, Richard Ashcroft and radiographer and skill mix expert, Robert Law. This article has never been published because it was not particularly politically correct and I was unhappy with the comments from one of the referees, which seemed to say that ethics were not a problem so shut up! We tried to provide an objective view of the effects of skill mix on the staff and patients and then to consider various ethical points that may be raised by the employment of staff in these new roles. There is no doubt in my mind that ethical problems in health care are being completely ignored by politicians and managers and even more so by the businesses that are taking health care over by stealth. The article is included in full here.

Skill Mix

Abstract

" Skill mix represents a major change in health care and ethical considerations need to be addressed. The reasons for advocating skill mix may be many and varied. These include: cost saving, lack of trained staff, excess of a different group of trained staff , improving the career prospects of a particular group and overall improved results. Effects on patients, staff doing skill mix, staff who previously did the work and staff who are doing the work left by skill mixers must all be considered. Problems of medico-legal responsibility must be addressed . By casting off old prejudices and embracing multi-disciplinary integration of staffing structures it is hoped that overall there will be considerable improvement in health care. Such improvement would not only justify skill mix but would make its adoption imperative. Relying on skill mix to provide cost savings or to replace staff shortages is more questionable and must be balanced against knock-on staff shortages and effects on other staff.

Introduction

Skill mix and modernisation are phrases used to describe a change in the pattern of care provision by the health service. In essence we are talking about one , perhaps more numerous, group taking over the role of another rarer and more expensive group of workers. Usually this consists of nurses, radiographers, paramedics or technicians undertaking tasks that have previously been the role of medically qualified staff.

A growing body of evidence has attested to the efficacy of such arrangements and there have been few reasoned objections. This paper looks at a different aspect of skill mix and poses the question: Does skill mix present new ethical dilemmas and what are the effects on the individuals concerned and on the population in general?

The reasons for advocating skill mix may be many and varied. These include:

- Cost saving
- Lack of trained staff
- Excess of a different group of trained staff !
- Improving the career prospects of a particular group
- Overall improved results

In this article we will discuss these reasons and whether they can be justified.

- **Cost saving**

Cost efficiency is often put forward as a good reason for undertaking skill mix. Superficially such saving may appear to be obvious. Thus a nurse or a radiographer seeing a patient rather than a doctor would cost less for the hours worked. But also to be considered is the speed of throughput. Can the nurse deal with the patient as fast as the doctor ? Can the ultrasonographer perform as many ultrasound examinations in a session as a radiologist ? Are the results as good or are there more later sequelae and finally referrals to doctors ?

Costs of training and costs of replacing the skill mix practitioner must also be considered. The results may show skill mix to be advantageous in every case but without this information it is not possible to tell whether skill mix results in saving or not. Problems of medico-legal responsibility must also be added into the cost equations.

- **Lack of trained staff**

This is a major problem throughout the National Health Service of the UK. For example, there are too few radiologists and the assistance of radiographers by skill mix is often not just a welcome bonus but essential if the work is to be completed. This can lead to a knock-on effect of shortage in the area from which the skill mix practitioner has been recruited

- **Excess of a different group of trained staff !**

In some countries there is an excess of trained staff in one particular discipline and retraining them for skill mix makes good sense. This is rarely the situation in the UK.

- **Improving the career prospects of a particular group**

Many paramedical groups find skill mix a rewarding experience. The increased responsibility and variety can be welcomed as a career expanding opportunity. Possible adverse effects on staff are discussed below.

- **Overall improved results**

By training paramedical staff to undertake more complex tasks usually performed by doctors there can be measurable improvements in patient care. This can occur because dedicated staff performing a task in which they are well versed will very soon be better at the tasks than trainee doctors and may, after a suitable period of training and experience, out-perform doctors who are only involved part-time in the subject.

Effects on patients

In order for skill mix to be ethical it is clearly important that patients are aware of skill mix and that it is not having a detrimental effect . They must be reassured that they are not having a second class service and any worries they have about being treated by non-medics must be addressed. This requires excellent information from audits of results and good communication skills on the part of the skill mixer. The provision of medical services by paramedics is, however, well established in many areas such as ambulance crews, district nurses etc. and there is no reason for skill mix to be unacceptable to the public if presented correctly.

Effects on staff doing skill mix

These effects are usually beneficial resulting in increased career opportunities and interest but there are several other considerations.

If a member of staff attempts skill mix but does not wish to continue in the process and wishes to return to his or her previous post this must be an available option and the staff member must be assisted in order that there is no sense of failure.

Continuing professional development is of considerable importance for skill mixers. A single skill work ethos is bad since at any time a change in medical practice could lead to a massive decrease in another technique. Thus a radiographer who has taken up barium enema work must continue to increase his/her skills in other aspects of gastro-intestinal work and also in general radiography since an increase in colonoscopy could lead to a massive decrease in enema requests. The need to retrain skill mix staff in such an eventuality must also be addressed.

Effects on staff who previously did the work

It is often the case that the staff who previously undertook the work taken on by skill mix are relieved because they were overworked. Thus a radiologist may be very grateful for shorter enema lists since the radiographer took an extended role or a casualty officers may be thankful for some decrease in the number of patients for their personal attention because nurse practitioners are seeing patients. In this situation it is very important to ensure that the introduction of skill mix has not resulted in a worsening of health care. Both the medical staff and the paramedical staff have a vested interest in skill mix continuing and without adequate checks it may be permitted to worsen care rather than maintain or improve the situation. Good audit and clinical governance policies will provide evidence to support the continuation of good skill mix and to suggest alterations when the skill mix is failing.

Staff may feel threatened by skill mix if they consider that an important part of their work has been or may be taken away from them. Skill mix may remove or decrease an opportunity for training of the original practitioners. Thus trainee radiologists may have less opportunity to train in ultrasound if the work is being performed by ultrasonographers.

Effects on staff who are doing the work left by skill mixers

There is rarely an excess of health care workers (although it can happen). Thus removing one member of staff to do skill mix can lead to an increased workload for the remaining staff. If radiographers take on radiologists work , who is doing the radiography? Are less qualified health care workers then going to be trained to do the radiography? What would the rest of the radiographers think of such a scenario?

Population

The effects on the population can include effects on overall morbidity and mortality. In addition there may be direct or indirect financial effects. These effects have not yet been robustly quantified but are part of the equation when considering the ethical status of skill mix.

Medico-Legal Responsibility

In many situations presently the skill mix professional relies on a doctor to take the final responsibility for an examination, investigation or treatment. This can be very difficult for the doctor when there are problems... it is, for example, much more difficult for a radiologist to interpret a radiographer's ultrasound examination than one he or she has performed. The liability for such examinations should reside more with the professions allied to medicine than the doctor. This question has not been resolved.

Unethical to Avoid Skill Mix?

If, as suspected, well-planned skill mix is affordable and can improve medical care, it may well be unethical to prevent its adoption. Vested interest by established groups such as doctors or nurses should not be instrumental in blocking what may turn out to be a vital development in health care.

Conclusion

Skill mix is part of the modernisation of health care systems worldwide. By casting off old prejudices and embracing multi-disciplinary integration of staffing structures it is hoped that overall there will be considerable improvement in health care. Such improvement would not only justify skill mix but would make its adoption imperative. Relying on skill mix to provide cost savings or to replace staff shortages is more questionable and must be balanced against knock-on staff shortages and effects on other staff."

In correspondence Richard Ashcroft sent me a number of references he considered relevant and added this comment " Interestingly, the skill mix literature is all about (a) downsizing or (b) cost-cutting or both. Not very much of it is about improving performance, or developing the skills of the staff!"

References 5,6 and 7 are about ethics but two of those were written by Ashcroft and myself. The rest[8-16] are as he says. He had found another 80 along the same lines.

Why are the hospitals so filthy and why is there such a problem with super-bugs?

Over the last few years there has been growing concern about the lack of cleanliness in our hospitals and the increasing risk of catching a so-called super-bug. Hospital acquired infection has indeed reached epidemic proportions and now kills a significant number of in-patients......and indeed many of our hospitals **are** filthy.

From the time of Florence Nightingale onwards the hospitals had prided themselves on their cleanliness. The relationship between dirt and disease had been well established and the way to deal with this was to keep everywhere in a spotless condition. The ward sisters (or charge nurses) kept the wards clean by inspecting the results of the cleaners' efforts and ordering them to redo any part that was unclean. If the sister felt that even more thorough cleaning was necessary or if the cleaners were not around, she would tell the staff nurses and student nurses to do the job. On many occasions she would roll up her sleeves and do the cleaning herself, thus setting an example for everyone. If a very dirty patient, such as a tramp, came onto the ward the nurses would strip of all the dirty clothes and thoroughly wash him or her, whether or not they objected.

This has all changed for the worse.

I HAD TO CLEAN MY WIFE'S WARD

Evening Post November 7th 2005 page 1
Bristol Royal Infirmary: patient's husband had to scrub away blood stains and dirt left un-cleaned by staff for at least four days.

I first noticed the change about 15 or 16 years ago when the chief executive of the local teaching hospital decided that, in order to save money, they would no longer get the windows cleaned. At about the same time, or slightly before, the same hospital out-sourced the general cleaning. As mentioned in chapter 7 the cleaning was now being done by a reduced number of the staff taken back on by outside contractors who paid, on average, 20% less. The ward sisters, graduates who were on the career pathway to a fully-fledged nursing management role, now had little or no control over the cleaning staff. The firms who had taken on the cleaning contracts found that they were being pushed to provide the services for too little money yet had to make a profit. Thus the cleaning became more and more skimpy. When, at about this time, I went into hospital for a minor operation we noticed that there was rat poison placed under my bed. A female patient suffering from recurrent post-operative abscesses was placed in the sideward with me. Not surprisingly I developed a post-operative abscess myself. Just a few years ago a medical colleague was admitted to a different local hospital suffering from heart trouble. When we visited her we noticed a filthy tissue on the floor of her sideward and I bent down intending to remove it. My ill colleague told me to stop.....she had noticed the tissue when she had been admitted five days previously and had watched as every day the cleaner had come into the sideward for just a couple of minutes, had mopped or brushed a very small area of the floor and ignored the gathering dust and the dirty tissue. Such was the cleaning of the ward. More worryingly in the shared bathroom used wet towels collected in a pile in the corner of the room all week. My colleague, pointing this out to the nurse in charge, expressed her concern about the infection risk. The nurse shrugged her shoulders, gave a look at her fellow nurses as if to imply that the patient was being awkward and replied 'So, what do you expect me to do about it?'

Political correctness is used as an argument with regard to unclean patients. These are now admitted into beds without the old-fashioned scrubbing. It is considered to be against the dignity and human rights of the patient to subject them to enforced cleaning of any sort. I believe this to be a let-out devised by nurses who never really enjoyed cleaning up such patients.... Is it not just as much against the human rights of the clean patients to have dirty smelly ones put in beds next to them or to have to use the beds after the dirty patients have soiled them?

UK HOSPITALS AMONG THE WORST FOR SUPERBUGS
BRITISH hospitals are among the worst

The increase in hospital-acquired infection is partly due to this. In addition bacteria develop resistance to antibiotics due to indiscriminate use. Contrary to the perceived ideas, I believe that much of this could be due to antibiotics used by farmers (in cattle food etcetera) rather than overuse by doctors, although the latter is a factor. Certainly there is a problem when patients do not finish their prescribed course of treatment. In Africa, for example, there is a major problem of resistant Tuberculosis because the patients frequently do not finish the treatment and resistance rapidly develops. These resistant bugs may then be brought in from overseas as well as evolve at home in the UK.

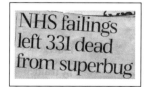

NHS failings left 331 dead from superbug

Crowded wards, a shortage of nurses and financial problems led to 1,176 people contracting Clostridium difficile over two and a half years at three hospitals in Kent. Managers failed to act, nurses did not wash their hands, bedpans were not decontaminated, beds were not cleaned. 90 patients were definitely killed by it and it was a factor in the deaths of a further 241 patients. The managers were too focused on targets. Ref[17]

In addition insufficient nursing care has increased the incidence of bed-sores, has permitted filthy patients to be admitted straight into the beds (as described above) and has seen several scandals in which the bed linen was not changed between patients. In one NHS

Trust (Maidstone and Tunbridge Wells) the nursing standards were so low and the staff numbers so depleted that the patients suffering from hospital-acquired diarrhoea were told to relieve themselves in their beds! The beds were so close together that patients in the adjacent beds had no chance at all…they also acquired the *Clostridium difficile* infection and developed diarrhoea. And enormous numbers of the patients died. The managers did not close the wards or stop admissions despite advice to do so. In a similar outbreak at Stoke Mandeville Hospital an enquiry by the Healthcare Commission again showed that the hospital was more concerned with meeting targets than dealing with infection.[18]

Hospitals ban tinsel to fight superbugs [19]

Managers do not seem to understand the plot. At the Cheltenham General and Gloucestershire Royal hospitals they have vetoed tinsel and paper chains at Christmas because of the infection risk. But as one of the trust's nurses stated ' The patient's love the decorations. ….if the hospital was cleaned in the first place there wouldn't be a problem'. Quite so.

Sir James Young Simpson had discovered in the 1850s that 40% of amputations in hospital led to death whilst only 10% performed outside hospital were fatal[20]. "Hospitals were like slums… patients were put into beds previously occupied…smelly … and crowded (with as many beds as possible squeezed into a large ward)." Despite the examples of Lister and Nightingale, this could be a criticism of many present-day NHS hospitals.

Can anything be done about the cleanliness problem? A one-off deep clean is no use. The hospitals need deep-cleaning every day. Here are some suggestions:

- Matrons should be put in charge of hospitals as previously. This has already been suggested but if enacted they must have power as well as responsibility. This power must include the ability to sack the cleaning staff if necessary and the companies employing them.
- Cleaning the wards should be a priority of each of the ward sisters. Again they need power as well as responsibility.
- Clearly more cleaning staff would need to be employed
- Mixed sex wards should cease to exist. They undermine patient dignity and they also prevent patients from undergoing their own ablutions with confidence.
- The minimum distance between beds should be increased
- Beds and their linen should be cleaned/changed between patients. This seems obvious but it is surprising how many cases I have heard of in which bed linen was not changed.
- The number of beds should be increased and bed occupancy decreased to the old level of around 70% thus providing the slack needed for cleaning and providing spare capacity when emergencies arise. Increasing the number of beds should also make some management tasks (bed allocation etc.) unnecessary and thus save money on management.

Chapter 14
Political whim and fancy

Disregard not a jewel because thou possesses it.
The Oeconomy of Human Life, translated from an Indian Manuscript, written by an ancient Bramin, Publishers John Donaldson, London MDCCLXXV (1775)

In an earlier chapter the NHS was described as a tremendous bargain. This is because the UK spending on healthcare has been considerably lower than those of other developed countries ever since the start of the National Health Service. We had, at one time, an excellent health care system at a very cheap price. The question was posed was "why have we so carelessly thrown it away?"

The problem has been that the spending was almost entirely on the part of the government. The NHS was seen as an enormous drain on the public purse. The more right wing governments must have looked in envy at the countries that ran their healthcare on a private insurance basis, fantasising how they could spend their extra money (More missiles? Tax cuts?) if they did not have to spend it on health. The left wing governments felt that they were not getting enough for their money and that if only they could control those wayward right wing doctors who were wrecking the wonderful NHS they would have a fairer system with better results and no spiralling costs.

These were, of course, fantasies. Even the USA with its private health care system, spends as much on health care from the government per head of population as we do in the UK. The difference is that in the USA the money is primarily spent on academic medicine and medical research and the majority of the spending on treatment comes from the patients' pockets (albeit a considerable proportion coming via health insurance schemes many of which are subsidised by employers-employee arrangements). In addition the income tax levels are considerably lower in the USA

To have stayed up with the other developed nations we had to spend money on healthcare. If it did not come out of our pockets as tax it would have had to come out as charity donations, insurance premiums or direct payment. Moreover if we had not been living in a Welfare State we would not have been willing to pay the level of tax that we do.

The doctors working in the NHS have not been particularly right wing. Whilst some are die-hard Tories there are also many staunch socialists, finding in the NHS the type of environment they desire. I suspect, however, that many doctors are middle of the road pragmatists like myself. As a member of the silent majority I have never joined a political party and the only party to which I have ever donated money was the ill-fated SDP.

The doctors and nurses may well have made up the majority of the wages bill in the past but they have certainly not been wreckers of the NHS. Without the enormous numbers of extra hours put in for love rather than for money, the NHS could not have succeeded as it did.

202

This is where the politicians made their big mistakes. Over the past 40 years since the first big reorganisation the successive government have acted out of politically driven motivation. The right wing has tried to bring in management and market economy and the left wing has tried to introduce control of the medical profession and to remove private medicine from within the NHS. The Blair government tried to do everything at the same time. They insisted on targets being met whatever the cost but demanded that the hospitals "come in on budget". They sent patients out from the NHS to have private medicine but paid for that care with NHS money. They told the patients that the choice is theirs when in fact there frequently *was* no choice.

They set up the 3 star hospitals as "Foundation Hospitals" when the statistics showed that such hospitals although showing fiscal rectitude were providing the worst healthcare.

On the plus side they pledged to increase spending on the NHS. This they did.

But, horror of horrors, instead of allowing this money to be spent by the NHS professionals on healthcare, the government introduced huge numbers of extra managers to check how it was spent, thus negating any advance they could have made. The new managers with new schemes, new audits, new risk management and new clinical governance simply created more work for the already hard-pressed clinical staff.

Gordon Brown's government has provided more of the same but in addition has set up another review. Gordon Brown recently said[1]:

"No institution touches the lives of the British people like the NHS. It is part of what makes Britain the place it is. Yet no modern health service that aspires to respond to its citizen's needs and expectations can afford to stand still. I believe we need to listen to patients experience and expectations to forge a new partnership with doctors, nurses and other practitioners and together produce a way forward that will lead to an NHS that is changing to be truly patient-led and ever more responsive to their needs."

This sounds like a person who is new to Government and had no previous influence on Government policy yet this is from the man who was in number 11 Downing Street until very recently and was in control of the UK's spending plans for the last 10 years.

 Alan Johnson, Health Secretary is even more worryingly out of touch:

"The last ten years have seen huge improvements in the NHS"

Clearly he has not seen all the headlines about patients dying from super-bugs or perhaps he is mixing up the very real improvements in medical science and attributing them erroneously to the NHS. It is true that the changes in the health system that have been introduced since the advent of the NHS have not been all bad. Astonishing advances have been made by the introduction of new medical science and technology into the system. Thus the NHS now provides transplant surgery, MRI scans and fertility treatment, major innovations that were not even dreamt of when the NHS was conceived.

But I know that this has been done despite the managers and despite the politicians, not because of them. The advances have been financed in exactly the way that they were 100 years ago ……by charity. It has never been enough to prove the medical value of such changes… we have had to demonstrate that they save money, that the public are demanding the services and that we can at least pay for the first five years running costs before the managers and politicians will permit these advances on the hallowed ground of the NHS. The very way in which the NHS has been set up tends towards the maintenance of the status quo rather than striving towards improvements.

When, by dint of enormous effort, we are able to set up a new service, such as MRI, despite the fact that the managers are never seen at fund raising events and try hard to stop its inception, they are right at the front when the centre is officially opened by the beaming local MP. The fund-raisers, pushed to the back, are rarely recognised publicly and it is the managers who these days receive the medals from the politicos.

What has gone wrong with the management?

To make this chapter particularly short I should perhaps have posed the question the other way round and asked what has gone right with management in the NHS? The answer would probably be: the first 25 years when the management, called at that time administrators, saw themselves as facilitators.

So when and why did it go wrong? This seems to have started at and around the time of the 1974 reorganisation of the health service. Whereas the doctors were wary of the changes, the administrators who stayed in the reorganised NHS appear to have embraced them. Presumably this is because power corrupts. However, as they took on their role of management progressively more with each subsequent reorganisation, they also became more and more aligned with and in the thrall of the Department of Health and the prevailing politics of the day. First with Blair and now Brown in fine dictatorial style the cabinet are no longer the power they were. Hence we reach the point that the management are the "police" of the government trying to force clinical staff such as the doctors, nurses or physiotherapists, to do the will of the prime minister.

Thus problems with the management can also be considered as being problems with British politics and, in particular, British government over the past twenty or thirty years.
The problems are so gross that it is hard to simply list them but here are a few of the major areas of concern:
- Severing of power from responsibility
- Health service management answering to the wrong masters (Government targets skewing medicine)
- Parkinson's Law and the Peter Principle in action. Enormous increase in numbers of managers
- The impossibility of running the NHS as a business

1. Severing of Power from Responsibility

With great power comes great responsibility we are told. But has this aphorism been forgotten? It is my belief that modern management and government are purposely ignoring the union of power and responsibility and that they have spent the best part of the last decade (or more) trying to sever the ties between the two.

Successive government and management dicta have purposely destroyed the bond between power and responsibility in the health service. It has become the norm to see accretion of power to the management whilst they demand increased answerability, productivity and output from 'pit face' workers such as the doctors and nurses.

I started in the NHS in the late 1960s when the power was held by the Consultants (vilified as little tin gods) and the Matron and her ward and theatre sisters (feared as dragons). The hospitals were administered by a medical superintendent (a consultant), the Matron and the hospital secretary (an administrator). But along with that power the Consultants, the Matron and Sisters also had the full responsibility. The wards were clean, theatre lists ran efficiently and the hospitals were well staffed.

I do not really have to remind you again of the present situation in the hospitals. The reports every day refer to the filth and grime, the methicillin resistant staph. aureus (MRSA) outbreaks, the wastage of operating theatre time and the human tragedies of cancelled operations and post code prescribing. We are told far too often that this is the fault of the doctors or a mistake on the part of a nurse or some other member of the healthcare team but how often do the managers take responsibility? There are now innumerable managers in the hospitals watching the medical staff, interfering with clinical as well as administrative decisions and there are further managers outside the hospitals in a variety of Trust HQs and health authorities watching the hospital based managers. Watching health authorities and making decisions on what can and cannot be permitted are health inspectors from the various bodies (CHAI, NICE etc.). There is no doubt that in the UK more money is being spent on health than ever before but it is disappearing into an ever-increasing morass of managerial control whilst less is actually achieved on the shop floor.

Please do not get me wrong: it is not all hopeless. There are still many achievements arising from the hospitals but the advances occur despite the management not because of it. Many are the times that I have been present at the opening of a new facility paid for entirely by voluntary contributions, only to find that the management have hijacked the opening ceremony, taking the glory and pushing the real contributors to the back.

Is this all the fault of the present government? No. The destruction of the NHS really started under Barbara Castle when, for ideological reasons, in 1974 she accepted the Salmon report (thus taking experienced nurses off the ward and turning them into a parallel line of surrogate managers) and in 1975 removed pay beds (severing private work from the NHS and removing an enormous source of funding). The Thatcher years did further harm with a variety of management changes. But the last eight or nine years have been the most damaging of all. The Blair government was wedded to the concept of severing power from responsibility. They constantly talked of devolving government to the people or to the provinces. In practice they held on to the power, put in place direct management control but devolved the responsibility. Thus when anything goes wrong it is the poor local person who is to blame but whenever he tries to change anything he cannot do so due to the managers above him (and the managers above them ad infinitum right up to the cabinet level and the Prime Minister). Brown has continued to dictate how the NHS runs in exactly the same Stalin-like manner.

All this has occurred at a time when the expectation of the patients has never been greater. In many ways this is the right thing. Expectations should be high! Medicine can now look after people in ways that would have been considered laughably ridiculous when I first started as a medical student. Many are the miracles that can be performed by modern medical science. We can transplant bits of brain material, fight disease with gene therapy, increase a person's leg-length, or operate internally through only a small puncture wound. We can look at the internal structures of the body in three dimensions, study an un-born baby as it opens its eyes and fight cancers with vaccines. These are marvellous developments. But overwhelmingly we find that we are fighting to maintain standards, that the drugs we can prescribe are limited by managerial dictum and far too frequently the decision is made on poor criteria such as the patient's postcode. The managers hide request cards, play with the waiting lists and prevent sound clinical decisions from being made. When the managers are caught at their tricks if admonished at all they are moved sideways or promoted. In the same situation a doctor would have been struck off.

Is this only happening in healthcare? No, of course not. It is occurring in all walks of life. The management are a new elite. Armed with an MBA they feel that they have the right to rule the world. Forget your six-year engineering degrees, your seven-year architecture training, and your fifteen years of medical training. Armed with an MBA you can walk straight in and start telling the professionals how to do their job. One of my trainees (after 14 years of medical training) was told on a management course that a manager did not have to know what a person's job entailed or have any knowledge of what they did in order to manage them. There is, so they believe, a managerial process, which is independent of the job being managed.

These beliefs, that the manager can manage without knowledge of the job in hand (using the managerial process) and that power can be accrued whilst devolving responsibility (the art of delegation) have got us into the fine mess we are in now. There are rising numbers of managers controlling all professions. In education you only have to look at the increasing number of managers in the schools. The teachers are being emasculated and the pupils are out of control. Even the examiners are being told that they must mark more leniently. The rail services are in a mess because the managers will not listen to the safety engineers. Or they listen and then don't act on the advice given (known as 'hearing what you say'). I have not even started on the impact of 'targets' which will be the subject of my next polemic.

But what results from this severing of power and responsibility? I am now going to present my own conjecture. I do not believe that in the long term they can be successfully severed. Without the power to undertake their profession the appointee cannot enact his or her responsibilities. Taking away the power from a medical doctor results in great inefficiency. To start with the doctor will not believe that he has lost the power. For example, he will continue to write prescriptions as he always did and may not notice that these are being countermanded by management. When he does notice he will either shrug his shoulders and deny responsibility (to the patient's detriment) or fight the management with dire effects on his health and working efficiency. The former doctor has hammered one more nail in the coffin of professional responsibility and may later be struck off because he has stopped caring enough. The doctor who fights the system is either suspended, becomes ill and retires or dies young.

The Lord's Prayer talks of the power and glory forever and ever. I believe it is the power and responsibility that should always go together. The professionals who have responsibility without power will find that they cannot do their job efficiently. The managers, like whores taking power without responsibility, will find that it catches up on them in the end when the public tire of their dictatorial ways and demand that the managers take responsibility for the mess they have created. Meanwhile as long as this cult of 'managerialism' continues we shall all suffer.

2. Health Service Management answering to the wrong masters and Government targets skewing medicine

Before the first Thatcher health revolution there were no staff widely known as managers in the health system. The management personnel were happy to call themselves administrators. It is true that the nursing profession had been twisted into a simulacrum of the civil service but the nursing officers were so busy trying to find a job to do that they had no time to call themselves managers and kept strictly to nursing problems. The good hospital administrators, often ex-army officers, saw their job as facilitating the care of the sick by helping the medical and nursing staff do their job. If the doctors had a problem they liked to help solve it.

This started to change in 1975 under the Labour Government when spending on health care got out of hand. The country was in financial difficulties, cuts had to be made and the administrators were told that they would have to make savings. However, whilst the administrators answered to the government via Regional and Area Health Authorities they were, in reality, more in awe of the Hospital Medical Committee, run by the consultants.

This changed abruptly with Thatcher's Griffith managers. The "internal market" and "self governing trusts" were her next reform. The Hospital Chief Executive was placed in managerial line of command above the Medical Director, who, in turn, was managerially over the Clinical Directors, who were over the consultants. The Chief Executive answered to the Department of Health rather than to the weak Trust Boards.

The government was delighted that at last they had managerial command over hospital doctors since this had not been achieved previously.

Under the Blair government this managerial control was considerably strengthened. Political imperatives, which would have been viewed with scorn and derision by doctors even as little as a decade ago, are now presented as a fait accompli. Targets are set for the medical staff by the government. Extra managers are appointed and drafted into the directorates to watch the performance of the clinical staff and check that they meet these targets.

Patients go blind waiting on NHS
Evening Post Tuesday July 22nd 2003
At least 25 patients have gone blind because their treatment was delayed as Bristol Eye Hospital tried to hit waiting list targets

Targets, many of them mutually exclusive, are the order of the day with our present government. Their impact on health care in the UK has been dire. We already had sufficient targets as provided by Hippocratic Oath and General Medical Council (GMC). Basically the duty of each doctor is to look after the health of each patient to the best of his or her ability. In addition to this, or perhaps instead, the medical profession is now expected to aim at a variety of politically inspired targets.

Predominant amongst these are the need to meet waiting list targets, reduce costs, stay in budget, increase throughput and assist in obtaining the cherished stars (or equivalent) for the employing NHS Trust.

I will now reproduce the text of my letter published in the Daily Telegraph₂,

"NHS caught between rock and a hard place
As a consultant at one of the 'no star' trusts , I would like to comment, in a personal capacity, on the table you published on July 25.(2002)
The areas in which my hospital, United Bristol healthcare, underachieved were the non-clinical targets, mainly waiting times (owing to lack of beds) and finance. In these we were rated bottom in the country. But in the essential clinical targets of negligence, death within 30 days of surgery (non-elective admissions) and emergency readmission to hospital, we had the best results in the country. You may have to wait at the UBHT but you do at least get the best possible treatment.
The clinical results of the three-star hospitals are much more variable, with emergency readmission a particular Achilles' heel.

Rewarding hospitals which are already able to meet their financial targets, and fiddling with the management of those who are not, may seem a sensible approach to government accountants but runs the danger of condoning poor clinical practice.

The medical profession is between a rock and a hard place. On one hand we are asked to observe good clinical practice and on the other to speed our patients through to reduce waiting times. Would you, as a patient, prefer to wait for safe treatment or be admitted quickly with a possible worse clinical result?

Many of my caring colleagues would rather be suspended for doing their best for their patients than struck off for negligence.

Prof Paul Goddard Consultant Radiologist UBHT"

This letter was followed up by a front page story in the Times newspaper pointing out that mortality figures were inversely proportional to star rating and a further report on the 4th page of the Financial Times[3] indicating that my opposition to the new consultants' contract was because it gave too much power to the managers who pursued targets set by politicians.

In May of 2003 I saw the my local MP, Valerie Davey, who had been looking into my assertions that the star rating system was praising and supporting the hospitals which did the worst clinical work. Moreover the proposed Foundation Hospitals would compound the problem since it was the 3-star hospitals which would become Foundation Hospitals and they were the worst offenders. In what way do the three star hospitals excel? In reducing costs and reducing waiting lists. These targets might coincide with looking after patients to the best of one's ability but it seems unlikely. After all it is easier to reduce waiting lists by operating on patients with varicose veins rather than the much longer surgery required for an aortic aneurysm. The Beveridge idea, that improved health care would improve the health of the nation so much that eventually less care would be needed, has long been exposed as the myth it is. Doing the best by your patients is expensive and is the opposite to reducing costs.

Ms Davey MP, agreed that my assertions were correct and stated that she would not be able to support the Government in their bill to introduce foundation hospitals. She subsequently abstained along with a number of other rebels.

Why do targets work against clinical efficiency? The most simple reason may be because they are set by the wrong people. Management understand management problems but they cannot understand clinical considerations without having undergone clinical training. Asking management to set clinical targets is akin to asking the cleaners to set targets for the physiotherapists. They can't do it so they simply set management goals and reward management results.

But there is another more fundamental possibility. An article in the Journal of the Royal Society of Medicine[4] suggested that the NHS, at least with regard to waiting lists, was acting in the manner of mathematical complexity at the edge of chaos and order. Such a system of self-organized criticality resists change and is most effective in the zone of complexity. In the area of order everything is too slow and too ordered. In the area of chaos too many conflicting things happen at the same time. Trying to control the system rather than letting it control itself changes the parameters and pushes the system unpredictably into chaos or order causing a dramatic loss of efficiency. Trying to control the NHS centrally by increased management may have completely the opposite result from that which is predicted. Increased order may result in greater accountability but considerably less output. Or, perversely, it may overwhelm the system in paperwork and result in chaos. Their suggestion was that increased funding and staff had to be done on a logarithmic basis (doubling, quadrupling etc.) rather than a few percent at a time or there was no realistic chance of shortening the waiting lists.

In discussion recently with people close to those who set the targets the question was posed: why should medicine be the only area of human activity which does not have targets?

My reply is that it is nonsense to suppose that medicine does not have targets or, for that matter, to suppose that there are specific aims guiding all other areas of endeavour. The GMC does set definite targets for doctors and our entire training is based around a set of ethics originally devised by Hippocrates. These ethics put the patient's wellbeing as the foremost target. For each individual patient we have to do our very best. Our overall results can be assessed from mortality figures (overall mortality, maternal death rates, infant mortality etc.) and life expectancy and our individual results can also look at error and patient satisfaction. These clinical targets are the ones that have been ignored.

3. Overwhelming numbers of managers

When everyone is somebody; Then no one's anybody   *from The Gondoliers by Sir W.S. Gilbert (Gilbert and Sullivan)*

Every day more hospital managers are appointed. Whilst some of them have significant positions with worthwhile work, many of them are completely unnecessary.
This is where Parkinson and Peter have their heyday.

Parkinson's Law
Work expands to fill the time allotted to it, or
The staff of an establishment expands even while the productivity remains constant or declines.
Peter Principle
In a hierarchy every employee tends to rise to his or her own level of incompetence.

There are huge tiers of managers with fancy title such as project manager, project leader, facilitator, collaborator, academic manager and such like. Many of these have never managed a project or facilitated anything. Their salaries are initially top-sliced and they are grafted onto departments and directorates without so much as a nod from even the clinical directors let alone the consultant staff who are actually running the department. These managers always have access to offices and secretaries whilst the medical consultants count themselves lucky if they can get such facilities at all. The car parks are full of their expensive cars and the poor doctors, who often have to travel between hospitals and rush hither and thither on emergencies, cannot find a place to park anywhere on the hospital precinct let alone in the places that only a few years ago used to be reserved for them. At the local district hospital (the one that used to be the Teaching Hospital) they have recently decided that any doctor who lives within a mile or two of the hospital will not be permitted a parking space unless he or she works elsewhere for more than 80% of the week. The inefficiency for doctors who have to travel between hospitals is not addressed.

There does not seem to be any commonsense in the way in which managers are deployed.

I will give you a small example that I am reliably informed is completely true.

Some years ago it was pointed out to a hospital consultant (Dr. A) that his local hospital did not have a Friends charity. He enquired into this and discovered the hospital had a large charity of special trustees. Their function was, however, rather different and did not include the usual Friends activities such as flowers in the entrance hall, raising sums for orthopaedic beds, the chapel and the like.

Dr. A spoke to colleagues and, with the chaplain and one of the surgeons, set up an independent charity as a Friends of the Hospital and started working to raise money. With a local member of the aristocracy kindly agreeing to act as chairman they raised a small but significant sum of money each year and spent it on flowers, orthopaedic beds, the chapel and similar items.

Then, a few years after the advent of Blair's esteemed leadership of the country, Dr. A went to a meeting of the committee and was surprised to see two managers present. They introduced themselves to the meeting and, via a power point presentation, told the Friend's committee about the management structure of the hospital. There they were on the management structure! To their surprise their small independent charity set up to raise money for the hospital warranted a position on the management structure! It is true that they were at the bottom but they did have their own manager and she was indeed talking to them. In the future, they were told, she would tell the Friends what to do, instruct them when to raise money and how to spend it. She answered to the hospital manager (the other manager present) who in turn answered to the chief executive of the hospital (who answered to the Dept of Health, which answered to Blair who answered directly to God, conveniently missing out the Queen).

At the end of the talk the Dr. A looked round at the committee of little old ladies, the few middle aged doctors, the single medical student and the affable aristocrat. They all looked shocked that their committee was to be managed in such a manner. The consultant asked if the manager for the Friends was in a salaried post. The hospital manager replied that of course she was paid. The Dr. A politely pointed out that the committee did not raise a huge sum of money and having a paid manager was rather excessive and probably not cost-effective.

211

Nevertheless, he was told, this is how it is going to be.

He then asked whether they understood the nature of voluntary work and they replied that, yes, they understood voluntary work. It was work for which the workers were not paid.

Dr. A then pointed out that indeed that was half of the equation. The other part was that the voluntary worker chose to do the work. They were masters of their own fate and they liked a say in what they did, where and when they raised the money and how they spent it.

The managers looked shocked at this.

I am informed that Dr. A next attested that there was another name for people who worked for free but did not do so by their own free will, who had others setting their goals and targets . They were commonly known as slaves.

I'm sorry to say that the managers did not take this banter at all well. They had rather got used to having their own way without argument.

This story illustrates several typical facets of NHS management.

1. Managers are frequently appointed to overlook areas in which they have no previous experience
2. By doing so they destroy the efficiency of the very area they are managing. Their usual response to this is to appoint further new managers and delegate the task to the new manager or to blame the staff they are managing.
3. Debate is not encouraged and staff who disagree with the managers are marked out as trouble makers when, in fact, they may well be very dedicated and just happen to be more knowledgeable than the manager.

The Friends of the Hospital did not need a manager. But then most departments in the hospital do not "need" a manager. The professionals, be they doctors, nurses, technicians or whatever, managed the hospitals perfectly well without a manager. However, in this age of accountability, managers are deemed essential and even if they fail completely this is overlooked so long as a good management structure can be demonstrated on paper.

Outside management consultants

When there is a problem in the public sector it is typical that a "management consultant" will be called in to analyse the situation. The management consultant comes in, consults briefly with the technical staff and notes down their answers to the problem, presents these to the permanent management as his or her solution and charges a truly exorbitant fee.

This practice continues partly because the management find it easier to accept a solution presented by a very expensive outsider than to ask their own experts. In fact they cannot easily ask their own experts because the line-managers in charge of them are also supposed to be experts but their expertise is in the wrong field. The permanent managers know this having appointed them on that very basis but cannot bypass them to get to the true experts without acknowledging the stupidity of their management structure.

Evening Post Tuesday October 7th 2003
The chief executive of North Bristol NHS Trust was given a £70,000 golden handshake even though the Trust was £44.3 million in the red

In general when there is a disaster the only managers who will be affected will be those with a medical post. Any service managers who do not hold another professional post will be promoted out of harms way or given a golden handshake despite their total failure. There does not seem to be an effective method of "striking-off" a manager in the way that there is for doctors.

Why is this the case? If you are a manager it is not really sensible to blame managers under you for any failing, If you do so, you may in turn be blamed for appointing them. You may indeed know that you are yourself to blame but you would not dream of letting anybody else know it. This policy holds all the way up to cabinet ministers who these days cling shamelessly to their posts when scandals engulf them. Matters which in the past would have led to an instant resignation are shrugged off as if they were the most minor of peccadilloes. Consider the examples of David Blunkett, Peter Mandelson and Estelle Morris in Blair's government and those of Wendy Alexander, Harriet Harman and Peter Hain in Brown's.

'You can't quit over donations row - or Harman may be next'
The Times Dec 4th 2007

They may then be placed in another important sinecure or make considerable sums of money by selling their memoirs or both.

Mandelson is now European Commissioner for Trade and Estelle Morris is now Baroness Morris of Yardley. Or perhaps more salient to the present book is the experience of Alan Milburn. Secretary of State for Health, until he resigned 'in order to spend more time with his family', he returned to help mastermind the last election campaign for "new" Labour. I know no direct details of his dealings but have noted the following reports on the Internet and in the newspapers. The readers must make their own judgments about their veracity.

I quote from a website[6] which detailed his activities around 2005.

"A big part of Alan's 'thinking' for the next election is increased use of private suppliers to provide public services. This may or may not be a good idea. But the Alliance Medical Saga should make instructive reading……..
Given that a key part of Alan Milburn's planning for New Labour's next term is greater use of private sector suppliers it is worth looking at his track record in this area.

There is a critical undersupply of radiology services in general, and MRI scanning in particular in the NHS. Many who work in the NHS, myself included, are not opposed to almost any means of expanding capacity including the use of private suppliers. However, New Labour has managed to spend a lot of money without much improvement.

Alan Milburn was paid £30,000 to sit on the advisory panel of Bridgepoint Capital who are part owners of Alliance Medical. Alliance Medical have been given £95 million of tax payers money in a 5 year deal to provide an MRI scanning service, increasing capacity by 15%.

In the first three months 16,317 scans were supposed to be carried out. In fact, only 9,406 MRI scans were performed. Results have been delayed for up to six weeks rather than 2-5 days as promised. Furthermore, the service cherry-picks the easiest cases which are reported by inexperienced radiologists who are then unavailable to discuss the results with clinicians.

This means extra work for NHS radiologists who are having to give second opinions on scans or arrange for repeat scans when Alliance Medical's work has been unsatisfactory.
Furthermore, Alliance Medical is outside the NHS clinical governance framework so no one knows who is accountable when mistakes are made. So much for New Labour's claims to put patient safety first.

Private services are brought in under the mantra of greater choice. However, patients are not given any choice and trusts are being compelled to use the service rather than improving their own services."

The story is extraordinary and one would be inclined to dismiss it as internet gossip but it is also recorded elsewhere as on the Telegraph Website[7].

Labour orders MP to keep quiet over Milburn scan deal

By Patrick Hennessy, Political Editor   27/03/2005
(Daily Telegraph website)

"The Labour Party has attempted to gag one of its own MPs who strongly criticised a £90 million deal between the NHS and a private health company linked to Alan Milburn, Labour's general election supremo. Kevan Jones, the MP for North Durham, was rebuked by local party officials after revealing that patients from his constituency were being sent 20 miles for private MRI scans, even though their own local hospital had a machine standing idle.

Mr Jones came out strongly in support of John Saxby, the chief executive of the University Hospital of North Durham, who complained about the purchase of scans from Alliance Medical, while his own NHS scanner was "considerably under-employed".

The row originally appeared to be little more than a local furore. However, it led to serious concerns in the higher reaches of the Labour Party because of the links between Alliance Medical and Mr Milburn.

Mr Milburn was paid £30,000 for a six-month stint as a consultant to the venture capitalists Bridgepoint, which owns Alliance Medical. While he was on the company's books, during the period between his departure as Health Secretary in 2003 and his return to the Government last September, the £90 million scanner deal was signed.
The contract was announced by John Hutton, the health minister and a close friend and former flatmate of Mr Milburn.

Mr Saxby originally wrote to Mr Jones, claiming that money poured by the Government into the private sector with the aim of reducing waiting lists, could have been better spent on the NHS.

Mr Jones went public with a furious assault on the policy of private-sector involvement in the health service, which had been championed by Mr Milburn when he was Health Secretary.

He described the situation that saw patients told to travel 20 miles to a hospital in Middlesbrough as "frankly ridiculous" and warned ministers to put their plans for a greater private-sector involvement "to one side".

He added: "If it is the case that the zeal of certain people in the Government to continually push the boundaries of the private sector in the health service has led to a poor service for my constituents, then I think it does need a closer examination."
His comments, The Telegraph understands, provoked a telephone call to the MP from a Labour Party official demanding an explanation and warning him that theyshould not be repeated.

Mr Jones last night refused to comment on the revelation that Labour had tried to lean on him. However, he insisted that he would continue to ask ministers questions about the scanner deal.

He said: "There are a lot of questions to be answered. I can't believe this arrangement is in the interests of patients in my constituency or anywhere else."
In total, he has tabled 20 parliamentary questions to health ministers.
While he was out of office, Mr Milburn had to manage without his former £71,433-a-year minister's salary. However, he made use of his extra spare time to earn £85,000 from speeches, articles and advice, including his Bridgepoint role.

Since his return, with the official Cabinet title of Chancellor of the Duchy of Lancaster, he has been paid £130,347 a year, a figure that has provoked a political row. The Conservatives argue that the taxpayer should not have to fund Mr Milburn's salary because he is engaged almost exclusively on Labour Party, and not Government, business".

Let me indulge myself and quote just one more report:

NHS Trusts dump Alliance Medical

Report by GMB(Britain's General Union www.gmb.org.uk)
Published: 08/06/05
GMB Congress in Newcastle upon Tyne told of litany of failures with private contractor Five NHS Hospital Trusts have refused to continue using the Alliance Medical Limited (AML) to scan their NHS patients even though last summer Ministers signed a contract to buy 635,000 MRI scans over the next five years at a cost of approximately £95 million.

You can find the full report on www.labournet.net/ukunion/0506/gmb2.html.

Doesn't it make you long for the days when the Secretary of State for Health after retiring from the job simply ignored all the health warnings from his own department and joined the board of a large Tobacco company ? (consider Kenneth Clarke).

At this point I would like the reader to understand that I am not suggesting that Alan Milburn has broken any regulations. It is my understanding that Milburn waited the statutory period before working for the medical industry and that all his outside interests have been correctly declared in the Register of Member's Interests.

There are many other references relevant to movement of NHS ministers and officials to be found on the internet and I have listed some in the references for this section[8-31].

I would point out to the reader that it is considered normal practice for government advisers and ministers to take on roles in business when they leave government positions and that this does not imply that there is any wrongdoing in such behaviour. Here are a few examples gleaned from the Internet[32].

Bill Moyes

Between 1990 and 1994, Bill Moyes was Director of Strategy and Performance Management at the management executive of NHS Scotland and a key advisor of Edinburgh Infirmary's PFI project.

He joined the British Linen Bank (a wholly-owned subsidiary of the Bank of Scotland), initially on secondment, in 1994 and set up their PFI advisory and equity investment team, which focussed on large deals mainly in health. In 1996, he was appointed a Director of the BLB in 1996 and, when it was absorbed into the Bank of Scotland, he became Head of the Infrastructure Investments Department.

From 2000 to 2003 he was Director-General of the British Retail Consortium. In 2003 the Secretary of State appointed him to be the new (and powerful) independent regulator of the NHS.

Simon Stevens

Simon Stevens was Tony Blair's senior health policy adviser at No.10 and policy advisor to two Secretaries of State for Health at the Department of Health. According to Private Eye (9th-22nd July 2004) he pioneered the NHS piloting of an American model of care provided to elderly patients, designed by United Health Group. In 2004 he left to become president of the newly established European subsidiary of United Health Group. It was set up by its US parent in order to build market share in the expanding European public health market.

Lord Hunt

Former Parliamentary Under Secretary of State, Department of Health. After leaving government in March 2003, Lord Hunt took a number of different positions including as an adviser for lawyers Beachcroft Wansbroughs (with a major interest in health) and for KPMG.

Sir Andrew Foster

Former Chief Executive at the Audit Commission for England and Wales (1992-2003) and before that Deputy Chief Executive in the NHS, Foster is now a non executive director with Nestor Health Care and Pruhealth, National Express and Liberata IT Outsourcing (all of them involved, or interested, in privatisation in one form or another). The audit commission is responsible for monitoring the performance of all health and local authorities.

All of this activity is legal and above board. I think we should all be grateful that their advice is so objective and clearly has the health of the nation as their main priority.

Management and meals
Ut quod ali cibus est aliis fuat acre venenum: What is food to one man is bitter poison to others
Lucretius 99-55BC (De Rerum Natura IV. 637)

The management for many years have had a bad attitude towards doctors and their food. This is wonderfully exemplified by the case discussed in chapter 11 of the brain surgeon suspended for taking extra croutons for his soup . This is but one example. The managers do not like doctors to be treated any better than other staff and to make sure that this is the case they treat them worse!

Food has always been very important to me, as it is to most people. When I was a student I considered mealtimes to be a great time for socialising as well as for sustenance. I noted earlier that when I first qualified as a doctor the NHS food was all provided free. In addition to three meals a day we received tea first thing in the morning before rising, coffee or tea at 11 am and tea at 3.30.

With the financial problems in the 1970s this situation was not going to continue for long.

Just after the Junior Doctors' Contract Dispute, in the Autumn of 1975, I was working at St Pancras Hospital, London (part of the University College Hospital Group). We had a proper doctors' mess and our meals were served to us three times a day. The food would not have been considered as gourmet but it was well prepared and the steward knew all of us, keeping food warm if we were late and looking after our meals if we were called away.

I found this particularly necessary since I could be called at any time, as could all of the on-call doctors. My rota at this stage averaged 100 hours a week, slightly less than my previous job but still very onerous. The nurses seemed to consider meal times to be a favourite time for calling us and the "emergencies" could rarely wait until the meal was finished.

The unit administrator decided that the hospital would save money by closing the mess and making the doctors use the general canteen. I politely went to ask the administrator whether or not there would be any arrangements to look after the particular needs of the doctors. I explained that we were in a different situation from the other staff since they all had regular meal breaks and were not on call during those times. We did not have that luxury, never got an hour off at lunchtime and were frequently called at breakfast and in the evening. If we had to queue for food at these times we would never be able to eat.

She laughed and replied that we would stay slim.

She laughed at a man working 100 hours a week, worried about his meals. Not a good idea.

I replied that if that were the case we would all have to leave our bleeps (pagers) with her during mealtimes, an hour in the morning, an hour at midday and an hour in the evening. We would expect her to deal with all emergencies and to take the full responsibility she so obviously enjoyed. I indicated that I would make this official union action and that she could be instrumental in setting off another dispute.

This immediately panicked her and she agreed to stop the cuts.

A few days later a particular consultant surgeon arrived in the operating theatre to do his own list. This was moderately surprising since his senior registrar usually did it. In fact it was only the second time to my knowledge that he had turned up in this way. (The first time was to question me about the junior doctors' dispute and on that occasion the Theatre Sister had asked him who he was).

This time he wanted to know why I was disagreeing with the unit administrator. I explained the situation and he replied that savings had to be made. Maybe, was my answer, but there are no savings being made here. I had carefully questioned what was to happen to the stewards and kitchen staff and the unit administrator had made it clear they would be redeployed in the main canteen. I postulated to the consultant that the main reason for the suggestion was so that the admin could take over our mess building for further administrative offices. I also wondered why they thought it was a good idea to make their savings to the detriment of the hardest working people in the entire hospital.

The consultant was taken aback that I was able to answer his points and agreed to look into them. Whilst I was at the hospital they did not close the mess but as soon as I left, they did …..and the mess building was immediately made into admin offices.

I remember a similar experience when working as a senior house officer in a very busy accident and emergency (A and E) department during the very hot summer of 1976.

The rotas were a considerable improvement on my previous 100 hours a week but they still included a "week of long nights". On these shifts I worked from 6.00pm one evening to 9.00am the next morning, without being permitted to leave the department. The canteen was right down the other end of the hospital and in eight months I only saw it twice. Food was therefore brought to us in the A and E department over the night shift and was indeed free.

After some months of this working well I turned up for a " long night". Midnight was the usual time for a short refreshment break after the first six continuous hours of work. On this occasion no food arrived. The nurses informed me that this had happened several times recently and that they had been obliged to send a porter out to buy food from a local take-away. Whilst waiting to see patients later in the night and early morning, I composed a short letter to the unit administrator reminding him of the necessity for providing food. The A and E department could not be left unmanned at any time and the stretch of 15 hours was far too long for someone to work without food. This letter was sent off straight away and within a few days I received a reply. The administrator agreed that the provision of food was essential and that the doctors could not leave the department. He also apologised for the lack of food and that he would do all in his power to make sure that this did not happen again. Whilst I was on for the next few nights everything was fine.

I came to the end of the night shifts and this was followed by a short vacation. My wife and I decided to spend the time in Wales and duly packed our bags, jumped in our twin exhaust piped, wire wheeled, fuel injected TR6.

Off we went. And the weather broke.

The summer had been the hottest on record but as soon as we reached Wales the weather broke and it poured with rain. I went down with a bad bout of tonsillitis and the holiday was ruined.

Returning to work, still feeling weak from the tonsillitis, I was straight back to working nights. No food. I asked the other staff what had happened whilst I was away. I was told that there had been no food and they had been basically informed that they would have to accept the situation. Having no success with the kitchens I telephoned the on call administration and politely explained the situation.

The conversation went something like this:

"No, there is no food. The night chef is on holiday."

"Could they not have prepared the food for us earlier?"

"Who the hell did you think you are demanding food? I really do not care that you are not allowed to leave the department. Now get off the line."

"I'll have to call you every 15 minutes until the food arrives"

"You can't do that. It's the middle of the night"

"Yes, it is for me too"

So I proceeded to call the administrator every 15 minutes. After five or six telephone calls he was getting desperate. I had learnt by then that he normally received no calls, that my behaviour was quite out of order, that he was definitely in charge of the catering section but that he had no desire to help us at all. The final conversation went something like this

"Excuse me but do you have a bread bin?"

"Of course I do"

"Any bread in it?"

"Yes"

"Any butter in the fridge?"

"Yes"

"Have you got a car?"

"Yes I have, why are you asking me this?"

"Are you physically well?"

"I am"

"Then please get up out of bed, make some sandwiches and bring them in to us"

"You can't speak to me like this. I'll get you sacked. You'll never work again"

"But it is possible for you to make us some sandwiches, isn't it?"

"It is but I have no intention of doing so."

"You must or you are showing yourself to be a total hypocrite"

I then read out the unit administrator's letter and the final section indicating that he would do all in his power to make sure that the lack of food did not happen again. The on call administrator by good fortune was indeed the author of the letter, something I had ascertained at the beginning of the evening. Since making sandwiches was in his power he either did it or showed himself to be a liar. Within 10 minutes a large tray of sandwiches was brought to the department.

Of course the consultant in charge of A and E was not happy to receive phone calls about my action and the next evening at 6.00 I saw him in the department. (It was one of the only two occasions that I saw him in A and E. Despite being in charge he spent all his time doing orthopaedic surgery, which was pretty typical behaviour until dedicated Casualty Consultants were appointed.) He admonished me for my actions and I replied that I would do it again unless we were either allowed time off for meals or the food continued to arrive. He replied that I had ensured that food would arrive whenever I was on call.

What do these stories tell us?

- I was (and probably I am still) a really awkward person especially when hungry
- That I was not the slightest bit afraid of administrators and at that time in the 70s neither were the other staff
- That they were already trying to cut down on supply of food to doctors even when that meant they could not work efficiently
- Hypocrisy was already creeping into the hospital administration. Say one thing but do another.

The unit administrator had made one mistake. He had written it down.

Did my intemperate phone calls have an effect on my employment? Luckily the answer is no, partly because I did not need the A and E consultant's reference and partly because the consultant was also not afraid of the administration. In fact I was next employed as a locum registrar in the same department.

If a doctor tried to do the same thing today he would be instantly suspended and it is highly likely that he would be sacked. It would not matter whether his complaint was just and he had good cause for being upset. Nor would it matter how hypocritical the manager had been.

After several 'reforms' we were obliged to pay for food unless we were regularly not able to leave a department for a meal break. The tea and coffee came directly out of our wages. But even this was apparently still not to be approved of. All the tea and coffee distribution ceased. Any tea on the wards between nurses and doctors was forbidden, ostensibly in order to make savings.

Further changes in health care more recently resulted in the introduction of 'multidisciplinary' meetings held over the lunchtimes. With no other time for the medical staff to eat the management were obliged to offer sandwiches and other refreshments. Just before I retired from the NHS they were busy reining back on the refreshments (either orange juice or teas but not both). My medically required dairy free food was also withdrawn at this time much to my annoyance.

If I felt this was bad it pales into insignificance compared with the experience of our surgeons. I have personally always admired their fortitude and stamina. One of the reasons that I became a radiologist rather than a surgeon was that I could not cope with the long hours in theatre and the physical tiredness it engendered.

Whilst most surgery may be fairly short there are surgical operations which will predictably take several hours in theatre. Some may take eight or twelve hours. It is of course imperative that the surgeon and anaesthetist do not leave the operating theatres during this time although he or she may require a short break. Traditionally they have received free sandwiches and tea provided by the catering staff. This enables them to work almost continuously at their life-saving tasks. Recently this facility has been stopped. No more free sandwiches for the surgeons even if they are undertaking a 12 hour operation! And no catering staff to make sandwiches even if the doctors are willing to pay!

The ostensible reason is cost-efficiency but I read an article in a freebee management magazine some years ago (I believe I was in the accountant's waiting room but I cannot be sure). This suggested quite another reason. The article stated that cutting down on "sandwiches whilst you work" and staff coffee and tea was simply poor management. The author was certain that the only reason it is actually done is to punish the recipient since the savings made were never significant and keeping the refreshments flowing kept the worker bees working. They were more productive when the free sandwiches and tea kept them gainfully employed.

This could be the reason in the NHS for removal of "in-flight" free food and beverages but I believe it is only part of the answer.

The management really do believe that doctors who disagree with them are wreckers of the management (and politicians') dream of a completely efficient NHS, so they are deemed to warrant punishment. In addition the managers cannot understand why doctors or other staff working at acute clinical work should be treated any differently from anyone else. They should take their lunch breaks and bring in their own food in a tuck box just like any one else. When the surgeons say that they cannot leave the operating theatre the managers think that they are just being prima donnas. Moreover any little saving on cost must be worth it even if it means that the number of operations has to be reduced.

Here of course comes another important point. Unless the case being operated on happens to feature in a named waiting list there is no reason for the management to worry whether the surgery happens or not. Long cases are certainly to be discouraged because 12 hours spent on one long complex case could have been much more fruitfully utilised, from the management viewpoint, reducing the waiting list by doing a large number of hernia or varicose vein operations and helping the hospital meet its targets. This is even more the case with the new tariff system since it is highly unlikely that the tariff would adequately compensate for the time spent on a very long complex case compared with the amount gained from rapidly processed simple cases.

But the doctors are not just like any of the other workers, or at least have not been in the past. It was important that we had our own dining rooms. Our crass insensitivity brought on by excessive familiarity with bodies and disease means that we are not really fit company for the common populace when we are eating. This is mainly because whilst we eat we will, oblivious to convention, insist on talking about disease and death, diarrhoea and vomiting. Making comparisons between foodstuffs and body fluids is a common medical sin. Our eating habits might also be a little strange. One excellent surgeon I know used to practice his dissection skills on his banana at every lunchtime!

222

Then again the lunch break for clinical doctors has always been a movable feast. There is no doubt that we all eat far too fast. As a junior doctor I had to eat whenever the opportunity arose and do so very quickly since I was liable to be called away at any moment. This was fine when we ate in our own mess dining room since the food was served immediately and kept hot for us if we were called away. In a large dining room the time spent queuing for food meant that you might be bleeped away before you were even served. Then it was back to the end of the queue when you returned (if you were able to do so). On many occasions I would receive my food, sit down to eat and be called to the telephone. Before I could turn round my untouched food would be cleared away!

This habit of discussing our work at the table did mean that we were able to refer cases to colleagues with ease, ask another expert's opinion on difficult problems and generally learn from the medical chatter around us. It was a sociable occasion that one could look forward to.

In my old hospital there is now no doctors dining room, no nurses dining room, no general staff canteen, no dining facility in the post-graduate centre and no social club. All of these facilities have disappeared over the last ten to fifteen years, as they have in many other hospitals.

Doctors as Managers
He who sups with the devil should use a long spoon
Referred to by Chaucer (The Squire's Tale, c1386) and Shakespeare The Tempest (1610)
"Dictionary of Proverbs and their Origins" by Linda and Roger Flavell (Barnes & Noble Books, New York, 1993))

My criticism of management may seem to imply that I am only critical of managers who do not have a medical degree or other practical health care experience. This is not the case. I am critical of all management which is undertaken outside the field of knowledge of the manager and which ignores the expert opinions of the practitioners. Changing nurses and doctors into managers is just part of the proliferation of managers in the NHS.

I first noticed this trend with the nursing officer grade. The nurses in the mid and late 70s were being promoted into management roles (then called administration) outside their experience. They then became a considerable nuisance since they interfered in ways that were inefficient and much resented. I have discussed this in the chapter on nursing.

With the medical profession I saw the same thing in action in postgraduate training. This time I realised that this was not happening by accident. It was a management ploy, carefully wrapped up as "policy". Let me give you an example of which I have been made aware. A programme director in radiology, an NHS consultant radiologist, was distressed to hear from a secretary in the deanery that the assistant or associate dean "in charge" of radiology was a dermatologist from a hospital over sixty miles away.

I was told by the programme director that he was distressed since dermatology is a specialty which has very little need to use radiology. He told me that he was not just distressed but also amazed. As Head of Training (the Royal College of Radiologists (RCR) term) otherwise known as Programme Director (post graduate deanery term) he was under the impression that he was in charge of the training of 40 trainees. Not only did he believe that he was in charge but he acted as if he was and was expected to do so. He arranged the teaching timetables, invited the speakers, organised the rotas, wrote the job advertisements and organised the short-listing meetings . He met the trainees regularly and helped sort out their job problems, received forty E-mails a day about the programme and wrote hundreds of letters to the RCR, Hospital Trusts, references to appointment committees, queries to the deanery etc. etc. He did this for the trainees and tutors in radiology in 10 different local hospitals. He also chaired the local training committee meeting, once a month, rotating the venue around the participating hospitals. He was, of course, expected to fulfil all his usual clinical commitments in addition to the training work.

It is true that there were important meetings at the deanery which he missed......because the deanery sent the invitations to him after the date of the meeting and, without access to a TARDIS (a time machine belonging to another Doctor completely), he was unable to attend.

So he then learnt that, though he was expected to do it all, there was somebody in charge of the radiology training and that it was not himself ! I was also very interested to hear that the programme director who told me about his situation received no payment for the extra hours he spent on the programme in addition to his normal duties but the associate/assistant dean received between £15,000 and £20,000 per annum!

And here is the rub. The managers purposely appoints and pays managers under them who come from the profession in a general sense but have no direct knowledge of the subject. He or she then forms a committee of these professional sub-managers, ostensibly asks their opinions but easily overrides them because they lack the critical information and experiential knowledge.

Does this only happen locally in deaneries? No, in the postgraduate medical world of the UK, it is the norm. Some years ago Lead Deans were appointed nationally for each of the specialties. **These deans were not allowed to be members of the specialty they represent!** The national dean for radiology was a chemical pathologist, an area of medicine that uses no radiology whatsoever.

The same thing is now happening in the hospitals. Chief executives are making it plain that they want the clinical directors to act as managers, not as doctors. They apparently purposely appoint consultants to be in charge of areas (now called divisions) in which the consultants have no clinical knowledge and once appointed, reinforce that they are to act as managers, not as medics.

It is the same thing all over again. The chief executive can hold a meeting of the clinical directors and tell them what they have to do. They will not be in a position to disagree since they will have little in the way of factual knowledge about the specialty they direct. He can then claim that he has the support of the doctors and the doctor/managers will try to enforce the policies on the unfortunate specialists. If something goes hopelessly wrong, as it will, the chief executive can point to the agreements made at the clinical directors meetings and walk away from the mess, leaving the doctors to take the blame.

Why are they doing this? The ostensible reason is that having specialists answering for their own departments leads to chaos since " they cannot see the wood for the trees" and they act in a too partisan manner. So woe betides a clinical director who learns too much about the specialty he is directing or the assistant dean who bothers to involve himself in the training.

The real reason is that it is a clever way of severing power from responsibility and at the same time the management can ' divide and rule'. The clinical directors/assistant deans take the responsibility of making the consultants toe the line and in return are rewarded by the chief executive and the medical director (or by the postgraduate dean). The clinical directors are, of course, doctors but they very quickly respond to the blandishments, admonitions or encouragement of the management and 'turn native', usually within a week or two. They then become a bigger problem for the consultants than the non-medical managers since arguing with them creates a miniature civil war. Only weeks before this same doctor was agreeing whole-heartedly with all the other consultants......it takes time for all the consultants to notice the change and if they, as a group, manage to control the clinical director it is easy enough for the management to insist that the director is changed.

Oh, by the way, what happened to the secretary in the deanery? They made her into a manager and told the programme director that he had to sign a piece of paper agreeing that she was his line-manager with regard to the training program. It also included a whole load of other obligations, which they wished him to agree to undertake with the penalty that if he failed they would remove some of the derisory sum of money they were providing towards *his* secretarial support. He refused to sign the paper but they still had to keep him on as programme director since at the time nobody else was willing to do all that work for no pay.

4. The impossibility of running the NHS as a business.

Due to the 'top down' or 'manna from heaven' style of funding there is little or no inherent incentive in the NHS, or anywhere in the Welfare State, to either save or make money. Every year the staff in the NHS are exhorted by their managers to "come within budget" or to "make a big effort to save money this year". If the department, directorate or hospital does indeed manage to come within budget they receive a 'cost improvement' the next year. This sounds like a reward for having done well but it is exactly the opposite. What it means is that the budget is slashed and they have to save even more money in the next financial year.

Conversely one may be unwise enough, as I have been in the past, to think that you are helping the department or hospital by raising money. This could be done by undertaking private work within the NHS thus bringing in much needed revenue to the NHS coffers.

I have even known medical staff to undertake such work for free thus ensuring that all the payment went into the NHS funds. Or money could be raised by taking on a research contract for a commercial concern, such as a drug company. This could raise funds for both the hospital and the university. Or you could simply raise money by standing outside the building shaking a charity tin. I have done all of these things.

If this fund raising, by whatever means, is acknowledged to the managers, it is very likely that the next year the amount you have raised will be put down *against* your budget. You will be expected to raise the same amount every year just to keep the budget stable.

Typical in all this is the process of robbing Peter to pay Paul. Whenever there is a government drive to promote a particular part of the health service other well functioning parts are made to suffer as money is withdrawn from them to pay for the latest fad. When cancer services are being supported the care of patients with chronic bronchitis suffers. When cervical screening is all the rage facilities for assessing needle biopsies are removed. The examples are endless and inherent in the system.

This is the basis of the problem of trying to run the NHS as a business. It is the antithesis of capitalism, running like a miniature version of the old USSR, which is not surprising since it was, in many ways, based on the Soviet system having been set up by people who admired and studied the communist healthcare model.

At risk of boring the reader I have to repeat: the NHS is the *opposite* to a business.

In a business the object is to make a profit by selling services or goods. You could be a manufacturer making a pair of Wellington Boots or an architect designing a building. In either case you need to bring in paying customers in order to keep the business going. Services and goods must be sold at a profit except in the occasional situation where a loss leader is affordable….. the loss leader is used to encourage the customer through the door and then other goods or services are sold to them at a profit. The more customers you can attract, each bringing a profit margin, the bigger and more profitable the business can become. Areas of the business which are the most profitable will provide the greatest reward for the staff and owners of the business and they are therefore encouraged. Areas of the business which are not profitable are encouraged to become so or they are shut down. In manufacturing the managers are aware of the fact that they cannot control all aspects of the business at a time and are therefore happy to delegate tasks to less senior staff who, by and large, are less educated and less knowledgeable but are able to manage an area under the more senior managers direction. Also throughout business as a whole the task is to take something less complex, such as crude rubber, and make it into something more complex, such as a Wellington Boot, thereby adding value to the product. An architect takes a piece of paper and with his skill, knowledge, pencils and rulers creates a design for a building. The plans produced are considerably more complex than the original blank sheet and the added value is obvious. At all stages the process is a human invention and is understood in its entirety.

So the main elements are

- *Making a profit by selling goods or services to paying customers*
- *The more paying customers, the greater the profit*
- *Profitable areas encouraged, non-profitable closed down*
- *Delegation to less senior and less knowledgeable staff is usually possible*
- *A product is a simple object made more complex by an understood process.*
- *Customers cannot have a product or service unless they are willing to pay.*

We shall compare this with the NHS.

Making a profit by selling goods or services to paying customers

Who are the customers in the NHS? Is it the patients or are they, as described earlier, the 'object made more complex or less complex'? Is it the government or the purchasing authorities? (Call them what you will but the various names over the last few years include primary care trusts, regional authorities, department of health, post-graduate deaneries). They certainly believe that they are purchasing health care and health training and talk as if they are the customer. Is the budget-holding GP the customer of the hospitals? But none of them really pay for the services provided. The true customer is the tax-paying public but their purchase of health care from the government is so far removed from the delivery that there is no correlation between supply and demand.

The more paying customers, the greater the profit

Quite the opposite: the greater the patient throughput the worse is the financial situation. The money arrives from the government and must be shared out to directorates. It has not classically moved with the patient. This has changed with the introduction of a tariff system resulting in a standard payment for a particular type of patient. This tariff system could be a step in the right direction but a standard tariff will bankrupt some hospitals whilst enriching others. Indeed many hospitals are now technically bankrupt and only keep going on loans. Skimming off the easy cases will leave the centres performing more difficult work struggling to cope on a reduced budget. Moreover tariff systems do not necessarily take into account the cost of training and research and they are costly to manage.

Profitable areas encouraged, non-profitable closed down

Services in the NHS that encourage more referrals will, as a result, have a waiting list. They will also cost more than unpopular departments. The less successful and less regarded a department, the less pressure there will be on the budget. An empty hospital is the cheapest to run! So busy staff are not rewarded and lazy staff are. In fact the less clinical work you do in the NHS the more time you have to go to endless meetings of management, audit, appraisal, governance or whatever and therefore to "join the party". This ought to have changed with the tariff system but facilities that are essential but only rarely used are never going to be profitable, even with the tariff system. They do still, by definition, remain essential and cannot be closed down. Some conditions are seasonal or occur rarely such as epidemics. To remove facilities for dealing with such conditions would make sense financially but does not make sense in healthcare terms.

Delegation to less senior and less knowledgeable staff is usually possible

The non-clinical management are the least educated amongst the professional staff in the health service. Whilst, not surprisingly, they can delegate management tasks to the more intelligent and better educated doctors and nurses shown as below them in the management pecking order, the clinical staff have no-one they can delegate to since the level of knowledge they possess is required in order to do the job. Taking up management tasks from the managers means that there is less time to do the actual process of healthcare. The managers for the most part do not understand the complexity and difficulty of diagnosing, treating and caring for patients.

In a normal business such as a factory the shop floor workers are the lowliest and least educated, able to do only the particular menial task they have been set. They answer to the foremen and shop stewards who have a management role over them. They in turn answer to the factory managers and union officials (again, better educated and more able) and at the top are the factory owners on one side and union officials on the other.

In the hospital setting the doctors and nurses are now often treated as if they are the lowest in the management order. A clinical manager may be appointed over them but that manager is frequently a doctor or nurse who was not particularly successful clinically or in research and is seeking success elsewhere by ' going into management'. Moreover they are often clinically trained in a completely different field. Above the clinical manager are one or two more managers who have no clinical or practical health care training at all and precious little qualification. Nowadays they do tend to have a Master of Business Administration (MBA), which takes between 18 months and two years to obtain. Above them are the politicians whose qualification is by election.

A product is a simple object made more complex by an easily understood process. The product is a human invention.

The human being is, without exaggeration, the most complex object in the known universe. Whilst the Milky Way galaxy has 10 billion stars, the human brain alone is known to have 10 billion nerve cells and over a trillion connections. We only understand a little about the workings of a human being and are frequently confounded by new variations of disease and abnormality. Professor Charles Dent of University College Hospital used to famously remark that whilst any one rare disease is rare, rare diseases are common. In addition any one patient may have multiple diseases. A sick patient is not a human invention and is an extremely complex object which the health service is trying to simplify by partially under-stood processes. There is as much art in medicine as there is science.

Customers cannot have a product or service unless they are willing to pay.

The whole original basis of the NHS was that it should be free at the point of use. Frankly it no longer is free in important areas such as the opticians, dentistry and prescriptions and it is in these areas that it is easier to define who is the customer and who is not. Generally speaking, however, the bulk of health care provided by the NHS is free and the patient can have the services without paying. I reiterate that the real customer for the NHS is the tax paying public and that they are buying the service from the government.

So why am I telling you all this? Simply put it is because the government believes that they can cure the problems in the NHS by drafting in more and more managers and by making the NHS 'run as a business'. The managers are led to believe that management techniques designed for industry will work in the British National Health Service. They will not. All of the management processes are designed to assist businesses which work in the opposite way to the NHS. The managers come in and start trying to put them into practice, discover they don't work and have to turn them topsy-turvy. The managers will not accept that health care is as difficult as the health professionals tell them. They do not like to listen to the doctors because they are frequently reminded of their own ignorance and interpret this as arrogance on the part of the medical staff. Moreover they have been taught in their management classes that the managers who oppose change are wrong and must be weeded out. It does not seem to occur to them that the medical staff have good reasons for questioning change. In medical science we are taught that we should only change our procedures when there is good evidence that we should do so. For some time the mantra in medicine has been that diagnosis and treatment should be 'evidence-based'.

Thus when told to change our practises by managers we question them and ask them to provide their evidence. This does not sit easily with the dictatorial-management style since they *have* no evidence and are only introducing the changes because they have been told that they have to do so.

They eventually believe that the doctors and nurses are wreckers of their perfectly run system and that the staff looking after patients are simply an unaffordable cost. The hardest working are punished, the experts are demoralised and the NHS simply absorbs more and more money for no discernable gain and many backward steps.

What's in a name?
"What's in a name? That which we call a rose
By any other word would smell as sweet."
Romeo and Juliet (II, ii, 1-2) Shakespeare

The title doctor used in the medical sense has been reserved for qualified medical staff registered with the GMC ever since the Medical Act of 1858. If another name had been chosen, such as Professor, Director, or whatever, it would have accrued the same cachet.

One such example is the title of Consultant. This was given to specialist doctors working in charity and local government hospitals before the NHS existed and it described exactly what they did. They came into the hospital to consult and often did that work for free. The name was carried over into the NHS and carried enormous respect. Unfortunately the title is not protected by the GMC in the same way as the name Doctor and over the last thirty years there has been an enormous explosion of people using this designation. Such people are frequently seen in the hospitals. The most obvious examples are the external management consultants who come in at the behest of politicians or management, usually have no understanding of the problems but write down the doctors' and nurses' solutions and present it as their own work.... At a huge expense.

It is the nature of the beast that the titles that go with respected posts are treasured by those who have them and envied by those who do not. At the hospital I worked for, until my early retirement, the name badges no longer carried the title doctor for medical staff.

On needing a change of badge I noticed this fact and, believing it to be a simple oversight, enquired of the badge-makers why this was the case., I was amazed to be told that it was deliberate policy and that titles such as doctor and professor were forbidden. They assumed that this was because they were considered as elitist. The job title, such as consultant or senior registrar, was included below the personal names along with the department in which the person was working. The badge-maker thought that this was sufficient but did agree that this did not necessarily mean that the holder of the badge was a doctor. Other members of staff, such as dentists, physicists and some nurses, also used the title of consultant....as well as management consultants, of course.

I have since learnt that there are other local hospitals which do not permit the use of the word *doctor* on the medical staff badges. But why ever not? People are always complaining that doctors do not introduce themselves well enough and the badge is an important identifying aid.

The answer lies once more with:
- envy on the part of staff who are not doctors (particularly management and senior nursing officers).
- the management desire to use non-medically qualified staff in the role of doctors (skill mix)

This is demonstrated in the story quoted from Hospital Doctor of December 15th 2005. It appears that at least two other hospitals have taken the opposite line of attack and have started the illegal practice of calling non-GMC-registered practitioners 'doctor associate'. It will be interesting to see whether or not they are prosecuted successfully given that a large number of 'alternative medicine' practitioners appear to use the title of doctor without any problem.

Hospital calls lay staff 'Dr'

December 15th 2005 Hospital Doctor page 3

BMA leader Dr Paul Miller was planning to report an NHS Trust to the police for giving non-medically qualified staff the title of 'doctor associate' or 'associate doctor'. At least two Trusts were giving staff misleading titles.
Medical Act 1983 makes it an offence for any person to pretend to be a registered doctor.

The Move Towards Privatisation of the NHS

Interestingly a number of the points I have been making in the book have been observed by the government. Although not attributing the problems to their own meddling some of the more astute amongst the politicians have realised that the problems do exist. They are, perhaps, at last losing faith in the Soviet style of meddling management.

It would be surprising if they did not notice this given that so many Trusts are facing cuts and the NHS is said to be a billion pounds overspent. The Trusts are overspent for a number of reasons including:

- costly initiatives to meet government targets such as waiting lists,
  salary increases above the level of inflation,
- employment of expensive temporary staff because of difficulties in recruiting permanent staff
- a further increase in the number of managers doing non-productive jobs

When the Trusts say that they are now working within their budgets careful analysis shows that this has been achieved by hiding the losses as loans and reducing costs by sacking large numbers of clinical staff.

Wards closed and staff cut as NHS cash crisis bites

Daily Mail, Thursday, April 13, 2006

Hospitals face more staff and drug cuts

...ttle up to 500 posts being shed to

Hospitals divert cash from patients to pay interest on loans

'Hospitals have run up debts of £1billion in a credit culture that threatens the future of dozens of NHS services'. Millions of pounds intended for patient care are being diverted to pay debts and interest payments. The Patients Association said that the revelations made nonsense of government claims that the health service is out of financial crisis. Sunday Telegraph Dec 9th 2007 page 18.

Whilst they are still constantly introducing new managers into the NHS, at the same time the government believes that they are moving away from the wasteful days of the past by further introducing the use of the private sector as a provider of services for health care. They now have faith that the private sector will provide major savings and still create a better NHS. Unfortunately the exact opposite is likely to be the case.

Private healthcare can indeed take a burden off the NHS. It does this when a patient pays to be treated privately in an independent hospital. In the past, paying patients produced a significant income for the NHS. Since 1976 and the removal of paybeds, this has not really been the case. Thatcher tried to reinstate paybeds but the private hospitals had established a foothold and private work in the NHS was in competition rather than enjoying the monopoly it previously held.

So why does the embracing of the private sector nowadays not represent a bonus for the NHS?

This is simply because it is the wrong way round. Whilst in the past private work brought money into the NHS from the patients and their insurers the latest schemes take money out of the NHS to pay for the work to be done privately. The Department of Health, via Nigel Crisp, has made it clear that they want at least 15% of NHS work to be done by the private sector by 2008. This would include work undertaken in treatment and diagnostic centres, in hospitals financed under Private Finance Initiatives (PFIs) agreements and directly in independent hospitals.

10   FEBRUARY 5 2006   SUNDAY TELEGRAPH

BUSINESS   business.telegraph.co.uk

The PFI industry has got us over a barrel

Sunday Telegraph Feb 5th 2006

The faith that private suppliers can undertake NHS work more efficiently than the NHS itself is simply extraordinary. Looking at the countries that run their health care systems with more competition and more private involvement always shows that they cost more than the NHS. PFI hospitals are all significantly smaller than their predecessors and cost more to run. This is not unexpected since the private partner has to make a profit to survive.

To help the private sector in this endeavour the government has brought in the tariff system mentioned earlier in this chapter: so-called payment by results. For the first time money actually follows the patient rather than the patient following the money. In itself this may well be a good idea but undoubtedly involves considerably greater bureaucracy and additional cost. It does not save money.

If the tariffs are set wrongly, which many say they have been, the system could be very harmful. Patients are not identical and so a system setting a national tariff for a particular condition, such as diabetes mellitus, may mean that complex diabetics cannot be provided with a service or that just one patient could bankrupt a clinic leading to it being shut down.

Teaching hospitals will struggle to deal with referrals, teaching will be squeezed yet again and independent clinical research will be impossible.

The private sector, which is expected to provide efficiency savings, will also be able to bid for the treatment of patients but they will not be controlled by the NHS tariff. At present I understand that they will be (or are) receiving more per patient than the NHS.

By " cherry picking" private hospitals are able to run at a profit, which is to be expected since they are businesses . Remember that most of the private hospitals do not undertake training and teaching, do not do significant research and refuse to deal with the more complex cases. Whilst these negatives do not endear themselves to a large number of NHS staff, I have to admit they do not worry me. The private sector provides choice for patients in the UK which the NHS, despite all the rhetoric, very rarely does. However, I do not see why they should be treated more favourably than the NHS using taxpayers' money. Nor do I agree that the privately-run Diagnostic and Treatment Centres should take the easy 20% of the NHS hospitals work whilst taking an even larger proportion of the NHS hospitals' budgets and leaving them to deal with all the complex cases.

Let us examine just one business case being put together for a local Diagnostic and Treatment Centre. The general manager in our department came to me in 2003 and said that once again they were asking him to provide a workable business plan for a Diagnostic and Treatment Centre to work with our hospital. It would be sited in South Bristol and take 20% of the workload from the Radiology Department. The money to run it would come from our budget and would initially be around 30% of our budget. The higher figure was necessary in order to pay for the equipping and building of the centre.
The specific question that the manager had was 'would this provide a training opportunity for specialist registrars?' In itself this was a sensible question since the work to be done at the centre was the more routine, straightforward work which was often undertaken by registrars. But they were only permitted to do this because they were being covered by senior colleagues. The consultants were available to answer any queries.

I suggested that the Diagnostic and Treatment Centre, because of the workload, would require between 20% and 30% of the consultant staff to run it in addition to junior medical staff. I also pointed out that we would have to reduce the workload at the teaching hospital in order that we would have time to do this extra work and that travelling between sites would further reduce efficiency. The manager had initially budgeted for one consultant but I considered we would need five. He thought that the work at the teaching hospital would automatically decrease. I pointed out that this was not the case since there would be capacity on the machines to do the work and there was always a waiting list. Until we had completely worked our way through the waiting list the work would continue at 100% capacity. Thus we would end up doing 100% work for 70% of the budget at one hospital and 20% of the work for the remaining 30% budget at the Diagnostic and Treatment Centre. I could not see how the figures could add up sensibly. Failure of similar centres elsewhere appears to be proving me to be correct.

There is almost no hospital development going on in the NHS right now which is not a PFI. Yet simple analysis demonstrates that the PFI system is much more costly than using the public purse directly and the deals done with the companies running the PFIs mean that the public's future has been mortgaged away. The NHS appears to have agreed to pay the companies set fees for an agreed number of cases (probably whether they are done or not) and to hand over the land at the end of the contracts. Money borrowed privately is always more expensive than money borrowed by the government but it does not appear as a government over-spend !

Alyson Pollock in her book entitled *NHS plc,* goes into considerable detail about the privatisation of the health service and I would recommend anyone who wishes to understand chapter and verse on this subject to read her book.

Why are the government moving in this direction? Is it because they have identified that all the extra managers are a burden on the NHS and that the system is failing or perhaps they believe that it has already failed? Do they still cling to the entirely mistaken idea that the doctors are wrecking the NHS and that this is the way to finally break the power of the medics?

In the next chapter we will look at the patients. Have the problems in the NHS all been due to the politicians, the managers, the doctors, dentists and nurses or are the patients also too blame? In the last chapter we will discuss where this is all taking us and what the future may hold for us. What will healthcare be like in 5, 10 or even 20 years time?

Chapter 15
What has gone wrong with the patients ?

Saints and sinners

For years now the medical profession has had to endure constant attacks from the politicians, the media and more recently their own patients. Despite the occasional example of a truly pathological doctor most of the criticism has been about the attitude of doctors and their inability to communicate. The essence of these attacks has been that the medical profession is ridden with uncaring, arrogant, overbearing creeps with a god-complex. In comparison the patients are portrayed as long-suffering saints. The nurses are pictured as wavering somewhere in the middle: sometimes portrayed as ministering angels but too often described as uncaring and callous (particularly the latter when looking after old people).

Well folks, I'm going to put a different story. It's the patients who are increasingly greedy and arrogant, aided and abetted by the politicians and media. It is the medical profession (including doctors and nurses and other health care professionals) who are the maligned altruists. Put even more simply, the patients are the sinners and the doctors are the saints. Hard to believe? Let us examine the evidence.

Despite propaganda to the contrary the vast majority of doctors have always worked well in excess of their contracted NHS hours. The extra work has mostly been undertaken for free......it has been, in effect, charity work. The hospital consultants are no exception. Studies have shown that on average they work 30% over their contracted hours[1,2] which is in complete contradistinction to the commonly held view that they spend all their time shirking NHS work and doing over-priced private work. As in all aspects of life there are occasional examples of lazy doctors but they are few and far between. In fact most doctors work far too hard and continue to work even when they are themselves ill....they take very little sick leave, most are unable to take their full study leave entitlement and many do not even take their full allocation of annual vacation.

But why the bad press and why have the doctors not fought back?

Increasing expectation on the part of patients has been fuelled by politicians.

The Department of Health has created a patient's charter, the GMC has laid down vigorous rules for doctors and numerous other bodies oversee, inspect, regulate and enforce the working practice of doctors. With appraisals and assessments, audit and clinical governance the medics have been worn down. All of these stress the rights of patients and responsibilities of doctors but none of them ever mention responsibilities of patients and rights of doctors.

Basically the doctors are not allowed to fight back. Doctors cannot respond to a patient's specific abuse without citing situations and clinical details, they cannot fight a politician's criticism without giving examples from their own practice. If they do they can be instantly struck off, suspended, sacked and legally humiliated since disclosure of clinical information is a breach of confidentiality. The usual response from a doctor is to say 'no comment'. This is not due to guilt or arrogance but a legal and moral obligation.

In addition there is a group of collaborators within the health service fighting against the doctors. The hospital managers are not all inherently antagonistic to the doctors but they are indeed trained to be so. They believe they are in a struggle for power and that they must win in order that the health service can be saved from the over-reaching grip of the doctors. Oh, that it was really the case! In truth the medics have little power, a lot of useful knowledge, far too much work and far too little time to do it in. The management like to present the situation as being something different from that which it is. They blame the doctors for their own mismanagement.

Why do the patients perceive the doctors as arrogant?
Often the reasons cited are that the doctor kept them waiting, did not listen or reply to them properly, was too brusque and did not give them sufficient time.

Let us take the outpatient clinic as an example. Thirty years ago the patients for a clinic were told the time that the clinic started and that they may have to wait for four hours (it was even suggested to some that they bring their own cushions and for entertainment brought their own books). All were expected to turn up, say, at around two o'clock and then they would be seen in turn until the clinic overran and finished at around 7.30pm. The patients, the nurses and the doctors were all exhausted but enormous numbers of patients had been dealt with most of whom expressed their gratitude and gave small presents to the staff.

Now the patients are booked with specific times (2.00, 2.15, 2.30 etc.). But many turn up late and even if the doctor is on time the patients are not. Some patients take more time than others leading to delays, notes and test are sometimes not available (further delay) and the two o'clock patient arriving at 3.30 still expects to be seen. This is, of course, inefficient but it does mean that the patients do not have to wait anywhere near as long as they used to and few doctors would really like to go back to the old system even if it was more time-efficient. Are the patients happier? No, not demonstrably so. In fact there are now many more complaints than there used to be and foremost amongst these is that the arrogant doctor kept them waiting. The assumption here is that the doctor *wanted* to keep them waiting as some display of his/her power over them. Nothing could be further from the truth. The poor over-worked doctor loves it when the clinic runs to time. Why wouldn't they, after all they are simply human (a bit more altruistic than most but still human) and keeping to time means that they can have a coffee or lunch break and that they might, for once, finish and get home on time.

What do the patients mean by unacceptable waiting? Surveys have shown that a large proportion of patients think that waiting even 15 minutes beyond their appointment time is entirely unacceptable.

Let me give you an example from my own experience. I will not disclose names so I reckon that I am immune from being struck off on this particular case. For many years I have assisted in raising money for scanners. On this particular day I was working in one of these charity provided scanners when the radiographer, the technician in charge of running the machine and also paid from charity funds, told me that a patient was complaining vociferously about being kept waiting. "How long has he waited?" I asked. "He is about five minutes behind schedule coming in to the scanner but we've told him that he will have to wait for another ten minutes," she replied. "We've also explained that an emergency patient had to be squeezed in,"she added, "and that his entire examination will, in all probability, still finish on time since there is some inbuilt leeway."

I went to talk to the patient. Now, many of the patients are suffering from brain damage from tumours and I thought perhaps that explained this patient's attitude. Keeping this in mind I was even more careful and considerate than usual when dealing with the patient. I explained again that he would only be 15 minutes behind, that he would leave on time and that it would not interfere with the quality of his own examination. I also explained that the scanner was provided by charity and that we were very pleased that we were able to offer him the service at all. I further reminded him that there was an emergency patient in there at the moment and that he now had less than five minutes to wait. His reply was vitriolic. He could not care less that an emergency patient was being scanned, he had an appointment time and that should be kept and he was not interested in the least with regard to how it was funded. The scan was his right and he wanted it now.

Luckily the discourse had taken up the waiting time and at that moment the radiographer cheerfully popped through and asked him to go with her into the scanner. This was greeted with more abuse. The results of the scans? Completely normal.

So what does this example show us?

Firstly that certainly some patients are not angels and they abuse their 'rights'. Is this a common experience and if so why don't the public hear about it? I'm afraid it is. A recent NHS survey showed that nearly 30% of staff had been harassed or abused by patients or the patients' relatives in the previous year. But this does not make the headlines in the same way that "Arrogant doctor nearly killed me" does.

Secondly it brings up a point put exceedingly well by Raymond Tallis [2] ... 'the patient is primarily self-interested and ...his or her self interest is potentially in conflict with that of other patients'. When one is ill one becomes more selfish not more saint-like whether you are an NHS or a private patient. We live in a fast food world and the patients want fast medicine.

"The doctors did not listen, did not explain the situation, were brusque and took too little time". The former is a complaint about communication. The latter (lack of time) is always going to be the case under our present health service and will only improve if there is a vast increase in staff or massive decrease in demand, neither of which seem likely. The brusqueness is a consequence of too little time and doctors fight hard to stop themselves from appearing rude, sometimes failing.

The communication problems It is almost impossible to communicate intelligently with a sick, worried patient. Doctors try very hard to do so. They are taught to listen, ask open-ended questions and provide understandable explanations regarding the patient's condition. But in my own long experience of doing procedures many patients, when they are anxious, literally cannot tell their right hand from their left. You ask them to turn left and they turn right. You ask them to lie down and they sit up. You ask them to stop breathing and they take a large breath in and out.

If they can't understand the simplest of instructions how can they understand a complex resume´ of their condition and the necessary treatment? The answer is that they can't. Fear makes fools of all of us. I have had several surgical operations myself and each time I have had utmost difficulty in understanding simple instructions, which I could have easily understood had I not been anxious and ill.

Are doctors poor communicators? I would argue that this is usually not the case. They are excellent lecturers (far better than any manager I have ever met), they are frequently great performers, good actors, good musicians and the life and soul of the party. They were the brightest of the bunch at school and despite the dimming effect of excessive study continue to excel until they meet the early demise that most doctors have due to stress and overwork. We are fighting hard to improve communication but it will never be easy. And in this context comes informed consent. Nowadays a signature is no longer proof that consent was given and the patients complain that they did not understand all of the words used or that an uncommon (less than 1%) complication was not remarked on.

In this situation I do not believe that informed consent is truly ever possible unless the patient has undergone the years of study that the doctor has….. and then read the same books and undergone the same training.

Does any of this matter? It most certainly does. As the esteem of doctors is knocked the number of students wishing to enter medical school also drops, the doctors themselves are disillusioned and will give up their extra hours of "charity" work and nearly all wish to retire early.

A change in the type of patient. Whilst I have been in Bristol there has been a considerable change in the pattern of diseases affecting the patients presenting to the Bristol Royal Infirmary. In 1976 there were 50 heroin addicts in Bristol and one estimate is now 8,000[3]. Bristol drug users are said to have an 80% prevalence of Hepatitis C and a high incidence of HIV infection. In 1990/91 there were just 50 admissions to the Bristol Royal Infirmary associated with drug misuse but by 2001/2 this had risen to 275.

The doctors are expected to treat the drug addicts in the same way as all other patients and to give them all the same options of treatment. In fact the GMC have been particularly strong on this point and at one time issued guidance indicating that the welfare of the patient must come before consideration of one's own safety. This prompted me to write to the President of the GMC urging a change in the rules:

To: Sir Donald Irvine
President of the GMC
178-202 Great Portland Street
London W1N 6JE

30.10.95
Dear Sir Donald Irvine

Thank you for sending me the latest guidance for doctors entitled "Duties of a doctor". This clearly represents a lot of work on the part of the GMC and you are to be congratulated for the clarity of most of the content.

I am, however, worried about the constant attention to HIV infection and the way in which preoccupation with HIV has somewhat misled the committee.

In particular the statement on page 5 of "Good medical practice" that "You must not refuse or delay treatment .... because you may be putting yourself at risk" is clearly included because of HIV. It is however a blanket statement that makes no sense.

Of course one should not delay treatment if the risk is only theoretical. But if there is a real tangible risk ignoring it will lead to two patients not one. It is not difficult to think of examples but here are a few possible risks :
- **being run over by vehicles on the motorway trying to help someone in an accident (this almost happened to me and one must be very careful to delay treatment until it is safe to provide it !!!)**
- **being shot at in a war,**
- **being attacked by a madman with an axe**
- **being pulled off the top of a building by a would-be suicide (surely best to wait until you can be strapped in safely before you try to reach the patient).**

In all of these situations, which are probably more common than HIV infection, it would be totally foolhardy NOT to delay treatment until the risk to yourself has been removed yet the doctor would be in breach of your latest missive. Please could you think again about such statements. It is probably true that all treatment of patients should be delayed until risks to the doctor that *can* be removed are removed. Indeed even with HIV infection it is often wise to consider the investigations and treatment in the light of the patient's condition and it may be sensible to undertake a slightly more expensive investigation that may not need an injection (eg unenhanced MRI) instead of the routine investigation (Computed tomography pre and post intravenous contrast medium) but again this could easily be construed as being against your guidelines.

It may appear that these considerations are only theoretical but in these litigious days it is very important that the advice from the GMC is sensible and fair. Please try to protect the doctors as well as the patients.

Yours sincerely
Paul R Goddard MD, FRCR Consultant Radiologist, Bristol Royal Infirmary, Chairman of the MRRA (UK)

I could have added other examples (e.g. danger of electrocution, danger of drowning) but the point was made. To their credit the GMC did change the guidelines slightly by adding a caveat in their latest version of the advice to the medical profession which can be found on their website: GMCGoodMedicalPractice.com

Decisions about access to medical care

....

8. You must not refuse to treat a patient because you may be putting yourself at risk. *If patients pose a risk to your health or safety you should take reasonable steps to protect yourself before investigating their condition or providing treatment.* (My italics and underlining)

Since I wrote the letter the number of patients presenting an inoculation risk has increased considerably. The Radiology Department are now frequently asked to use their skills in draining abscesses in drug addicts whereas even ten years ago it was an unusual and rare occurrence.

The Radiology Department is right next to the Accident and Emergency (A and E) Department and walking through to Radiology, particularly when the hour is late, has the sensation of running a gauntlet as one passes the inevitable posse of drug addicts and alcohol abusers. I am aware of how exposed and vulnerable one often felt as a casualty officer, having worked as a senior house officer and registrar in accident and emergency. These days to do such a job must on occasions be genuinely frightening and I glad that it is something I do not have to do ever again.

So are all doctors saints and all patients sinners? Not really. There is a mix of saints and sinners amongst them all. There are many delightful patients or we would have stopped working almost before we started. Doctors are just human beings albeit more public-minded than most. Patients are understandably selfish and sometimes aggressively so. But politicians and the media have enjoyed turning the appreciation of the situation topsy-turvy and this will end up to the detriment of all.

NHS Constitution

A draft constitution for the NHS was unveiled on the 60th anniversary of the founding of the National Health Service as part of Lord Darzi's review of the NHS. (see www.ournhs.nhs.uk/). A constitution was first suggested in 2006 by then Health Minister, Andy Burnham, and resurrected by Gordon Brown in a New Year address to the NHS on January 1st 2008[4]. The constitution[5] will "guarantee minimum standards of care" including all patients being able to register with a GP and not having to wait longer than 18 weeks for an operation. In return the patients will be told that they must keep appointments and not be violent or abusive to staff. It will not determine what services are available, free the NHS from political control or initially be enshrined by law. Rather it draws together the rights that already exist. As an idea it is excellent but it sounds much like the unenforceable Patient's Charter and may once again fuel expectation without providing the means of fulfilling it.

Chapter 16
State Medicine: The Future
Conclusions and predictions, possibilities and certainties
General Summing-Up

A wise man that had it for a by-word, when he saw men hasten to a conclusion,
'Stay a little that we may make an end the sooner.'
Francis Bacon 1561-1626 [1]

Having analysed the history of State Medicine, examined the rise and fall of health services and looked at aspects of the present NHS can we draw any conclusions and make any predictions? Was the Kennedy Report correct in determining that 'clinical freedom' was at the heart of medical problems or does this simply echo George Bernard Shaw's typical left-wing mantra that 'All professions are conspiracies against the laity'?

I have presented evidence to the effect that the NHS was a flawed experiment from the very beginning. However, despite the initial compromises, or maybe even because of them, it served the people of Britain exceedingly well for the first half of its existence and the doctors were the mainstay of its working practice. The NHS only started to become a problem when there was a worldwide recession in the mid seventies and the NHS 'ran out of cash'. At this time a series of 'reforms' were put into action, which unfortunately served to make the otherwise efficient system work inefficiently. The various governments have continued to make major changes every other year or so since then. These have progressively moved the NHS away from the original nationwide comprehensive free health service provided in 1948 and have hampered the organisation with an ever-increasing burden of management and regulation.

Particularly worrying have been the changes in care for the weakest in society. The elderly needing long-term care have only a proportion of that care provided by the State. That care is means-tested and under the control of Local rather than National Government. Many old people, although severely disabled or demented, are living in nursing homes and providing the majority of their living and nursing expenses from their savings. If they were previously living at home alone they may have been obliged to sell their property when they moved into the nursing home. If they run out of money they may be made to move into whatever accommodation the Local Government decides. This is not exactly what the octogenarians expected when they voted for the Labour government 60 years ago and it is not what they were promised. The mentally ill have been just as badly treated. It was clear to anyone who had an ounce of imagination that 'care in the community' was obviously going to be 'neglect on the streets'. Many of the previously institutionalised have been pushed out to fend for themselves in a rough, unkind world.

The acutely ill are sometimes fortunate enough to be treated adequately in the NHS. They may receive hospital treatment for free if a bed can be found for them. It is likely that they will be sent out too soon, they will be in danger of hospital-acquired infection and emergency readmission is now common. Cancer sufferers will, however, have to look carefully at their own treatment since they may or may not get the best treatment for their condition. They will not necessarily have this explained to them since the Trusts do not like the doctors speaking 'out of turn' even though the GMC maintain that the patient should receive all the information. Important drugs may be denied them depending on their postcode or other arbitrary factors. Fat people and smokers may be denied treatment unless they mend their ways.

The salary and contracts for doctors and other staff now vary depending on the different countries of the UK so the word National no longer refers to a uniform British provision of the NHS on the staff side, if it ever did. In fact the contracts of the doctors vary between different Trusts even within the same city and the concept of National negotiations has long gone even though lip service is paid to it.

Dentistry is hardly provided on the NHS at all and it appears that under the new contract some treatment even under the NHS costs the patient the full amount, or may even subsidise other patients by paying 110%. Prescriptions are now free in Wales and soon will be in Scotland but not in England.

So has the NHS failed and is there an alternative?

The NHS clearly is functioning and provides the bulk of healthcare in the UK. However, I am sorry to say that the evidence shows us that the NHS has indeed failed in its attempt to be a national comprehensive free service. Once we realise that it may be easier to look at what can be done about it.

In asking whether there is an alternative the assumption is that we either have the NHS or a completely different system. The government have been trying to take the NHS down a middle road in which private healthcare is embraced and the patients are given a choice. Unfortunately all the systems they have tried cost considerably more than the present NHS and vastly more than the old NHS pre-reforms.

I believe that a National Health Service in which the majority of the costs are borne by the tax-payer is essential for several reasons:

If we are to care for the most disadvantaged in our society and to provide at the very least a safety net for the rest we must provide the service out of some form of taxation or compulsory insurance. The latter is, of course, just taxation under another name. The prime

242

example of a nation from the developed world using *private* health care systems is the USA. There healthcare is very patchy but they still provide a considerable service from the State via the University and Veterans health services.

Essential research and training is best undertaken with national supervision. At present whilst research has predominance in the universities it has lost much of its place in the NHS. Unfortunately training has little kudos in either the NHS or in many of the universities. The new contracts for doctors discourage training roles. The Consultants' contract is particularly bad in this regard with little time given to train the juniors and consultants expected to do this training out of hours whilst the juniors are paid to listen. But this is a major role of the NHS and we must train our own staff and not expect that we can rely on pinching staff trained overseas.

Privatisation of the NHS

The systems being put in place to privatise the NHS are being done in quite the wrong way if the system is to survive at all. Using tax-payers money to arrange operations privately is bound to cost more, as is the obsession with private finance initiatives (PFI) whatever the latest buzz word used.

Predictions and personal experiences

It seems clear that we will have more and more headlines detailing the closure of hospitals, rationing of services and pillorying of doctors. The politicians will blame the medical profession for refusing to 'modernise'.

The medical profession is already adapting to the new role. The young doctors, perhaps quite sensibly, refuse to work with the dedication of the old doctors. They seem to be asking 'If they are going to be treated badly even though they work their very hardest, why work so hard?' I have even been told by junior doctors that my work ethic was a bad example. They tell me that the desire to finish the day's work however long it takes must go unassuaged. When five o'clock comes it is time to leave whatever has happened to the patients… the work is now done on more of a shift basis and if continuity suffers why should they care. Certainly the managers do not worry so why should the doctors?

I used to smile wryly at the junior doctors who would take the lift (elevator) rather than the stairs and then announce that they had to leave at 4.55 to go to the gym but perhaps they are the ones who fit into the new world of British medicine.

If this is the case, and it does seem to be, then the future for healthcare in the UK is even more bleak. The doctors who stay in the service and do not join the 25% dropping out will have few of the features we admired in the doctors of the past. Already the profession has rebelled against the long hours and even stabilising an acutely ill patient or finishing the emergency operation after hours, will be considered an anathema.

The number of doctors graduating from medical school may well be increased dramatically but if they all desire to work short hours, or even part-time, their net input to medical services will be very small.

At present the service is being held together by a relatively small number of doctors working with the old feelings of duty that are akin to a guilt complex. These doctors are mostly over fifty or close to it and they are rapidly reaching an age when they will be forced to slow down, retire or die. The effects of continuing change, public antagonism, rising patient expectation and lowering of status in the hospitals has been very detrimental on the well-being of these older consultants. When they have gone the remaining doctors will not be able to cope with the level of work in the NHS. Many will not even try. The politicians have attempted to recruit doctors from overseas with a poor degree of success since there really are too few doctors anywhere on the planet and our conditions are not so conducive to most foreign graduates that they would want to come here. Unless the anti-doctor attitude is changed soon the recruitment to medical schools will continue to be difficult and an increasing percentage will dropout for more lucrative employment in the City. The older doctors will retire early and the few remaining caring doctors will suffer badly from overwork and stress.

The business of turning doctors into managers and thus turning them against colleagues and the encouragement of 'competition' and 'the market' within the NHS has been very detrimental for the more altruistic amongst the staff and beneficial for the more selfish practitioner. In the past it was typical for many altruistic people working in the NHS to feel that their work was a ' calling' similar to a religious occupation. They felt that they were benefiting mankind. This attitude was encouraged by the older staff and even spilt over into private medicine where it was considered the norm to treat anybody who worked in the health service and their families, for free. Interestingly this courtesy was usually extended to the clergy and their families. This may have been the final legacy from the days when the medical staff were clergymen and rather neatly ties up the pastoral and faith side of medicine with the scientific side.

These days have gone.

Over the past ten years I have documented cases where medical colleagues, usually with a management role, have turned on other medical colleagues and denounced them to higher levels of non-medical management. After inquiries it is most unusual for the accusations to be substantiated but the doctor picked on in this way has usually been taken away from work for a substantial period.

As discussed in Chapter 11 the typical behaviour of the management is to suspend the argumentative doctor with no reason given initially. They then trawl through notes and question other staff in order to find a reason for the suspension. Typical findings may be that the clinician in question made a few clinical mistakes. Failing this they will try to say that doctor was either racist or harassed the secretaries. In one recent case they even suggested that the doctor harassed the secretarial staff *by being overheard arguing with a manager*! They tried to substantiate this ludicrous argument by asking the secretarial staff in question to write complaints about the doctor. When they refused to do so the management became quite angry. The original complaint put by the argumentative doctor was never addressed, which is typical. The response is always the same; shoot the messenger.

In another case a doctor was suspended after complaining about thousands of unreported films being locked away from inspectors.

This suspension was reversed in order for the doctor to be called in to do a complex procedure and then re-instated.

He was finally sacked. The reason given? 'Serious deficiencies in his behaviour with colleagues'. Presumably by annoying them when he pointed out that work had not been done when it should have been[2]. The doctor failed at a High Court hearing to have his dismissal reversed.

The NHS was built on the goodwill of the staff working for it. This is now spread very thin. The most important role in the NHS has always been that of the doctors. They are now under attack in so many different ways that they dare not speak their minds and simply wish they were not working for the over-bearing megalith of a near-monopoly employer that the NHS has become. All the changes envisaged by the political parties seem to involve the same ordering around of medical staff and, as mentioned earlier, the management recruit doctors and succeed by divide and rule and the poorest of management techniques.

I predict that the doctors will not accept this in the future and that there will be serious problems in providing sufficient medical manpower to even staff a skeleton NHS.

The pre-registration house officer

Recently at a university party we were told by a pre-registration house officer that things were becoming progressively worse in the NHS. She had to search around the wards for simple basic equipment such as syringes and they all spent a lot of time chasing paperwork. The supposed shortening of hours due to the EU working time directive had not reduced hours at all. She was obliged to do 15 hours a week 'voluntary' work unpaid and to tell no-one in case she got the team into trouble. On her monitoring form she had to put fewer hours than she actually did, her salary was being decreased and she was worried about 'blowing the whistle' because of the effect on future employment. She loved the work but not the conditions.

Things have turned full circle back to the poor state of affairs when I was a house officer and the junior doctors were afraid to complete their overtime forms. In those days we could at least look forward to a period of respect and good pay, either as GPs or consultants.

Will skill mix or advances in medical science save the day?

The assumption that other staff can fill in for doctors and take over aspects of our work is only partially true and that truth is present in only the most trivial aspects. Yes they can 'take blood' and sew people up under supervision. They always did when I was first working in the NHS and it is good that they are doing so again.

No they cannot diagnose and treat patients in the comprehensive way that doctors can. At least they cannot do so without the same knowledge that a doctor has. If they *can* be trained to the level of proficiency required to do just that without a full medical training it calls in question the whole point of that training. If they do, indeed, need a sufficient level of knowledge that they can pass the same examinations and do the same job as a doctor then in all fairness they *are* doctors whether they were nurses or radiographers or whatever in the first place. And in any case they are in short supply just as doctors are.

The examples of NHS Direct and NHS walk-in centres provide a salutary lesson. Well-trained nurses have been taken away from their productive nursing role to provide a triage service on the telephone for NHS Direct. The cost has been huge and the results have been poor. The £80 million used to set up the service in 1998 could have been much better spent helping the beleaguered casualty departments or supporting over-worked GPs (pages 144, 145, NHS plc Allyson Pollock). By 2003 forty-two NHS walk-in centres, also run by nurses, had been set up and these had not been integrated with GP surgeries, were much more expensive than the GP out of hours service and far less effective than the under-funded battlefield of an Accident and Emergency Department. Meanwhile the hospitals, short of nurses, have had to rely on expensive agency staff or have recruited overseas nurses.

So we cannot expect that the day will be saved by skill mix.

Can other advances such as telemedicine help?

Yes they can, for example dermatology or radiology can be partly conducted remotely using digital images. Where there is a shortage of specialists this can be very useful. It does not provide the hands-on aspects of the profession and it still costs money. The medical practitioners expect to be paid wherever they are in the world and as telemedicine becomes more widespread the places providing a cheap service will gradually raise their prices. There are many other ethical issues raised by telemedicine some of which are addressed in our paper on the subject[3].

246

These uses of telemedicine can raise as many problems as they solve. Whereas it was acceptable for a GP to provide a dermatology diagnosis in the past, in the future the tele-dermatology option may be considered the standard.

Can medical tourism help?

There has been an undoubted rise in standards of other health services around the world compared with our own. An increasing number of patients are now looking abroad for private healthcare when they cannot afford the same in the UK. In addition the NHS has sent some patients abroad for treatment. This 'medical tourism' could reduce the burden on the NHS but is probably more than offset by the large numbers of people migrating to this country or visiting for healthcare reasons.

Can 'alternative' or 'complementary; medicine help?
What is the role of new-age healing?

Recently there has been a move to include complementary medicines in the NHS.

Most of the complementary medicine techniques have been around for hundreds or thousands of years as we can see by reading the earlier chapters of this book. Where they have been scientifically proven and tested many of the techniques have already been assimilated into modern medical practice. If they have not been adopted by modern medicine it is usually, but not always, because their effectiveness is questionable.

Thus many of the effective herbal medicines have been purified and de-toxified becoming in the process the basis of modern pharmacology. The results from the remaining herbal remedies which have not been adopted and researched by pharmaceutical companies are usually equivocal and hampered by a reluctance on the part of some herbal practitioners to test their use in a scientific manner. There are, however, major research projects looking for example at products from the rain forests, at the use of honey in patients with methicillin resistant staph. aureus (MRSA), at the effects of snake venoms and a host of other biologically active preparations available from natural sources.

There is still more to learn from herbalism but it is not the panacea that some believe it to be. Herbal medicines can suffer from variability in potency and purity and a lack of understanding of drug-interactions. Many are genuinely potent drugs and their use should be considered in the light of this knowledge. My experience of herbalists, admittedly limited, is that they are extremely knowledgeable about the effects of the herbal drugs but much less clued up on diagnosis. If they were able to work more closely with first class diagnosticians both parties may benefit.

Some branches of alternative medicine, such as osteopathy, have proven effective in specific circumstances such as acute backache of musculoskeletal origin. The techniques used have been accepted by conventional medicine but we are being asked now to embrace the explanations given for the manipulation effectiveness. This we cannot do since osteopaths, chiropractors and physiotherapists all use approximately the same manipulation and massage but have different explanations as to why they work. Since they cannot all be right and since the theories have not been shown to predict the outcome the best we can do at present is to accept that the techniques are sometimes effective. The theories make predictions that long term courses of treatment are required for a large number of musculo-skeletal problems. These predictions have not been well proven and should thus be ignored until shown conclusively. Better research into the reasons for the effectiveness of the treatment is required in order that the patients who would benefit most can be selected for treatment and those who may be adversely affected by manipulation, massage etc. can be excluded.

Homeopathy has not been shown to work any better than an equally well-presented placebo and trials are required before the NHS should further take up these techniques. This does beg the question as to whether or not medical staff should be allowed to give placebos (such as the old pink medicine and tonics). At present they have been removed from the national pharmacopoeia but if the placebo effect is accepted in homeopathy why can it not be accepted in general medical practice?

Acupuncture is undoubtedly helpful for many people with pain, although it is not uniformly successful. There is considerable debate over how it works with no scientific evidence for the Traditional Chinese Medicine belief in 'energy flow' around the body. Possible mechanisms include pain-gate theory (stimulation of alternative nerve fibres reducing the flow via the pain carrying nerves), stimulation of endorphins (natural pain killing substances in the brain), hypnotic suggestion and placebo effects[4]. The latter two explanations would not explain anecdotally reported successful pain relief in animals treated with acupuncture whereas the pain gate and endorphin release mechanisms perhaps would. It is possible the effects in human beings are achieved by a combination of all of these mechanisms. Some research seems to show that the exact positioning of needles is not as essential as acupuncturists believe raising further doubts over the effective mechanism.

Some new age healing techniques have not been studied scientifically in any way and embracing them into the NHS would simply be foolish until they have been shown to work. Practitioners of these methods have been making a living out of gullible sick people and should be prosecuted for making excessive claims.

The reassuring bedside manner of the old clinician was in itself an important part of the cure. As a result of litigation (and its avoidance) doctors are now obliged to present to the patient all of the possible side-effects or possible complications of a treatment regime. For some patients this is entirely acceptable but many others, probably the majority, wish that the doctor could just give them the treatment and assure them that all will be well. This seems to be what alternative practitioners with little or no training are now able to provide whilst fully qualified doctors are no longer permitted to do so.

'Alternative' or 'complementary' medicine is not really an alternative to conventional medicine. So-called 'Western' medicine, whilst still having something to learn from these

248

other techniques, has already absorbed the better and more proven parts of 'complementary' medicine.

New-age medicine cannot effectively replace the NHS.

Why have we reached this parlous condition and are there any options left for the NHS?

Partly medicine has been a victim of its own success. Partly the problems have occurred due to meddlesome interference by politicians and managers.

The successes have been obvious. Transplant surgery, anti-cancer drugs, stem cell research and magnetic resonance imaging are just a few of the miracles of modern medicine. As more can be done medicine inevitably costs more also.

The interference by politicians and the connivance of the managers has created enormous funding problems over and above the medical inflationary costs. Rationing and non-medical control of clinical decisions have reached a peak since the recent medical scandals and the equally scandalous and biased inquiries into them.

It is a surprising paradox that in the 4th or 5th richest nation we are debating whether a healthcare system that is the cheapest in the developed world can be afforded. I would have thought that there is a lot more slack in the wealth of the nation before healthcare provision in the UK is really unaffordable. The problem is, perhaps, whether the public is prepared to pay for their healthcare via taxation and will they continue to be happy to do so when it is clear that there is significant wastage due to private profit-taking or management incompetence. Will they rebel, via the voting booth, when they find that the rich, the fat, the old and the chronically sick are all excluded?

As stated earlier in the book, if rationing is necessary this is something which should be debated openly and without rancour. The politicians should stop trying to blame the doctors for doing excellent work and start a proper discourse with all who are involved but particularly the tax-payer, the patient and the doctor.

It is not altogether certain that rationing is inevitable. The costs have risen very quickly but much of this is due to unnecessary management, foolish duplication and expensive innovation. It may be that the new generation of doctors would be unable to manage their own rotas, their own operating lists and their waiting lists without the administration telling them what to do but this is what we did, amazingly efficiently, before the managers intervened and doctors are very adaptable creatures who could no doubt take up these tasks again. Having a manager in pharmacy cutting down the number of tablets on a prescription may save money from a Hospital Trust bill but just increases the bill from the GP side when the remainder of the pills are obtained via the surgery and a more-expensive high street pharmacy.

Prescriptions of Herceptin denied

A DRUG that dramatically reduces the chances of breast cancer returning will not be prescribed on the NHS in Bristol until it has been licensed by the Government.

Unlicensed breast cancer drug 'not on Bristol NHS'.

Evening Post Oct 20th 2005 p 5

A drug that dramatically reduces the chances of breast cancer returning will not be prescribed on the NHS in Bristol until it has been licensed by the Government but it is available on the NHS in some parts of Somerset, Devon and Cornwall.

Preventing a patient with carcinoma of the breast from receiving Herceptin may indeed save a few thousand pounds but at the expense of letting the patient die. Now that the patients are becoming aware of what the managers are doing they are suing for the right treatment. What is more they will win since the European Convention on Human Rights includes the 'right to life' and refusing a patient effective drugs on the grounds of cost would undoubtedly contravene the patient's rights.

So we can expect many more newspaper headlines about the breakdown in healthcare and some of the more perceptive of the Press will gradually begin to realise that it is not the doctors who are the villains. All along we have been trying to do the best for our patients even when we have been thwarted by cuts and set-backs. In the future this will be more apparent and the meddlesome politicians will not get their own way for ever. It is undoubtedly the case that the government will produce more and more spin about the increasing amounts they are spending on the NHS whilst the workers at the pit-face will see less funds available for actual healthcare. But their ploys will be rumbled.

So what is the answer?

There is no single answer to the problems. There may be, however, an answering strategy.

First of all the public must be made fully aware of the problems. These are not small and they will not go away by ignoring them.

If people still desire to have a National Health Service this should be made clear. Certainly many people are sickened by the dictatorial nature of the present government. The opposition could take note of this. The present managerial dictatorship does create a natural opposition which is liberal democracy.

The opposition should join forces to fight the Nanny State mentality of New Labour and the NHS could be assisted by this. The Liberal and Conservative parties are still fighting a battle with each other that was over one hundred years ago. The Liberals believe that they are standing up for the workers, which is indeed the role they had in the 19th century. The Tories (Conservatives) believe that they are the party of the business owner, again the role they had in the 19th century. The effect of the Liberal party is to split the vote and thus to keep the dictatorial Labour party in power.

Despite recent advances in the opinion polls, mainly due to a series of problems besetting Brown's administration, the Conservatives have an uphill battle to overcome the way in which Labour can be elected with a minority vote. In my view the Conservatives and the Liberals should join forces to fight the absurdly dictatorial so-called socialists of New Labour. This would mean that the Conservatives would have to be more liberal thinking and the Liberals more responsible but we might get a good government out of such an alliance. In truth the Conservatives and Liberals are more alike now than they ever have been. We need the business sense of the Tories and the free-thinking of the Liberals. What we do not need is the dictatorial moral high-ground of the socialists.

My best answer would be to take the NHS back to the simple administrative position of the early years. Loosen up on the doctors and let the doctors take up their previous position of individual management and remove completely the layers of line management.

To encourage the sale of medicine from within the NHS (i.e. bringing private work into the NHS) could be useful perhaps by partially subsidising private insurance. Allowing private medical insurance against tax could do this. This might help to persuade people to put money into their own health care plans and if it was only redeemable within the NHS the profits would end up back with the NHS thus supporting it.

Private hospitals are being encouraged by both the Socialists and Conservatives at present. Doing this with Government money is not a good ploy unless they are also encouraged to pay their way on training and research. The private sector cannot be expected to take on these roles willingly or to provide long term chronic or complex care. Thus the private sector is not *per se* an alternative to the NHS.

But turning the clock back is never really possible so the strategy may have to be different.

I repeat that we do need a National Health Service and that involving the doctors in this debate is essential. Many will not be free to engage in this debate due to the nature of the new doctors' contracts.

Such is the dilemma which we find ourselves in. The very people who have been trained to understand all aspects of healthcare are unable to take part in the debate about what that healthcare should entail without putting their employment at risk in a very nasty manner.

But if they do not speak out the employment of all the NHS staff will inevitably be at risk.

Options, Predicted Outcomes and Conclusions

So what are the options for the NHS?

Whilst being at risk of repetition I will outline possible options for the NHS.

Option 1 The New Labour Approach

We continue down the present route of increasing management and out-sourcing to the private sector.

Prediction

The NHS continues to bumble along becoming progressively less efficient and more expensive. It will be further burdened by the rising number of managers and many of these will be controlled by the profit-motive rather than healthcare provision since they will be employed by private profit-making concerns. The doctors will find themselves in conflict with managers on an ever-increasing number of occasions until most of the experienced, caring doctors have been removed by the system.

The type of care provided to the patients will be limited by rationing. This will not be done via consultation with patients but by the independent executives running the healthcare consortia looking at the costs and making fiscal rather than clinical decisions. Patients will frequently resort to the courts using human rights arguments to back their case and on individual occasions they will win. Overall the effects on healthcare will be dire and it will be obvious to everyone that there is no true National Health Service anymore.

The middle classes, aware of these problems, will turn more and more to health insurance. Meanwhile the doctors working in the private sector will be controlled with increasing rigor so that the patients will not be able to choose their doctor either privately or in the NHS, let alone have a 'choice of four hospitals' as promised by the present government.

Just when the patient needs their private insurance they will find that it has reached its limit and runs out. Most private insurance does not cover chronic sickness and long term care. But then nor does the NHS now: so just when you need it, it's not there!

Option 2 Even greater privatisation of NHS

Much the same as the above but the outsourcing to the private sector is increased.
This is favoured by some Conservative supporters.

Prediction

The same as for the New Labour approach but the crisis hits earlier. The hidden costs not covered by the private sector are in particular the chronic and more complex patients, the training and research. In addition the private companies, not unreasonably, do want to make a profit. Even if the outsourcing costs no more than the equivalent NHS treatment there will be problems with this approach.

A crisis in the training of doctors for routine surgery and other hands-on specialties would hit the NHS very early on. The staff employed privately would either find that they are short-staffed compared with the NHS or underpaid.

The overall costs of the NHS/private consortia would spiral out of control within a year or two unless a very rigid rationing regime was instigated making healthcare even less comprehensive.

Option 3 'Turning back the clock'

As such this is impossible but the approach would be to overnight remove all managers apart from a skeleton staff of wages clerks. Return control of the hospitals to consultants and nurses with a committee of consultants, senior nurses (including a new Matron) and other senior hospital staff (senior physiotherapists etc.) in charge.

Clinical directors would be told to go back to their medical jobs. Business managers would be made redundant. Staff would run the hospitals on a consensus basis as they did thirty years ago.

Prediction

There would be initial chaos since the doctors and nurses are no longer used to running the hospitals themselves. It is my prediction that this chaos would be short-lived and much less profound than the collapse which is already on its way under the present schemes. All collection of data apart from simple mortality and readmission figures would have to cease as would all the unnecessary committee meetings, the repetitive audits, clinical governance and risk assessments.

There would be an initial blip of cost in the first year as the managers were made redundant but by the second year the cost-savings would be enormous.

The new venture could be called something like the NHS Co-operative. Patients agreeing to be treated in NHS Co-operative Hospitals and surgeries would have to sign an agreement that they would accept arbitration and no-faults compensation for any mistakes.

Since this would be a genuine change from present policies I would advise that any action of this sort involves genuine pilot studies and proper research before implementation. I do believe that it would be very popular with the staff and patients.

Option 4 Private Medicine

Private medicine is already available for the wealthy but could be subsidised for the not-so –well-off by giving tax incentives.

Prediction

If this were the only approach the private sector would flourish at the expense of the NHS. The poor, elderly and chronically sick would be left in the NHS and the private sector would 'cherry pick' the easiest cases. This would also be expensive in lost revenue to the NHS and training and research would suffer.

Option 5 Charity or Voluntary Hospitals

This is another 'turning the clock back' option but in this case the period chosen is pre-NHS. The hospitals could be run on a voluntary basis with consultants working in the private sector for money and in the voluntary hospital for free. Patients could be asked to provide as much or as little towards the cost as they could afford. A variation on this could be to 'means test' the patients and make the payment compulsory

Prediction

Although up until fairly recently many doctors did work 15 to 20 hours a week unpaid I expect that the days when they would work in a different 'charity' hospital substantially for free are over.

Asking patients to pay something small when they attend Casualty or out-patients and fining those who do not attend appointments (without providing a suitable reason or giving notice) might cut down on wasted time and opportunity. It might also persuade people that medicine does have value since one of the problems at present is that many patients do not set a value on medical services because they have always received them for free.

Option 6 A combination of the above approaches

Prediction

This could be considered as liberalisation of British Healthcare. Private health providers would be allowed to compete on equal terms with NHS Co-operative suppliers. All providers of health care would have to include training, research and treatment of the difficult and chronic cases as part of their programme. An overall commitment to a fair National provision would be necessary so that there was not over-provision in rich areas and under-provision in poor areas. The false accounting that gives PFIs advantages would have to be removed since tax-payers would be paying for the work and the government would be guaranteeing the throughput and overall costs. If the NHS Co-operative hospitals and surgeries wished to promote private work in their own hospitals they could be encouraged to do so and tax breaks for specific NHS Co-op private insurance could be provided by the government alongside similar policies for the private hospitals. The mortality figures and readmission rates could be compared for the different systems providing they were treating comparable cases.

Conclusion

The National Health Service has reached crisis point and over the next few years will collapse unless radical solutions are sought. This rise and subsequent fall of State medicine is perhaps historically inevitable but we should learn from previous mistakes. Liberalisation of healthcare provision as opposed to the present managerial and capitalist dictatorship may be a way of saving the day.

Whatever is done it will cost more money in the short term even if it saves more lives. Perhaps there is a chance that freeing healthcare from its politically correct, Soviet style management will lead to fiscal savings in the long term. Whether or not a State decides to have a State-run health care system always comes down to hard cash in the end.

Time alone will tell.

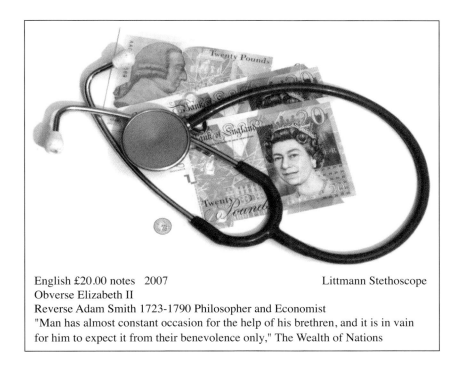

English £20.00 notes 2007   Littmann Stethoscope
Obverse Elizabeth II
Reverse Adam Smith 1723-1790 Philosopher and Economist
"Man has almost constant occasion for the help of his brethren, and it is in vain
for him to expect it from their benevolence only," The Wealth of Nations

References
Part 1, Chapter 1: The Rise of State Medicine: A Chronology and Critique

1) Essays, 560, of Studies, by Francis Bacon
2) Concise Oxford Dictionary of Current English, Oxford Univ. Press.8ᵗʰ edition 1990
3) www2.sjsu.edu/depts/museum/hippoc.html
4) Asimov, I., (1982). *Asimov's Biographical Encyclopedia of Science and Technology* (2nd Revised Edition). Garden City, New York: Doubleday
5) Alice Kehoe *Shamans and Religion: An Anthropological Exploration in Critical Thinking*
6) en.wikipedia.org/wiki/Shamanism
7) Lewthwaite, "South Africans go on witch hunts. (La Guardia, "South Africa's non-political witch-hunts," *The Daily Telegraph*, September 9, 1998
8) www.gendercide.org/case_witchhunts,html
9) www.sjsu.edu/faculty/watkins/sumer.htm
10) www.infoplease.com/ce6/people/A0822568.html
11) http://en.wikipedia.org/wiki/Hammurabi
12) History of medicine, school science.co.uk
13) Tharwat Mohammed Halwani, Mohamad Said Maani Takrouri: Medical laws and ethics of Babylon as read in Hammurabi's code (History). *The Internet Journal of Law, Healthcare and Ethics*. 2007. Volume 4 Number 2www.ispub.com/ostia/index.php?xmlFilePath=journals/ijlhe/vol4n2/babylon.xml
14) www.indiana.edu/~ancmed/meso.HTM
15) www.indiana.edu/~ancmed/egypt.HTM,
16) www.egyptologyonline.com/treatments.htm
17) Bryan, P.W. *The Papyrus Ebers* (Geoffrey Bles: London, 1930)
18) The Art of Medicine in Ancient Egypt p13 (The Metropolitan Museum of Art, New York, Yale University Press 2006)
19) The contagiousness of childbed fever": a short history of puerperal sepsis and its treatment eMJA 2/16 December 2002 *Med J Aust* 2002; 177 (11/12): 668-671)
20) www.in-ta.net/info/aesculapius
21) en.wikipedia.org/wiki/Sophocles
22) Wages Through The Ages: The Ethics of Physician Income www.llu.edu/llu/bioethics/prov2_93.htm David Schiedermayer
23) F. Kudlein, "Medicine as a 'liberal art' and the question of the physician's income," Journal of the History of Medicine, October 1976: 448-459
24) Plato's Republic, 346D
25) Ancient Athenian Plague Proves to Be Typhoid By David Biello Scientific American.Com Jan 25ᵗʰ 2006 www.sciam.com/article.cfm?articleID=000BF619-9B78-13D6-9B7883414B7F0135 and Dentistry 16 Feb 2006 p15
26) en.wikipedia.org/wiki/Herodicus
27) http://en.wikipedia.org/wiki/Thrace
28) Gangopadhyaya, Mrinalkanti. *Indian Atomism: History and Sources*. Atlantic Highlands, New Jersey: Humanities Press, 1981
29) www.healthsystem.virginia.edu/Internet/library/historical/artifacts/antiqua/alexandrian.cfm University of Virginia
30) www.egyptianholiday.net/kom.htm
31) Egyptian Time Scale by G.M.James, Clinical Press Ltd. Bristol, England
32) en.wikipedia.org/wiki/Traditional_Chinese_medicine
33) The Medical Classic of the Yellow Emperor, Produced by Beijing Foreign Languages Press, Translated by *Zhu Min*.
34) www.townsendletter.com/Dec2002/artemisinin1202.htm
35) Western Medicine, an illustrated history, editor Irvine Loudon. Oxford Univ. Press
36) www.hyperhistory.com
37) www.medhunters.com/articles/timelineCelsus.html
38) Celsus on line: http://penelope.uchicago.edu/Thayer/E/Roman/Texts/Celsus/home.html
39) www.newadvent.org/cathen/03731a.htm
40) Josephus, *Jewish Antiquities*
41) Pliny, Letters, transl. by William Melmoth, rev. by W.M.L. Hutchinson (Cambridge: Harvard Univ. Press, 1935), vol. II, X:96,
42) Tacitus, Annals 15.44, cited in Strobel, *The Case for Christ*, 82
43) *The Babylonian Talmud*, transl. by I. Epstein (London: Soncino, 1935), vol. III, Sanhedrin 43a, 281, cited in Habermas, The Historical Jesus, 203
44) www.probe.org/content/view/18/77/
45) Matthew Chapter 10 verse 8 Authorised Version of the Bible
46) The Holy Bible illustrated, William Collins, Sons and Co. 1872
47) Matthew 22:19, Mark 12:15, Luke 20:24
48) Personal communication from Barry Clayden, MD Coincraft
49) Matthew 17:24-27
50) P25 Seaby Coins of England Standard Catalogue 1996
51) Matthew 21:12
52) Matthew 26:15
53) Exodus 21:32
54) The Law of Moses Chapter VII in Bible and Spade by Stephen L Caiger DB first published by the University Press, Oxford 1936. This Edition prepared for Katapi by Paul Ingram 2003 www.katapi.org.uk/BAndS/ChVII.htm
55) en.wikipedia.org/wiki/Bladud
56) Martial, Epigrams 8.74
57) Gargilius Martialis, Preface, 7
58) Bristol Medico-Chirurgical Journal Vol 14 1896 pages 114 and 115
59) http://en.wikipedia.org/wiki/Galen
60) www.med.virginia.edu/hs-library/historical/antiqua/galen.htm
61) Charles Singer, A Short History of Anatomy from the Greeks to Harvey, Dover Publications,Inc.,1957, p. 48
62) Pp 24 and 40 Seaby Coins of England Standard Catalogue 1996

Chapter 2: Medicine in the Middle Ages

1. The Ostrogothic Kingdom and the Byzantine Reconquest 220-225 Atlas of the Roman Empire Cornell and Matthews, Phaidon, Oxford.
2. en.wikipedia.org/wiki/Decline_of_the_Roman_Empire
3. Edward Gibbon, The Decline and Fall of the Roman Empire (1776)
4. Social England, Vol 1 1893,pp173-174, Cassell and Company Ltd.)
5. www.huttoncommentaries.com/ECNews/SuperVolc/Krakatau/Krakatau1.htm
6. www.physicsforums.com/archive/index.php/t-90232.html\
7. http://www.lanl.gov/news/index.php?fuseaction=home.story&story_id=111
8. http://gchbryant.tripod.com/Articles/darkages0999.htm
9. Lester K. Little, ed., Plague and the End of Antiquity: The Pandemic of 541-750, Cambridge, 2006. ISBN 0-521-84639-0
10. Rosen, William. Justinian's Flea: Plague, Empire, and the Birth of Europe, Viking Adult, 2007. ISBN 978-0670038558.
11. en.wikipedia.org/wiki/Plague_of_Justinian
12. Josiah C. Russell, "Population in Europe:, in Carlo M. Cipolla, ed., The Fontana Economic History of Europe, Vol. I: The Middle Ages, (Glasgow : Collins/Fontana, 1972), 25-71
13. www.loyno.edu/~history/journal/1996-7/Smith.html
14. Medical History: Plagues and Epidemics Miguel A. Faria, Jr., www.uwmc.uwc.edu/csepa/mhall/IGS/Plagues/SAP/Justinianplague.htm
15. Social England, Vol 1 1893,pp173-174, Cassell and Company Ltd
16. Phoenix p 2 P320 Nov 2007
17. www.travelchinaguide.com and en.wikipedia.org
18. The Physician and the Health Professions in Medeival Islam.Bull. N.Y. Acad. Med. 47.1088-1110, 1971
19. Contributions Of Islam To Medicine www.islam-usa.com/im3.html
20. Al-A'Sar Y.H.: Lights on History, of Science. Famous physicians of the Eastern part of the Arab World. Hospital Medical Practice, Cairo, Egypt 1:14-29, 1971,
21. Min-Kin J.S.: The World of Moses Maimonides: Thomas Yoseloff Inc. New York, 1968
22. en.wikipedia.org/wiki/St_Bartholomew's_Hospital
23. http://www.kented.org.uk/ngfl/subjects/history/medhist/page16_hospital.html
24. Shakspeare and the Medical Sciences Bristol Med.Chi.J. Vol 5 pp 225-256 Dec 1887
25. www.general-anaesthesia.com
26. Chaucer www.fordham.edu
27. everything2.com/index.pl?node=Physician
28. Chaucer's Doctour of Phisyk Bristol Med Chi J Vol 12 p156 1894
29. urbanrim.org.uk Brian Williams, 1997 and 2004
30. Creighton, Charles (1965), A History of Epidemics in Britain Vol I: From AD 664 to the Great Plague (2nd ed), with additional material by DEC Eversley, EA Underwood, and L Ovenall, London: Frank Cass. (This work was originally published in 1891.)
31. Gottfried, Robert S (1978), Epidemic Disease in Fifteenth Century England: The Medical Response and the Demographic Consequences, Leicester: Leicester University Press.
32. Gottfried, Robert S (1983), The Black Death: Natural and Human Disaster in Medieval Europe, London: Robert Hale
33. Shrewsbury, John Findlay Drew (1970), A History of Bubonic Plague in the British Isles, Cambridge: Cambridge University Press
34. Bencao Gangmu: Compendium of Materia Medica (6 vols.) By Li Shizhen Publisher: Foreign Languages Press (October 2003.)
35. en.wikipedia.org/wiki/Artemisinin
36. www.mirabilis.ca/archives/001027.html)
37. medicinenet.com

Chapter 3: Medicine in the Early Modern Period

1) An outline history of medicine Philip Rhodes Butterworths 1985
2) Wikipedia.org/wiki/renaissance
3) Western Medicine, Irvine Loudon , p195. OUP
4) Chambers Journal vol x 1859 pp56,57
5) Elizabethan Age, Life in an age of adventure, Alison Plowden, Reader's Digest p 193
6) Social England Vol IV p153 Cassell and Co Ltd. Published 1895
7) Brittanica Online
8) www.Luminarium.org
9) Chronicle of the World, p641-643
10) Social England Vol IV p286 Cassell and Co London 1895
11) Social England Vol IV p317-318 Cassell and Co London 1895
12) www.surgical-tutor.org.uk/default-home.htm?surgeons/hunter.htm~right
13) Western Medicine An illustrated history Irvine Loudon Oxford Univ Press 1997 p 319
14) The Age of Napoleon page 325
15) Priestly, Lavoisier and Scheele from Resuscitation Greats Edited by Baskett and Baskett, 2007 Clinical Press.
16) Concise Oxford Dictionary
17) The Age of Napoleon pp392-393
18) Genitourinary medicine and surgery in Nelson's navy,J C Goddard Postgraduate Medical Journal 2005;81:413-418pmj.bmjjournals.com/cgi/content/abstract/81/957/413
19) Health and Medicine in Britain since 1860, Anne Hardy, Palgrave, 2001
20) www.realclearpolitics.com/articles/2006/03/abdul_rahman_and_the_future_of.html
21) Western Medicine, Irvine Loudon, p98
22) Daily Telegraph P1 Saturday Oct 13, 2007 Post strike poised to end after Royal Mail talks
23) Western Medicine An illustrated history Irvine Loudon Oxford Univ Press 1997 p 198
24) en.wikipedia.org/wiki/Florence_Nightingale
25) www.agnesscott.edu/lriddle/women/nitegale.htm
26) Western Medicine An illustrated history Irvine Loudon Oxford Univ Press 1997 pp115,201
27) www.which.co.uk/reports and BBC News 24 Monday, 31 October 2005
28) www.victorianweb.org/history/chad1.html
29) The Cholera Years. Rosenberg, Charles E. Chicago: The University of Chicago Press. 1962.
30) Snow, John. Snow on Cholera. New York: The Commonwealth Fund; London: Oxford University Press.
31) Bristol Medico-Chirurgical Journal Vol. 16 1898 p 28

32) www.bbc.co.uk/history/historic_figures/pasteur_louis.shtml
33) French face a snub as they seek the return of Napoleon III, Daily Telegraph 10.12.2007 p18
34) en.wikipedia.org/wiki/Alexandre_Yersin
35) Perry RD, Fetherston JD; Yersinia pestis--etiologic agent of plague. Clin Microbiol Rev. 1997 Jan;10(1):35-66. [abstract]
36) Health and Medicine in Britain since 1860, Anne Hardy, Palgrave, 2001p16
37) www.gober.net/victorian/reports/housing.html
38) Winter 1994 , Future Health, Canadians for Health Research
39) http://campus.udayton.edu/~hume/Lister/lister.htm
40) Health and Medicine in Britain since 1860, Anne Hardy, Palgrave, 2001p18
41) Typhoid fever; its nature, mode of spreading, and prevention.William Budd London, Longmans, Green & Co. 1873
42) Bristol Medico-Chirurgical Journals 1886-1903
43) Health and Medicine in Britain since 1860, Anne Hardy, Palgrave, 2001p32

Chapter 4: Modern medicine and the build up to the UK National Health Service

1) Health and Medicine in Britain since 1860, Anne Hardy, Palgrave, 2001
2) Strand Magazine vol II 1891 Street Corner Men pp260-265
3) Clinical Image Management, Department of Radiology, Penn State University College of Medicine http://www.xray.hmc.psu.edu/rci/ss1/ss1_2.html
4) Bristol Med Chi J.Vol. 14 1896 p 112
5) Bristol Med Chi Journal Vol. 14 1896 pp 238-239
6) Developments in Magnetic Resonance 1.3 1996 pp 69-74, Clinical Press
7) www.thebakken.org/library/books/20n.htm
8) Charity and the London Hospitals, 1850-1898 Keir Waddington Boydell and Brewer Ltd
9) Crown and Empire, Glimpses of Royal Life by A E Knight, SW Partridge 1902 pp159-160
10) The London Hospital, Fred A. McKenzie, Windsor Magazine 1901-1 pp 49-58
11) Notes on Plague in Bristol in 1916, Lieut-Col. D.S. Davies, Bristol Med-Chi J. Vol XXXV No 132, pp2-4 April 1917
12) The prevention of sepsis in war wounds, with special reference to the Carrel-Dakin Method, James Swain Bristol Med-Chi J. Vol. XXXV No 133 pp68-80 July 1917
13) Western Medicine An illustrated history Irvine Loudon Oxford Univ Press 1997 p321
14) www.med.uni-giessen.de/itr/history/inshist.html
15) Nobel Lectures, Physiology or Medicine 1922-41 Elsevier, Amsterdam 1965
16) www.nobelprize.org/medicine/laureates/1939/domagk-bio.html
17) Red Medicine: Socialized Health in Soviet Russia Published in 1933 By Sir Arthur Newsholme and John Adams Kingsbury
18) www.marxists.org/archive/newsholme/1933/red-medicine/
19) Health and Medicine in Britain since 1860 pages 126 & 127
20) Health and Medicine in Britain since 1860 Anne Hardy p112
21) www.remember.org/educate/medexp.html
22) en.wikipedia.org/wiki/Nazi_human_experimentation
23) www.germanculture.com.ua/library/weekly/aa020200a.htm
24) www.ushmm.org/research/doctors/index.html
25) Children of Hippocrates: Doctors in Nazi Germany Jack S. Booze The Annals of the American Academy of Political and Social Science, Vol. 450, No. 1, 83-97 (1980)

Chapter 5: The Welfare State

1) Social Statics, or the Conditions Essential to Human Happiness IV.30.16
2) UK census 2001 (projected to 2007 by the author)
3) From Cradle to Grave: fifty years of the NHS, Geoffrey Rivett ISBN 1 85717 148
4) Modern History Sourcebook: Social Insurance and Allied Services, 1942. (Beveridge Report)
5) The Compleat Angler, Epistle to the Reader I.21
6) www.bupa.co.uk/about/asp/history/index.asp
7) 'Patients broke down my door Wednesday, July 1, 1998 Published at 13:38 GMT 14:38 UK BBC News .The NHS at 50
8) www.medibroker.com/gloss.html
9) Resuscitation Greats by P and T Baskett Clinical Press, Bristol
10) Royal Pharmaceutical Society of Great Britain
11) www.bma.org.uk/ap.nsf/Content/FundingPrescriptionCharges
12) Colin Fox on the Scottish Socialist Party website
13) RNIB web site www.rnib.org.uk/xpedio/groups/public/documents/PublicWebsite/public_gettingeyetest.hcsp#P101_5553
14) Scotland brings in free eye tests news.bbc.co.uk/1/hi/scotland/4865828.stm
15) Doll R, Hill AB. The mortality of doctors in relation to their smoking habits. Br Med J 1954;228:1451-5. PMID 13160495. Reproduced in: BMJ 2004;328:1529-3. PMID 15217868.
16) Doll R, Hill AB. Lung cancer and other causes of death in relation to smoking. A second report on the mortality of British doctors. BMJ 1956;233:1071-6. PMID 13364389.
17) Doll R, Peto R, Boreham J, Sutherland I. Mortality in relation to smoking: 50 years' observation on male British doctors. BMJ 2004;328:1519-33. PMID 15213107
18) Professor Sir John Charnley B. M. Wroblewski Rheumatology 2002; 41: 824-82
19) http://news.bbc.co.uk/onthisday/hi/dates/stories/july/20/newsid_3728000/3728225.stm
20) NHS plc by Allison Pollock pp 91,92 Verso
21) Pharmaceutical Society of Great Britain

Chapter 6: Reorganisation and industrial action in the 1970s

1) Royal Liverpool Children's Inquiry Chapter 6
2) Healthcare Finance Management Association hfma.org.uk
3) Reorganising the National Health Service: An Evaluation of the Griffiths Report by Manfred Davidmann 1984
4) www.chronology.ndo.co.uk/1975-1984.htm

5) K.D. Ewing and C.A. Gearty *The Struggle for Civil Liberties: Political Freedom and the Rule of Law in Britain, 1914-1945)*
6) The junior hospital doctors' pay dispute 1975-1976: an analysis of events, issues and conflicts. Susun Treolar, Brisbane *J Soc Policy.* 1981 Jan;10(1):1-30.
7) 1979: Public sector strike paralyses country, news.bbc.co.uk/onthisday/hi/dates/stories/january/22/newsid_2506000/2506715.stm
8) http://libcom.org/history/1978-1979-winter-of-discontent
9) Changing Working Lives, Royal College of Radiologists 2005

Chapter 7: Fundamental Changes in the NHS

1) There are Bad Times Just Around The Corner by Noel Coward
2) en.wikipedia.org/wiki/Margaret_Thatcher
3) You Never Give Me Your Money on Abbey Road by the Beatles (Lennon and McCartney)
4) Management and Competition in the NHS 2nd edition by Chris Ham, Radcliffe Medical Press 1997
5) WHO 2002
6) Pharmaceutical Society of Great Britain
7) Eleanor Rigby on Revolver by the Beatles (John Lennon and Paul McCartney)
8) www.pfc.org.uk/medical/pchrt-el.htm
9) Department of Health. Raising standards across the NHS. A programme of rewards and support for all NHS Trusts. London Department of Health 2002

Chapter 8: How does the NHS compare with the Health Services in other Countries?

1) World population prospects the 2006 Revision, United Nations, www.un.org/esa/population/publications/wpp2006/WPP2006_Highlights_rev.pdf
2) en.wikipedia.org/wiki/List_of_countries_by_life_expectancy
3) 10 August 2001 Independent
4) BMJ 2001;323:307-310 Comparative efficiency of national health systems: cross national econometric analysis David B Evans, , Ajay Tandon, , Christopher J L Murray, , Jeremy A Lauer
5) news.bbc.co.uk/1/hi/health/4098810.stm
6) U.S. Census Bureau, International Database.
7) Press Association Friday November 14, 2003 SocietyGuardian.co.uk
8) BBC News 28th Nov 2005
9) en.wikipedia.org/wiki/Japan
10) Victor Rodwin. Health Care in Japan. New York University. Retrieved on 2007-03-10.
11) Health Insurance: General Characteristics. National Institute of Population and Social Security Research. Retrieved on 2007-03-2
12) www.nchc.org/facts/France.pdf
13) http://riviera.angloinfo.com/information/1/healthinsure.asp
14) Elizabeth Docteur and Howard Oxley, "Health-Care Systems: Lessons from the Reform Experience," OECD Health Working Papers 9, Organization for Economic Cooperation and Development, 5 December 2003.
15) http://riviera.angloinfo.com/information/1/healthinsure.asp
16) http://www.egide.asso.fr/uk/guide/vivre/soigner/regimes.jhtml
17) Laurentius, first physician to Henry IV of France, in his work DeMirabili Strumas Samando, Paris, 1609
18) The Sovereign Remedy Touch-Pieces and the King's Evil Noel Woolfe The British Association of Numismatic Societies, Doris Stockwell Memorial papers No.4
19) www.amergold.com/vault/20FrancGoldAngels.php
20) http://en.wikipedia.org/wiki/Healthcare_in_Cuba
21) Cubans Show Little Satisfaction with Opportunities and Individual Freedom World Public Opinion. 10 January 2007
22) Commitment to health: resources, access and services United Nations Human Development report
23) http://en.wikipedia.org/wiki/Che_Guevara
24) ("The World Health Report 2006 - Working together for health.")
25) (www.nchc.org/facts/cost.shtml)).
26) America's lost children, Robert Adler, New Scientist 3 November 2007 p22
27) www.amergold.com/vault/uspeacesilverdollars.php
28) wikipedia.org/wiki/Touch_Pieces
29) en.wikipedia.org/wiki/Indian_Head_cent
30) www. discountcatholicproducts.com
31) Ball TS, Alexander DD. Catching up with eighteenth century science in the evaluation of therapeutic touch. Skeptical Inquirer 22(4):31-34, 1998.
32) Rosa L. Survey of Therapeutic Touch "Research." Loveland, Colorado: Front Range Skeptics, 1996.
33) Rosa L, Rosa E, Sarner L, Barrett S. A Close Look at Therapeutic Touch. JAMA 279:1005-1010, 1998. To obtain a reprint of this article, send a self-addressed stamped envelope to the National Therapeutic Touch Study Group, 711 W. 9th St., Loveland, CO 80537.
34) Lundberg GD. Editor's note. JAMA 279:1040, 1998.
35) USSR, A Concise History pp262-267, Basil Dmytryshyn, Charles Scribner's Sons New York 2nd edition 1971
36) Chronicle of the World, Derrik Mercer, editor, 1996 DK Publishing
37) The Medical Survey Mission on behalf of the Committee for Co-operation for the Elimination of Nuclear Weapons in the Ukraine, Consultative Report to the Crown Agents from Dr. Paul Goddard BSc, MBBS, DMRD, MD, FRCR (12.12.94)
38) Russian Cocktails W.C. Fieldsikov, Vice Vol. 13 number 4 pp 50-51
39) Dying Too Young in the Russian Federation: http://go.worldbank.org/C8ZON4IGB0
40) The United Nations Office for the Coordination of humanitarian Affairs in the Russian Federation said in their August 2007 bulletin
41) (Preserving disorder: IMF policies and Kenya's health care crisis *Soren Ambrose (2006-06-01)* *www.pambazuka.org/en/category/features/34800*
42) Elizabeth Mwai, "Ignore the World Bank on health, says minister," The Standard (Nairobi), March 7, 2006
43) en.wikipedia.org/wiki/Swaziland
44) New Scientist p12 7th October 2006
45) www.un-bg.bg/index.php5?l=2&p=4&
46) en.wikipedia.org/wiki/Health_care

47) Go anywhere in the EU for free treatment The Sunday Telegraph 25.11.07 p10
48) www.ehic.org.uk/Internet/home.do
49) osha.europa.eu/legislation/standards
50) www.iso.org/iso/home.htm
51) Record numbers go abroad for health, The Sunday Telegraph page 1 Oct 28th 2007
52) http://www.envirosecurity.org/ges/TheUtilityOfForceByGeneralSirRupertSmith.pdf
53) The Utility of Force: The Art of War in the Modern World: Rupert Smith Allen Lane

Chapter 9: Successes in the present day NHS but also ethical dilemmas in a rationed health service.

1) Prevention and health: everybody's business 1976 HMSO ISBN 0 11320188 5
2) Ethical dilemmas in a Rationed Health Service P Goddard and R Ashcroft, Rad March 2000 pp35 –36
3) The Lancet 2002; 359: 1877-1890
4) Lancet 2002; 360: 1531-1539
5) Science 2004; 303: 1838-1842
6) www.ucl.ac.uk/whitehallII/
7) The Lancet 2005; 365: 1139-1146
8) Nature 2006; 440: 1217-1221

Chapter 10: The Medical profession and the NHS: what went wrong?

1) www2.sjsu.edu/depts/museum/hippoc.html
2) The duties of a doctor registered with the General Medical Council
3) Medical Annual 1947, Wright, Bristol p 166
4) Stressed U.K. Doctors Turn to Drugs, Alcohol http://alcoholism.about.com/b/a/016143.htm   August 08, 2003
5) BBC news Wednesday, 5 October 2005 bbc.co.uk
6) cebmh.warne.ox.ac.uk/csr/resdoctors.html
7) Birmingham Post 06/13/05

Chapter 11: Medical Error and Negligence, The Witch-hunt and Suspension

1) Errors in Three Medical Eras: A Necropsy Study. Sonderegger-Iseli K, Burger S, Muntwyler J, et al. The Lancet. 2000;355(9220):2027-2031
2) Goddard P, Leslie A, Jones A, et al. Error in radiology.
   Br J Radiol (England), Oct 2001, 74 (886) p949-51
3) Inter-observer variation in interpretation of chest X-rays. Article Source: Scott Med J 1990 Oct;35(5):140-1 Author(s): Shaw NJ; Hendry M; Eden O
4) Double-contrast barium enema studies: effect of multiple reading on perception error. Article Source: Radiology 1990 Apr;175(1):155-6 Author(s): Markus JB; Somers S; O'Malley BP; Stevenson GW
5) Interpretation of abdominal CT: analysis of errors and their causes. Article Source: J Comput Assist Tomogr 1997 Sep-Oct;21(5):681-5 Author(s): Bechtold RE; Chen MY; Ott DJ; Zagoria RJ; Scharling ES; Wolfman NT; Vining DJ*
6) A negative double-contrast barium meal--qualified reassurance. Article Source: Clin Radiol 1987 Jan;38(1):49-50 Author(s): Arfeen S; Salter RH; Girdwood TG
7) Accuracy of radiological diagnosis in the Casualty Department of a children's hospital. Article Source: Aust Paediatr J 1984 Aug;20(3):221-3 Author(s): Masel JP; Grant P *
8) Errors at knee magnetic resonance imaging: true or false? Br J Radiol 1995 Oct;68(814):1045-51 Author(s): Mackenzie R; Keene GS; Lomas DJ; Dixon
9) Error rates in Australian chemical pathology laboratories Mounira Khoury, Leslie Burnett and Mark A Mackay *Medical Journal of Australia* 1996; 165: 128-13
10) Effects of restructuring on the performance of microbiology laboratories in Alberta Archives of Pathology & Laboratory Medicine, Mar 2000 by Church, Deirdre L, Don-Joe, Connie, Unger, Barbara http://findarticles.com/p/articles/mi_qa3725/is_200003/ai_n8900647/pg_5
11) Do computer generated ECG reports improve interpretation by accident and emergency senior house officers? S Goodacre, A Webster, F Morri *Postgrad Med J* 2001;77:455-457 (July)
12) Ergonomics of digital imaging SP Prabhu, S Gandhi, PR Goddard. *Br J Radiol.*2005; 78: 582-586
13) Brussels Sprouts p 9 Private EyeNo.1198 23 Nov-6th Dec 2007

Chapter 12: Why do some doctors find it so hard to work in the present political climate?

1) Learning Through Indigenous Proverbs and Myths www.missiology.org/animism/Learning/proverbs.htm
2) Financial Times November 1st 2002 page 4
3) Consultants paid more for less, by James Kirkup, Daily Telegraph, page 1 Nov 22 2007
4) www.hefce.ac.uk/research/assessment/
5) www.hero.ac.uk/rae/PanGuide/Guide/guide2.htm
6) www.nhi.clara.net/shipman0.htm
7) www.the-shipman-inquiry.org.uk/
8) Daily Telegraph Friday December 10th 2004 p 8).
9) BBC News 30 Jan 2001, Fury over Alder Hey report.
10) www.edinburgh.gov.uk/libraries/ historysphere/burkeandhare/burkeandhare.html
11) The Human Tissue Act 2004 (Ethical Approval, Exceptions from Licensing and Supply of Information about Transplants) Regulations 2006, ISBN 0110745523
12) Self-inflicted Stab Wound Causing Aorto-Right Ventricular Fistula Goddard P., Jones AG and Wisheart JD British Heart Journal (1981)Vol 46,101-103)

13) The Bristol Royal Infirmary Inquiry, by COI Communications□CM 5207(I) ISBN 0-10-152073-5 The Stationery Office Limited and www.bristol-inquiry.org.uk/final_report/rpt_print.htm
14) Kennedy, Ian, The Unmasking of medicine: based on Reith Lectures.Allen & Unwin London, 1981
15) Br Med J (Clin Res Ed). 1981 July 25; 283(6286): 306–307 Review of The Unmasking of Medicine by David Greave
16) Dead bodies scandal: return of the living dead by Dr Michael Fitzpatrick www.spiked-online.com/Printable/00000000543D.htm
17) Allyson Pollock NHS Plc p115
18) BBC News Friday, 29 September, 2000, 02:17 GMT 03:17 UK Bristol 'had double normal death rates' news.bbc.co.uk/1/hi/health/947204.stm
19) Report slams hospital shortage BBC News Tuesday 4 March 2008 21:36

Chapter 13: Dentistry and Nursing

1. Evening Post page 25 October 25th 2005.
2. Hamlyn Encyclopedic World Dictionary
3. Nurses' perceptions of the British hospital nursing officer .J Adv Nurs. 1980 Nov;5(6):613-23 Heyman B, Shaw M
4. How do registered nurses think and experience nursing. A phenomenological investigation. I Graham J Clin Nurs. 1994 Jul;3(4):235-42).
5. Ethical issues in Teleradiology RE Ashcroft and P R Goddard BJR 73 (2000), 578-582
6. Ethical dilemmas in a rationed health service Rad March 2000 pp35 –36 P Goddard and R Ashcroft
7. Hinderer DR Hospital downsizing: Ethics and employees. J Nursing Administration 1997; 27(4): 9-11
8. Johnson RS, Berger CS The challenge of change: enhancing social work services at a time of cutback. Health & Social Work, 1990; 15(3): 181-190
9. Ocker BM, Plank DM The research nurse role in a clinic-based oncology research setting. Cancer Nursing. 2000; 23(4): 286-292
10. Richardson G Identifying, evaluating and implementing cost-effective skill mix. J Nursing Management 1999; 7(5): 265-270
11. Calpin-Davies PJ, Akehurst RL Doctor-nurse substitution: the workforce equation. J Nursing Management 1999; 7(2): 71-79
12. Richards A, Carley J, Jenkins-Clarke S, Richards DA Skill mix between nurses and doctors working in primary care-delegation or allocation: a review of the literature. Int J Nursing Studies 2000; 37(3): 185-197
13. Glance LG The cost effectiveness of anaesthesia workforce models: A simulation approach using decision-analysis modelling. Anesthesia andAnalgesia 2000; 90(3): 584-592
14. Robinson PJ, Wilson D, Coral A, Murphy A, Verow P Variation between experienced observers in the interpretation of accident and emergency radiographs. Br J Radiology 1999; 72(856): 323-330
15. Young S, Brown HN Effects of hospital downsizing on surviving staff. Nursing Economics 1998; 16(5): 258-262
16. Hunter DJ The changing roles of health care personnel in health and health care management. Social Science and Medicine 1996; 43(5): 799-808
17. Daily Telegraph 11.10.2007 p 1
18. Daily Telegraph Nov 16th 2007 p 18
19. Daily Telegraph 10.12.2007 p 13
20. Doctors Doing Harm since Hippocrates, p 180 David Wooton,OUP 2007

Chapter 14: Political whim and fancy

1. Wednesday 4 July 2007 13:00 Department of Health (National) Shaping health care for the next decade Government News Network
2. Daily Telegraph, 2.8.2002
3. Financial Times p4 November Tᵗ 2002
4. M Papadopoulos et al Journal of the Royal Society of Medicine Volume 94, December 2001, pp613-616)
5. Hamlyn Encyclopedic World Dictionary: Edited by Patrick Hanks
6. www.dontvotemilburn.co.uk/id1.html
7. www.telegraph.co.uk/news/main.jhtml?xml=/news/2005/03/27/nmilb27.xml&sSheet=/news/2005/03/27/ixnewstop.html.
8. [Publication date: 27/4/2005] 'UK Connections: Access and Influence' by Steve Davies [Date URL accessed: 1/8/2005 | Source ID = 8530] The Guardian
9. [Publication date: 1/12/2003] 'Hospital bidder accused of interests conflict' by Terry Macalister http://www.guardian.co.uk/business/story/0,,1096833,00.html [Date URL accessed: 2/2/2005 | Source ID = 12936]
10. The Guardian [Publication date: 16/8/2004] 'Plan to end Whitehall sleaze rule Path eased to private sector jobs' http://politics.guardian.co.uk/whitehall/story/0%2C9061%2C1284021%2C00.html?79% 3A+Uk+news+-+guardian+-+do+not+use [Date URL accessed: 3/2/2005 | Source ID = 12957]
11. Red Pepper [Publication date: 1/7/2004] 'Know your enemy: Health Lucre' http://www.redpepper.org.uk/KYE/x-kye-July2004.html [Date URL accessed: 3/2/2005 | Source ID = 12960]
12. Advisory Committee on Business Appointments [Publication date: 1/7/2004] 'The Advisory Committee On Business Appointments Sixth Report 2002–2004' http://www.cabinetoffice.gov.uk/publications/reports/acba/sixthrep.pdf [Date URL accessed: 1/3/2005 | Source ID = 13186]
13. The Guardian [Publication date: 16/8/2004] 'Increase in ministers and officials barred from taking advantage of former jobs' by David Hencke http://www.guardian.co.uk/print/0,3858,4993930-103685,00.html [Date URL accessed: 1/3/2005 | Source ID = 13188]
14. Private Eye [Publication date: 4/3/2005] 'Many Happy Returns' http://www.guardian.co.uk/print/0,3858,4993930-103685,00.html [Date URL accessed: 4/3/2005 | Source ID = 13219]
15. Building [Publication date: 23/1/1998] 'PFI UPDATE - NEW ERA FOR PFI HOSPITALS' http://www.guardian.co.uk/print/0,3858,4993930-103685,00.html [Date URL accessed: 14/3/2005 | Source ID = 13240]
16. House of Commons [Publication date: 28/1/2005] 'Register of Members' Interests (Session 2004-05)' http://www.publications.parliament.uk/pa/cm/cmregmem/050128/memi02.htm [Date URL accessed: 23/3/2005 | Source ID = 13304]
17. House of Lords [Publication date: 22/3/2005] 'Register of Lords' Interests' http://www.publications.parliament.uk/pa/ld/ldreg/reg01.htm [Date URL accessed: 23/3/2005 | Source ID = 13305]
18. The Observer [Publication date: 25/11/2001] 'Fury over Blair ally's NHS cash: Peer's firm charges millions for nurses' by Antony Barnett http://observer.guardian.co.uk/print/0,3858,4306882-102279,00.html [Date URL accessed: 30/3/2005 | Source ID = 13315]
19. Evening Standard [Publication date: 18/6/2001] 'Reed spin-off's union boss' by Robert Lindsay http://observer.guardian.co.uk/print/0,3858,4306882-102279,00.html [Date URL accessed: 5/4/2005 | Source ID = 13316]
20. Financial Times [Publication date: 19/2/2004] 'Gershon cost cut' http://observer.guardian.co.uk/print/0,3858,4306882-102279,00.html [Date URL accessed: 30/3/2005 | Source ID = 13317]
21. Financial Times [Publication date: 9/6/2003] 'A new openness to high-flying outsiders' by Nicholas Timmins http://observer.guardian.co.uk/print/0,3858,4306882-102279,00.html [Date URL accessed: 5/4/2005 | Source ID = 13318]

22.   Daily Mail   'Milburn 'gag' storm' by DAVID HUGHES   http://observer.guardian.co.uk/print/0,3858,4306882-102279,00.html [Date URL accessed: 5/4/2005 | Source ID = 13319]

23.   SUNDAY TELEGRAPH   [Publication date: 27/3/2005] 'Labour orders MP to keep quiet over Milburn scan deal' by PATRICK HENNESSY   http://news.telegraph.co.uk/news/main.jhtml?xml=/news/2005/03/27/nmilb27.xml&sS heet=/news/2005/03/27/ixnewstop.html [Date URL accessed: 30/3/2005 | Source ID = 13320]

24.   New Statesman   [Publication date: 23/8/2004] 'Alan Milburn's family life'   http://news.telegraph.co.uk/news/main.jhtml?xml=/news/2005/03/27/nmilb27.xml&sS heet=/news/2005/03/27/ixnewstop.html [Date URL accessed: 30/3/2005 | Source ID = 13321]

25.   Guardian   [Publication date: 25/6/2004] 'The spoils of office: Like their Tory predecessors, former New Labour ministers are now dining off corporate consultancies' by Kevin Maguire   http://politics.guardian.co.uk/print/0,3858,4956116-107865,00.html [Date URL accessed: 30/3/2005 | Source ID = 13322]

26.   Building   [Publication date: 6/6/2003] 'AMEY TO BUY BACK TUBE STAKE: SUPPORT SERVICES GROUP AMEY WILL BUY BACK ITS £ 60M STAKE IN THE LONDON UNDERGROUND PPP. THE ANNOUNCEMENT CAME AFTER AMEY'S SALE TO SPANISH CONTRACTOR FERROVIAL WAS CONFIRMED LAST THURSDAY' by Mark Leftly   http://politics.guardian.co.uk/print/0,3858,4956116-107865,00.html [Date URL accessed: 5/4/2005 | Source ID = 13323]

27.   Business and Industry Public Private Finance [Publication date: 1/6/2003] 'LGA slams education LIFT model'   http://politics.guardian.co.uk/print/0,3858,4956116-107865,00.html [Date URL accessed: 30/3/2005 | Source ID = 13324]

28.   Contract Journal [Publication date: 29/5/2003] 'FORMER PFI CONTRACTOR LEADS SCHOOLS REBUILDING' by John Leitch   http://politics.guardian.co.uk/print/0,3858,4956116-107865,00.html [Date URL accessed: 5/4/2005 | Source ID = 13325]

29.   Building   [Publication date: 9/8/2002] 'WE CAN WORK IT OUT' by Phil Clark   http://politics.guardian.co.uk/print/0,3858,4956116-107865,00.html [Date URL accessed: 5/4/2005 | Source ID = 13326]

30.   HMSO   [Publication date: 26/6/2003] 'Governing by appointment' by House of Commons Public Administration Select Committee   http://www.publications.parliament.uk/pa/cm200203/cmselect/cmpubadm/165/165.pdf   [Date URL accessed: 20/4/2005 | Source ID = 13403]

31.   Red Pepper [Publication date: 1/7/2004] 'Healthy lucre' by Solomon Huges   http://www.redpepper.org.uk/KYE/x-kye-July2004.html [Date URL accessed: 22/4/2005 | Source ID = 13447]

32.   www.againstcorruption.org/BriefingsItem.asp?id=12433

Chapter 15: What has gone wrong with the patients ?

1)   WR Burnham Federation of the RCP Census 2000 Clinical Medicine 2202 2(1)7-8
2)   Raymond Tallis , Hippocratic Oaths , Atlantic Books
3)   Drug Users at Montpelier, Montpelier Health Centre Report 2005, page 40,41).
4)   NHS Constitution urges good health, Ben Russell, The Independent Tuesday 1st Jan 2008
5)   NHS Constitution to be unveiled, Porter & Smith, Daily Telegraph pp1&2 25th June 2008

Chapter 16: State Medicine: The Future

1)   Francis Bacon 1561-1626 (Essays 25 'Of Dispatch')
2)   www.drrant.net/2006/08/dr-otto-chan.html
3)   Ethical issues in Teleradiology (Review Article)*Br J Radiol* 73 (2000) 578-582 R Ashcroft and P Goddard)
4)   New Age Healing, page 71,Reader's Digest 1992

Bibliography

The Age of Napoleon, Alistair Horne

The Art of Medicine in Ancient Egypt (The Metropolitan Museum of Art, New York, Yale University Press)

Bristol Medico-Chirurgical Journal

Concise Oxford Dictionary of Current English, Oxford Univ. Press.

Chronicle of the World, Derrik Mercer, editor, 1996 DK Publishing

Doctors Doing Harm since Hippocrates David Wooton, OUP 2007

From Cradle to Grave: fifty years of the NHS, Geoffrey Rivett ISBN 1 85717 148

Health and Medicine in Britain since 1860, Anne Hardy, Palgrave, 2001

Hippocratic Oaths: Medicine and Its Discontents by Raymond Tallis

The Moral State We're In by Julia Neuberger, Harper Collins London 2005

An outline history of medicine by Philip Rhodes Butterworths 1985

NHS plc, the Privatisation of Our Health Care by Allison Pollock, Verso

The Phoenix by Coincraft

Resuscitation Greats by P and T Baskett Clinical Press, Bristol

The Rise and fall of Modern Medicine, James le Fanu, London 1999

Seaby Coins of England Standard Catalogue 1996

Social England, Cassell and Company Ltd

Western Medicine, Irvine Loudon, OUP

Index

Index

Index

Index

Index